Growing California
Native Plants

California Natural History Guides: 45

Growing California Native Plants

Marjorie G. Schmidt

Drawings by Beth D. Merrick

UNIVERSITY OF CALIFORNIA PRESS
Berkeley Los Angeles London

University of California Press
Berkeley and Los Angeles, California
University of California Press, Ltd.
London, England

Schmidt, Marjorie G
  Growing California native plants.

  (California natural history guides; 45)
  Bibliography: p.
  Includes index.
  1. Wild flower gardening—California. 2. Botany—
California. 3. Plants, Ornamental—California.
I. Title. II. Series.
SB439.S33   635.9'51794   78-62845
ISBN 0-520-03761-8
ISBN 0-520-03762-6 pbk.

CONTENTS

ACKNOWLEDGMENTS

This book is dedicated to my husband, Willard E. Schmidt, whose patient assistance, and at times severe criticism has kept me on my toes. It is also dedicated to kind friends and relatives whose faith in my ability to complete this work has sustained me. My appreciation to those who have shared their knowledge and experience is deep and sincere. Many years of garden experience with native plants have been the basis for this book, but even as I rush toward the deadline, new selections and cultivars are appearing regularly. A new assessment of the role of native plants is being made, for their value to the countryside, as well as for their ornamental purposes.

To the following I wish to acknowledge special thanks for supplying needed information and assistance: Wayne Roderick, Director of Regional Parks Botanic Garden, Berkeley; James B. Roof, Director Emeritus, Regional Parks Botanic Garden, Berkeley; John Dourley, Superintendent Rancho Santa Ana Botanic Garden, Claremont; Dara Emery, Propagator, Santa Barbara Botanic Garden, Santa Barbara; Kenneth Taylor, Nurseryman, Aromas; Elizabeth McClintock, Curator Emeritus, Botany, California Academy of Sciences, San Francisco; Lee W. Lenz, Director, Rancho Santa Ana Botanic Garden, Claremont; Robert Smaus, Associate Editor, Home Magazine, Los Angeles Times; and John T. Howell, Curator Emeritus, Botany, California Academy of Sciences.

ABOUT PLANT NAMES
AND TERMS

The only way to be certain of correctly identifying a plant is to learn its botanical name. Every plant has a two-part botanical name: first the capitalized name of the genus which identifies a large group of related plants, and second the name of the species which identifies the particular type of plant within the group. For example, the genus *Pinus* includes several kinds of pine, with a specific designation, such as *Pinus ponderosa* for Ponderosa Pine. The genus and species may have common names, generally traditional and well established for trees, but not always so for other categories of plants.

Common names are usually easier to remember and may indicate something of the plant's characteristics. If an outstanding feature has made a common name logical, such as "shooting stars" for species of *Dodecatheon,* the common name is useful. But some popular names are only used locally, others are used for more than one plant, and some plants have many common names, such as *Pseudotsuga menziesii* which has more than twenty names, although Douglas Fir is the one most used. I have tried to find the most suitable common name to help encourage uniformity, and to reduce misunderstanding. Unfortunately, where there is no universally accepted common name, one has to be contrived and it seldom pleases all concerned.

Terms used in this book include:

CULTIVAR: A cultivated plant distinguished by certain characteristics which, when reproduced, retain these characteristics. Cultivar is a contraction of "cultivated variety" and should be distinguished from a naturally occurring "botanical variety."

If a cultivar is derived from a single species its origin is clear. If it is derived from two or more species under carefully controlled conditions there should be no doubt of its ancestry. However, if a cultivar has been selected from one or more naturally occurring hybrids of uncertain origin, or from mixed plantings, or if poor records have been kept, it will be impossible to determine its ancestry with any accuracy. In this book, cultivars are referred to the species from which they are thought to be derived whenever possible. In some cases this may represent only the opinion of some workers in the field.

CLONE: The term used for plants that originate from a single individual, and that are reproduced by vegetative means: cuttings, budding, or grafting.

Cultivars and clones usually have an English name indicating a selected horticultural form of a plant.

SUBSPECIES and VARIETY are terms used by botanists to indicate some variation in form or structure of plant species. The terms are practically synonymous.

1. THE CASE FOR NATIVE PLANTS

California became known as the land of flowers from the time the first explorer set foot here. Explorers and others who followed were amazed by the wide range of plant types, including trees, shrubs, perennials, bulb plants, vines, succulents, grasses and nonflowering plants. They soon discovered that, while some of these plants were similar to those of their homeland, many were new to them.

Today this magnificent native flora, whose esthetic value gives the California countryside much of its distinctive beauty and attraction, is threatened. The rapid increase in population has changed and disrupted the habitat of all wildlife, particularly of wild plants. Inflated land values, lack of planning and zoning for the future, and the supposed time-honored "rights" of land developers complicate efforts to protect native species. Several actions can be taken to save the native plants. The most important in the opinion of naturalists is to preserve habitats by setting aside wild lands where typical, rare, or endangered species occur in some concentration. On protected lands, native plants can remain undisturbed in their natural state and available for study. Living collections of representative species in horticultural institutions provide further insurance that no species will become totally extinct. More important is to use attractive and suitable native plants as garden materials. Most will flourish with much less attention, will enhance the garden, and be more in keeping with the terrain than most exotics. Much has been lost from the once extensive and glorious flora of my home state of California. We can never fully replace such losses, but we can protect and encourage the use of our remaining treasure of native plants.

DISTRIBUTION

We cannot give more than a brief idea of the nature, distribution, and complexity of the California flora here. Certain broad features are obvious, especially the magnificent forests of most mountain regions and of the northwestern coastal section of the state. Some of these forests, especially at higher elevations, are a mixture of needle-leaved evergreens, while in other places the conifers are mixed with broadleaved trees. Foothill regions are mostly dominated by oaks and their attendant shrubs, herbaceous plants, and grasses. Low hills, valleys, coastal plains, deserts, and mesas each have their own wide assortment of colorful plants, especially annuals, which bloom abundantly in spring and form vast mosaic carpets. Some native plants are found only near watercourses, in meadows, and other moist places where they bloom freely over long periods to form wild gardens of great beauty. Drought-tolerant and firm-leaved shrubs, forming dense thickets known as chaparral, are the dominant plants on many arid hills and low mountains. Many plants are restricted to localized sections within these broad areas, such as alpine regions, bogs, talus slopes, rock crevices and ledges, and serpentine slopes. Such restricted plants often require special attention when brought into cultivation. Gardeners need to know that many of the natives now in cultivation derive from California's most extensive geographical feature, the foothills. Adaptable plants have also come from mild, coastal regions, low-elevation valleys, from meadows and streamsides, and elsewhere. Plants from these areas, along with a few from localized places, are the easiest natives to grow in most California gardens, and some became popular garden subjects before the turn of this century.

FACTS AND FIGURES

California has 5,027 species of native plants belonging to 1,139 genera (Robert Ornduff, *An Introduction to California Plant Life,* Berkeley, 1974). About 2,000 of these native plants are endemic, that is, they are restricted to a single locality or habitat. Several genera contain large numbers of California species. For example, *Mimulus* (monkey flowers) includes 77 species, many of which are also endemic. Several trees and shrubs are among the rarest of the endemics, including Giant Sequoia *(Sequoiadendron giganteum)*; Torrey Pine *(Pinus torreyana)*; Bristlecone Fir *(Abies bracteata)*; and the lovely Tree Anemone *(Carpenteria californica)*. These have been popular garden plants for many years and two, the Giant Sequoia and the Tree Anemone, are widely grown in England.

For more detailed discussion of plant distribution, consult *Terrestrial Vegetation of California,* edited by Michael G. Barbour and Jack Major (John Wiley and Sons, 1977). This large book is the work of many authors and gives a systematic and scientific description of the native vegetation. It includes a full color map, which can help develop more detailed understanding of plant distribution.

See Appendix, pages 330–332, for detailed descriptions of Plant Communities, which are referred to throughout this book.

TAMING WILD PLANTS

Bringing wild plants into cultivation involves finding those with adaptable traits and discovering how they might be improved, when necessary, by a breeding program. This effort to bring plants into gardens is very old in the history of man's endeavors to enhance his surroundings. Many of California's wild plants which already had desirable qualities were brought into cultivation as early as the late 1700s, when explorers sent seeds and cuttings to their home countries. Gardeners in the British Isles, especially, have deep admiration for many of our native plants, and have sought to make them conform to their climate, either by creating suitable situations, or by crossing species to create adaptable new forms. These forms are well suited to English gardens, and we can follow the same pattern of crossing, selecting, and testing to find the most adaptable natives for our own conditions.

LACK OF INTEREST IN
NATIVE PLANTS

A newcomer to California may well ask why much of this superb heritage of native plants has failed, until recently, to become popular garden material. The reasons are many, and in spite of renewed interest, some still prevail. Most of California's early settlers had little time to be concerned with wild plants. Early gardens usually contained favorite plants brought by the settlers, who didn't attempt to cultivate the strange, native plants of the West. The first nurseries, some well established by the mid-1800s, imported plants rather than encouraging the use of native ones. Even now few nurseries carry a full complement of native plants, and the gardening public has failed to show a sustained interest in them. Another deterrent is the competition of highly cultivated plants which are so readily obtained from professional growers. Gardeners seeking to observe native plants grown with suitable companions find few examples, except in some of the horticultural and botanical institutions. And further, very little publicity is given even to those natives which have been refined for garden use, and there is no agency concerned primarily with testing and introducing native plants to cultivation.

NEED FOR LITERATURE ON GROWING NATIVE PLANTS

Lack of literature on the propagation and culture of native plants, especially from personal experience, has to a degree worked against their becoming popular. Only a few books are concerned with growing western wild plants, and while they discuss certain aspects, only rarely do they include detailed records of propagating and growing. There is little in any literature that evaluates the merits of native plants as garden materials. Some information can be gleaned from leaflets of horticultural institutions, government and university publications, catalogs, plant society publications, and popular garden magazines. Except for the magazines, much of the gardening public is not aware of these publications. In many instances the gardener needs good field notes on soil, exposure, sun/shade situation, and details of a plant's appearance throughout the seasons. Eye-witness accounts of the occurrence and distribution of wild plants before large-scale land disturbance are rare, although impressions of some of the more spectacular plants are recorded in old books and journals. There is a large selection of handbooks available to aid in the identification of native plants, but most are confined to specific regions. The bibliography at the end of this book lists publications that I have found most useful.

EARLY HORTICULTURAL HISTORY

The recorded history of the use of California native plants in gardens is sparse and sketchy. Interest in this flora began long before statehood, as the early explorers came to recognize this wealth of wild plants. For about two hundred years many of the most beautiful of these plants have been cultivated in Europe, especially in England, Scotland, France, Germany, and recently in Holland. Seeds, bulbs, and plant materials were collected and sent abroad where they became much loved and highly respected garden plants. The Pink Sand Verbena *(Abronia umbellata)* was thought to be the first California plant grown in Europe, from seed collected near Monterey about 1786. David Douglas was one of the best known of the early botanical explorers, and probably sent more seeds and specimens to Europe than any other person. But in California, until very recently, concern for native plants did not keep pace with the European enthusiasm.

HORTICULTURAL BEGINNINGS

The original settlers and Mission Fathers learned some practical uses for native plants from the Indians, who had long been familiar with the food plants, medicinal plants, and plants with a variety of uses for such things as basket materials, ropes, clothing, etc. By the early 1900s a small selection of native trees and shrubs were considered worthy of a place in gardens, including: Coast Redwood *(Sequoia sempervirens);* Matilija Poppy *(Romneya coulteri);* Island Tree Poppy *(Dendromecon harfordii);* Hollyleaf Cherry *(Prunus ilicifolia);* Toyon *(Heteromeles arbutifolia);* several of the California lilacs *(Ceanothus* spp.); and evergreen sumacs *(Rhus* spp.). Agricultural development was proceeding rapidly, attended by the introduction of exotic and often weedy grasses, perennials, and several trees. Thus, Oleander (*Nerium* spp.), eucalyptus (*Eucalyptus* spp.), and the Pepper Tree *(Schinus molle)* became so firmly established that it is difficult to convince newcomers that these are not native to California. Even before this period, John Muir, the most respected of early conservationists, expressed the sentiments of many when he deplored the invasion of man's activities in forests and in the Great Valley "bee pastures."

PIONEERING ACTIVITIES

Records of the early settlement periods are scant, but several dedicated people were proceeding without much fanfare to help Californians become acquainted with their wild plants. To them it seemed logical and practical to use the plants that graced the hills and canyons, and we owe these far-sighted plantsmen a debt of gratitude for their persistence.

These native plant enthusiasts were either botanists, nurserymen, or home gardeners, most of whom did their own seed collecting and propagating. One of them was Theodore Payne of Los Angeles, in whose name a native plant foundation has now been established. Another was Carl Purdy, who had deep interest in native bulbs, and whose writing and nursery business helped Californians become interested in the best of these plants. Louis Edmunds collected and propagated many outstanding natives in central California, as did Kate Sessions in the San Diego area. Howard E. McMinn of Oakland performed a similar service for native shrubs. His lecturing and writing brought a better understanding of their value to landscaping. Perhaps the most famous native plant advocate during the 1930s and 40s was a woman, Lester Rowntree, who often travelled alone into the high Sierra to collect seeds of rare and lovely native plants. Countless other dedicated people have contributed to the present knowledge of native plants. Today, many young horticulturists are studying the countryside, and the possibilities for useful native plants, determined to fill the gaps where knowledge and experience about them are still missing.

The early history includes several instances of rare plants being rescued from destruction. One, at least, was highly dramatic when almost the last tendril of the San Francisco Manzanita *(Arctostaphylos hookeri* ssp. *franciscana*) was snatched from the old Laurel Hill Cemetery in San Francisco. Several other rare plants were also rescued from the path of progress and subsequently made available to gardeners: Nevin's Barberry *(Berberis nevinii),* whose original habitat in the San Fernando Valley is now covered with houses; the pretty Wavyleaf Ceanothus *(Ceanothus foliosus* var. *vineatus)* of Sonoma County; the Dwarf Pt. Reyes Lilac *(Ceanothus gloriosus* var. *porrectus);* and the lovely San Diego Ceanothus *(C. cyeanus).* These and others have been preserved to enrich western gardens.

BOTANIC GARDENS

The first big upswing of activity toward a better understanding of native plants began in the 1920s with the establishment of the first botanic gardens, and the beginning of some public and private plant collections. Santa Barbara Botanic Garden was organized in 1926, and Rancho Santa Ana Botanic Garden in 1927. The Tilden Park Botanic Garden was founded in 1940 with plants arranged in seven major divisions. At Mills College in Oakland, the Joseph McInnes Memorial Botanical Garden features woody plants of California and the Pacific Basin. The Saratoga Horticultural Foundation, organized in 1951, selects and tests plants of superior quality, including many native ones. Their program has produced named forms in the following genera: *Arctostaphylos, Ceanothus, Garrya, Berberis, Rhamnus,* and others. Strybing Arboretum in Golden Gate Park now has a section devoted to a wide assortment of native plants in their most suitable situations. Many universities have botanic gardens with large plant collections, which frequently include some native ones. The University of California Botanic Garden in Berkeley, established in 1891, is one of the oldest. Much basic work in the process of refining native plants is conducted in these institutions, although it remains on a relatively small scale. Propagating, testing, and selecting takes time, and it may take many years to judge the merits of the plants being tested. Each step must be recorded to share the benefit of experience in successes or failures. Most of these institutions are open to the public, and have guided tours and educational programs, so gardeners can observe well-grown natives in compatible groupings. In my opinion California needs even larger botanic gardens, in which complete collections of native plants can be accommodated and their many uses thoroughly investigated.

CALIFORNIA NATIVE PLANT SOCIETY

Another important step was taken in 1965 with the founding of the California Native Plant Society, whose paramount purpose is to preserve wild plants. Many chapters have been organized throughout the state, and these conduct field trips to study common, rare, and endangered species, and to promote appreciation for and understanding of native plants in relation to the total environment. Joining this society is one way to become involved in the welfare and continued existence of the wild flora.

The following chapters are based mainly on my personal experiences and on frequent observations of cultivated natives in botanic gardens, nurseries, and arboretums. It is hardly possible for any one person to have grown every likely candidate from among the possibilities, but I have been on intimate terms with at least 200 of them. My experiences include gardening in central California and in the mountains of the northwestern section of the state at 3,000 feet elevation. In general, the failures are few and the successes many, giving the gardener courage to dig further into the delights of native plant study and experimentation.

2. GETTING STARTED

The native plants of California are much too numerous and varied to allow any simple assessment of their garden value. For use in the garden, they can be divided into six categories—annuals, perennials, bulbs, vines, shrubs, and trees. Only a few in each of the chosen genera can be described here, and some equally worthy ones have been left out. The appropriate garden situation, and most suitable companions for each selected example is suggested, but many other combinations, either with natives or with old garden favorites, are possible.

This chapter on getting started is designed to aid the beginner by suggested procedures and examples gleaned from personal observation and experience. Some steps may seem elementary to the experienced gardener but, since there are so few publications available for guidance, I have tried to supply the fundamental, necessary details. Perhaps this chapter should be called ''making the most of the environment,'' since it contains a strong appeal to keep existing plants where possible, to preserve whatever remains of local wildflowers, and so to create an environmental garden of pleasing western style.

DESIRABLE TRAITS

In choosing native plants for garden use, certain guidelines can be followed. An ornamental plant should have some, or maybe all, of the following qualifications: foliage of good substance and color, flowers in acceptable colors or in abundance to enhance the plant, colorful fruits or interesting seed vessels, plus some off-season attraction such as colored foliage in autumn. These features should be combined with a neat appearance and nonrampant growing habits. In addition to these

9

ornamental qualities, plants should also be adaptable to cultivation, or at least to show some tendency to accept garden conditions. For a few, special requirements may have to be satisfied, such as selected exposure, special soils, or the need for a dormant period. Most of these desirable traits are present in the native plants which have persisted in gardens over the years.

SOME BEGINNING STEPS

For the newcomer to California, or the beginner who knows little of the native plants, there are a few preliminary steps.

1. Make use of every opportunity to observe well-grown natives, in home gardens, collections, botanic gardens, or where they have been used in large-scale plantings.

2. Decide on your garden plan to suit the situation, amounts of light and shade, availability of water, and life style of your family. If the garden is to be watered throughout the year, choose plants known to be adaptable, especially hybrids and cultivars (cultural varieties maintained as a nursery stock). If there is a sunny section which can be devoted to drought-tolerant materials, consult the long list of natives accustomed to sun and dryness. For a shade border, many woodland, meadow, and streamside plants will be suitable. If the garden plan is formal, use native plants of known refinement which have no untidy or rampant habits, preferably those which have a steady, uniform growth rate.

3. The ideal way to get acquainted with native plants is to observe them in the wild. If you can't visit the plants in their own homes, attend wildflower shows where they are exhibited and identified by both botanical and common names. An outstanding event of this kind is the Spring Blossom and Wild Flower Show held in Golden Gate Park in San Francisco, with displays from horticultural institutions as well as from home gardens. Chapters of the California Native Plant Society sponsor or aid in organizing wildflower shows all over the state and the one in the Oakland Museum in April is outstanding.

4. As already noted, finding published information on propagating and growing native plants takes diligent investigation of many kinds of publications. Every scrap of personal experience is important. Keep a notebook of your procedures

in propagating and handling native plants, and you will soon have an accumulation of useful information and a record of the plantings. This book grew from my voluminous garden notes and records, which contain hard-won, practical information as well as more whimsical data, such as how early the Baby Blue-Eyes *(Nemophila menziesii)* bloomed in the spring.

5. Finding a source of seeds and plants can begin with a search of nurseries, both local and those which advertise in garden publications. Most nurseries now stock cultivars, since these are apt to give a good garden performance, along with some of the adaptable species. Sometimes specialty nurseries stock unusual plants, including natives, or are in touch with collectors of wild plant seeds. Other sources are the several plant societies devoted to a single genus, such as wild forms of lilies or irises. They have seed and plant exchanges which include some rare or not usually obtainable materials. Many horticultural societies and botanic gardens have seed listings and plant sales, but the only way to get some of the natives you want is to collect seeds yourself. Always spend time observing a plant and its habits before bringing it into your garden.

DIGGING WILD PLANTS

You may be tempted to take plants from the wilds, but this is against the law in California, and in most other states, without a permit. If a collected plant fails to grow, both the plant and the seed which it would have produced are lost. Laws against digging and cutting wild plants were passed to stop the destructive breaking of branches for berries and greenery, and the digging which threatened to destroy stands of rare native plants.

It is true that land development, logging, grazing, fire, and other activities have destroyed many precious stands of wildflowers—a bitter thing to botanists and naturalists, but considered to be unavoidable in the course of events. In some cases where land development or road building is in progress, uprooted plants can be rescued. When this can be done, be prepared with plastic bags, or with cans for immediate potting. Keep any rescued plant moist and sheltered until danger of wilting has passed. No matter how tough and drought tolerant a native plant might be in its own habitat, it must have care following transplanting and occasional attention until it becomes established.

PREPARATION FOR PLANTING

Any kind of planting needs thorough soil preparation to insure proper conditions for vigorous growth. Uncultivated soil will contain weed seeds that must be destroyed, either by weed killers or by wetting and turning the soil. Soil amendments are generally necessary, or desirable, to improve the physical structure and water-holding capacity of the soil. These amendments may be the final product, known as humus, of once-living plants and animals. They are provided by leaf mold, peat moss, manures, composted vegetation, sludge, and nitrogen-fortified ground barks. Uncomposted soil amendments rob the soil of nitrogen as they break down, so nitrogen must be added when they are used. Nitrogen can be supplied by ammonium sulfate, used according to directions on the package. Top soil is often imported to new homesites, and it may bring in different but equally obnoxious weed seeds.

Turning and working the soil is the traditional method of preparation. However, for native plants it is just as feasible to dig a hole for each plant, especially where a large area is being planted to all native materials. Dig the hole a little wider and deeper than the root system, mix organic materials with the soil, wet thoroughly, and allow to settle before setting in the plant. New gardeners often spend needless time removing small stones from the soil. Small stones and pebbles in the soil help provide the drainage that is vital for most native plants.

EXISTING FLORA

If you are lucky enough to find remnants of the wild flora on your property, it is practical and logical to use them as a nucleus of your garden. Some heavy brush or highly invasive plants may have to be removed, but a careful survey of existing plants should be made before having them all bulldozed out. One of the common tragedies of the California countryside is the devastating removal of all living plants, which leaves dry, baked soil open to weed invasion and erosion. Laws seem unable to stop this kind of "progress," but a new home-owner can refuse to invest in such mutilated land. Where native vegetation remains, it should be observed over a period of several seasons to discover flowering, fruiting, or otherwise useful or ornamental plants. A new season may bring colonies of annuals, perennials, or handsome bulb plants. Where manzanitas, coffeeberries, or other evergreens of uniform growth habit occur, some should be retained either as a hedge or as permanent background materials. Tree seedlings and large shrubs may have awkward or dead limbs or be straggly in appearance, but they will emerge as useful plants when trimmed or thinned. A sympathetic appraisal of existing native plants can discover a ready-made garden framework. Carefully selected additional materials can create a distinctive landscape and a smooth transition to the surroundings.

INITIAL PLANTING

After the soil is prepared, planting can begin according to the season and the garden plan. In open, sunny areas a wide assortment of annuals, both native and garden favorites, can be seeded directly. The wild annuals can be used in naturally occurring combinations, such as California Poppies with small, blue lupines. Or they may be used in grand and colorful mixtures, or in masses of a single species for patches of a solid color. Native annuals may also be used in mixed flower borders, open slopes, little colonies in rock gardens, and a few in woodland gardens.

Plants of a permanent character, including trees, shrubs, and evergreen or herbaceous perennials, should be set out from mid-autumn until the following spring. These should be compatible in size, flower color, period of bloom, and cultural requirements, with special care taken in their choice if they are to be used in an established garden. These native plants may be chosen for their flowers, for colorful fruits or interesting seed vessels, or for contrast in foliage shape and color. Deciduous materials may be used with evergreen plants by selecting those whose early leaf emergence will be especially intriguing against evergreen trees and shrubs.

Native plants which require specialized treatment can be added later when you are sure that you can satisfy their requirements. Many of the small bulbs and certain of the alpine plants require coarse soil and a summer dormant period, while others of woodlands need filtered shade and will tolerate year-round watering.

NATIVES FOR PARTICULAR USES

Native plants which can be used for special kinds of planting, for specific purposes and situations could easily fill another book. An all-native plant garden is possible but seldom to be recommended except for country or vacation homes. Most gardens can be a mixture of wild and cultivated plants, carefully chosen to suit the garden plan. Plants with similar cultural requirements should be kept together. Forming compatible combinations is one of the keys to successful cultivation of native plants. Brief examples of garden situations and suggested native materials follow.

Drought-Resistant Border

Sunny, semi-dry borders where water is given only to get plants established are important in California gardening. Drought-resistant natives chosen from the list in the back of the book can save water, since they require very little once they are established. Such plants need only a minimum of water and cultivation, but should have some advance soil preparation and mulching during hot weather. A self-sufficient border of native plants, especially one that is presentable through the years, is a very satisfactory achievement. For example, a blue-and-gold border can be planned, using Mexican Fremontia *(Fremontodendron mexicanum),* or California Fremontia *(F. californicum),* with California lilacs, such as Ray Hartman Lilac *(Ceanothus griseus × C. arboreus* 'Ray Hartman') or Louis Edmunds Lilac *(C. griseus* 'Louis Edmunds') for a wealth of blue flowers to contrast with the yellow saucers of the fremontias. Selections from the genera of penstemons *(Penstemon),* sages *(Salvia),* blue-curls *(Trichostema),* and bush poppies

(Dendromecon) will give a long succession of flowers to enhance the color scheme. As soon as the border is well established, some of California's adaptable bulbs can be planted in open areas where sun and semi-dry conditions will suit their requirements. Selections can be made to suit the landscape plan from other genera, including lupines *(Lupinus)*, woolly sunflowers *(Eriophyllum)*, wallflowers *(Erysimum)*, buckwheats *(Eriogonum)*, and monkey flowers *(Mimulus)*. You can also choose from the wide assortment of drought-tolerant shrubs, including manzanitas *(Arctostaphylos)*, California lilacs *(Ceanothus)*, mountain mahoganies *(Cercocarpus)*, and garryas *(Garrya)*. In open spaces or pockets among the more permanent plants, sun-loving native annuals can be broadcast for spring color, or to carry out or extend the color scheme. In establishing a dry border you are limited only in your ability to find available plants, or in learning to propagate them from seeds or cuttings.

Shade Garden

The California countryside offers a wide assortment of native plants that prefer shade. They are usually water tolerant and adaptable to cultivation, and may be used with old garden favorites that have the same requirements. The ideal situation is where some sunlight is filtered through trees or large shrubs, or where there is morning sun to encourage flowering of plants such as wild irises and columbines. Where there is dense shade from buildings, fences, or tight hedges, only a green, leafy cover can be expected. Prime among carpeting plants is Evergreen Currant *(Ribes viburnifolium)*, whose trailing branches form a leafy, aromatic cover. Other shade-loving plants which afford either interesting foliage, flowers, or fruits include selections from the following: the inside-out flowers *(Vancouveria* spp.) for their lacy, apple green leaflets; the spreading, wild gingers *(Asarum* spp.); the delicate Pacific Bleeding Heart *(Dicentra formosa);* and fragrant Yerba Buena *(Satureja douglasii)*. A few carefully selected bulbs may be used in shady situations, including lilies *(Lilium)*, fawn lilies *(Erythronium)*, woodland mission bells *(Fritillaria)*, and the exquisite fairy lanterns in *Calochortus*. There is a wide choice of shade-loving shrubs to be found in the listings. Three outstanding examples are Salal *(Gaultheria shallon),* California Huckleberry *(Vaccinium ovatum),* and the lovely Western Azalea *(Rhododendron occidentale).* All of these need an acid, humus soil.

Rock Gardens

Rock gardeners have been especially enterprising in seeking native plants of size and character to be used among boulders, on terraces, slopes, rock walls, or in raised borders. These should be dense and compact plants, of trailing, creeping, or mounding habit, in particular some of the low shrubs and perennials having firm, evergreen foliage. Choice alpines from such genera as *Phlox, Arabis, Arenaria, Sedum, Silene,* and *Eriogonum* may frequently be found in nurseries. These are plants from many habitats, including ledges and crevices of boulders, rock faces, gravelly places, talus slopes, and sea cliffs. They are accustomed to sharply drained, and lean or porous soil, correct exposure, free circulation of air, and for a few, a summer dormant period. These and many others keep their attractive appearance through the seasons, but they should not be put in competition with aggressive plants that could detract from their diminutive charms.

Small City Garden

Most city gardens are hemmed in by buildings and fences, and watered throughout the year. Only those natives of known adaptability and water tolerance should be used. Furthermore they should be plants of moderate growth rate, with firm, evergreen foliage, and flowers or fruits which present no prolonged untidy period. Two beautiful shrubs in this class are Huckleberry *(Vaccinium ovatum),* and Glossyleaf Manzanita *(Arctostaphylos nummularia),* both requiring woodsy, acid soil. Other shrubs which might be suitable are selected forms of Sierra Coffeeberry *(Rhamnus rubra),* which drapes so engagingly over boulders along Sierra streams, or Boxleaf Garrya *(Garrya buxifolia),* a five-foot shrub of the north Coast Ranges. An outstanding cover plant of moderate growth rate is Marbleleaf Ginger *(Asarum hartwegii),* whose large, round, dark green leaves are mottled with very pale green. Some leafy plants of fine shape and color from the redwood region, where they are accustomed to almost constant moisture, will accept the close conditions of a city garden. Suggested plants include: alum roots *(Heuchera),* Sugar Scoop *(Tiarella unifoliata),* the round, lobed leaves of miterworts *(Mitella),* or the clover-leaved Redwood Sorrel *(Oxalis oregana).*

Foundation Planting

Although few native plants have been tested for planting close to buildings, several evergreen shrubs of tidy habit are suitable for this purpose. Nevin Barberry *(Berberis nevinii)* is an excellent example. It has an interesting prickly foliage pattern, reddish berries, and a quite dense growth habit. Another useful shrub is Coast Silktassel *(Garrya elliptica),* with its wealth of decorative winter catkins. Two others that have been used occasionally on walls are Tree Anemone *(Carpenteria californica)* and Alderleaf Mountain Mahogany *(Cercocarpus betuloides* var. *blanchaea).* The Mountain Mahogany is particularly attractive trained on a house wall where it provides an open, leafy framework.

Natives for Hedges, Screens, Dividers

The use of native shrubs and trees for hedges, screens, and dividers is not well documented. Plants used for hedges should have firm, evergreen foliage and should take well to pruning and training. Hollyleaf Cherry *(Prunus ilicifolia)* is an outstanding example. It has long been used for hedges and is adaptable to twice yearly pruning. The related Catalina Cherry *(Prunus lyonii)* is much taller and is often recommended as a tall divider. Drought-resistant candidates include selected California lilacs, manzanitas, coffeeberries, and one or two of the evergreen sumacs. Wax Myrtle *(Myrica californica),* with its rich, dark green leaves, makes a fine dense hedge for moist situations. For many years the Monterey Cypress *(Cupressus macrocarpa)* has been used to provide a windbreak for row crops. Thorough testing of other natives, small conifers, broad-leaved plants, and possibly a few deciduous ones, will provide us with additional reliable material for hedges, dividers, or background.

Natives for Specimen
or Accent Plants

A number of evergreen shrubs and small trees of uniform growth rate already mentioned may be used for these purposes. Two of these are the Tree Anemone *(Carpenteria californica)* with its wealth of white saucer-flowers and Southern Fremontia *(Fremontadendron mexicanum)* or one of its new forms which are almost everblooming. Summer Holly *(Comarostaphylos diversifolia)* is valuable for its red berries against firm, dark green foliage, as is the Toyon whose large berry clusters remain intact through the winter. The large buckwheat, St. Catherine's Lace *(Eriogonum giganteum),* provides spectacular, flat sprays of oyster white flowers, and the selected Sentinel Manzanita *(Arctostaphylos densiflora* 'Sentinel') is valued for an abundance of pearly pink flowers in February.

Ground Covers

Low-growing native shrubs and perennials of quite dense habit are suitable, and a number have become popular ground covers. Plants used for this purpose should be neat through the seasons, have foliage of firm substance, and pleasing shades of green. Some are native to dry hills and may be used with drought-tolerant materials, while others are woodland plants, suitable for shaded areas. Foremost is the wide assortment of selections and cultivars of manzanita and California lilac, creeping or mat-forming plants useful in home gardens as well as for large-scale landscaping. Some of these native ground covers may also be used for edging, curbings, and parking strips, as well as for ground or slope covers where grass cannot be used.

Good Companions

Throughout this book many pleasing and compatible plant combinations are described from my gardening experiences. Some are groupings of natives entirely; others combine native plants with old garden favorites. Combinations are almost unlimited and seasoned gardeners will have worked out their own favorite compatible groups. A spring garden under deciduous trees should have a selection of Pacific irises in delicate colors to complement primroses, violets, and scillas. Ancient oak trees deserve thoughtful underplanting. The choices from among natives are numerous, but Pt. Reyes Ceanothus *(Ceanothus gloriosus)* and Evergreen Currant *(Ribes viburnifolium)* are especially appropriate. The large yellow daisies of Sea Dahlia *(Coreopsis maritima)* with the vivid blue of California Gilia *(Gilia achillaefolia)* form an equally colorful and sparkling combination in a sunny border. My summer dry border gains a rare luminous quality from the combination of its rich blue-purple bells of Elegant Brodiaea *(Brodiaea elegans)* with Azure Penstemon *(Penstemon azureus),* whose flowers are a similar shade. An engaging and colorful combination occurred one autumn when a late planting of Desert Bells *(Phacelia campanularia)* provided a vivid blue carpet under a birch just as its leaves turned pale gold. Many other groupings can be worked out by massed plantings of a single color or combination of flower colors, or with contrasting foliage colors and shapes.

Dry Garden

Rather than invent a dry border, I will describe my semi-dry one as so-far developed in my mountain property at 3,000 feet elevation in the northwest Coast Ranges. This section is about 90 feet long and 24 feet wide, has a southwestern tilt, and is in sun for most of the day. With one or two exceptions it is an all-native border, designed chiefly to test the drought tolerance of desirable local natives and others with the same qualifications from elsewhere. Planting is far from complete and probably never will be. I have plans for adding several species of *Eriogonum* (buckwheat), among others which will be compatible with the existing plants.

The plants that originally grew here include Bowl-Tubed Iris *(Iris macrosiphon),* Slender Iris *(I. tenuissima),* California Goldenrod *(Solidago californica),* Coyote Mint *(Monardella villosa),* and two young Madrones *(Arbutus menziesii).* Several local manzanitas have appeared and flourished, including Green Manzanita *(Arctostaphylos patula),* Hoary Manzanita *(A. canescens)* (see Pl. 5B), and Common Manzanita *(A. manzanita).* Here and there are volunteer Garry Oaks *(Quercus garryana)* planted by gray squirrels and still slender with a few short, side branches. Handfalls of the dainty Tolmie's Star Tulip *(Calochortus tolmiei)* occur here and there, and will eventually be gathered to the front of the border and planted between iris clumps. Also tiny, but with flowers in bright yellow, is the Sierra Star Tulip *(C. monophylla),* planted a few years ago near a violet-blue Bowl-Tubed Iris.

A few rooted cuttings of Creeping Sage *(Salvia sonomensis)* were set out here, and now meander extensively through the foreground plantings. They require some clipping when they threaten to overrun other plants. Three lupines, one evergreen and two herbaceous, have performed very well. Two of them flower over a long period, from early May into June. First is Silver Circle Lupine *(Lupinus albifrons* ssp. *flumineus),* evergreen and mat-forming, with small, silky, pale green leaves and solid spikes of blue-purple flowers. Second is another local species, Broadleaf Lupine *(L. latifolius),* a pleasant, free-flowering plant with many spikes in shades of medium to pale blue. Locally it inhabits forested flats, and several varieties are widely distributed in the state. The third is not common in California and not quite so adaptable, except under almost totally dry conditions. This is Felted Lupine *(L. leucophyllus),* whose every part is furry-silky with shaggy hairs and with stout, white-felted stems. It should be used more for its handsome foliage than for its flowers, which are a nondescript pinkish or lavender and age almost immediately to a rusty brown.

Through all of this area, rich and vibrant shades of blue are provided by five kinds of penstemon, including the sparkling Azure Penstemon *(Penstemon azureus),* the dependable Foothill Penstemon *(P. heterophyllus),* a similar local form, New Penstemon *(P. neotericus),* and the Small Azure Penstemon *(P. parvulus).* To the rear rises the tall, spectacular Palmer's Penstemon *(P. palmeri),* with its large, tubular flowers in clear shades of pink. In addition to these plants that have value for interesting foliage and well-colored flowers, this border is also a treasury of precious native bulbs. Most of them thrive here with sun, lean soil, and a dormant period in late summer. Several mariposa tulips were brought from my former garden, including White Mariposa Lily *(Calochortus venustus)* and the bright yellow Gold Nuggets *(C. luteus)*. These bulbs, a few kinds of brodiaeas, and a small colony of Scarlet Fritillary *(Fritillaria recurva),* are content with the well-drained soil and a minimum of water. Several species of wild onions *(Allium)* will be added when I can obtain them. Toward the far end of the border, receiving practically no water, are three spreading plants of Western Squaw Carpet *(Ceanothus prostratus* var. *occidentalis).* Two were grown from cuttings and one from seed, all from plants which decorate dry road banks at about 4,000 feet elevation. They began to flower and set seed after about the third year of growth. This variety is very similar to the Sierra form, with the same lustrous, dark green, toothed leaves, only slightly smaller, and the same rounded flower clusters, varying from white, to lavender, and to deep violet-blue.

My object in keeping water to a minimum in this border is to learn how plants will perform. I water it deeply every two weeks, from the end of the rainy season until mid-July, allowing for seed setting. By late August most plants appear a bit taggy, the Broadleaf Lupine has long since gone dormant, and the penstemons do not provide a second blooming as they might with ample water through the summer. I call this border semi-dry because it does have some summer water, but only about half the amount usually given to a flower border. For my purposes it is nearly self-sufficient and requires little attention except for removal of dead flowers and foliage.

Coastal Garden

Another native garden is well under way in a different situation, near the coast of southern California. It is on a west-northwest slope with sun most of the day, and receives a minimum of water. Several California lilacs, particularly *Ceanothus papillosus* var. *roweanus* × *impressus* 'Concha', form an almost solid background with bright blue flower clusters in spring set off by the yellow daisies of Sea Dahlia *(Coreopsis maritima),* and orange California Poppies *(Eschoscholzia californica).* Selected native iris bloom four to five months of the year, and provide enough seedlings to cover large spaces. There is a surprising assortment of shrubs, each with some feature of special interest: Bladder-Pod *(Isomeris arborea)* with a long blooming period followed by large, inflated pods; Island Bush Poppy with a long season of open, clear yellow flowers; and two sages, Cleveland's Sage *(Salvia clevelandii)* and Purple Sage *(S. leucophylla),* with bright blue or purple flowers and pungently fragrant foliage. Some deciduous shrubs provide early flowers, including the Fuchsia-Flowered Gooseberry *(Ribes speciosum)* and Red Flowering Currant *(R. sanguineum).* Although the gardener has used a variety of native annuals among the permanent plantings, these have not reseeded as expected, and are gradually being replaced by a selected form of Coyote Brush *(Baccharis pilularis* 'Twin Peaks'). It is fast growing, with or without water, and is considered to be indestructible. Other shrubs and perennials are used in this garden, but the ones described above are among the easiest to grow in this area and of the greatest ornamental value.

Natural Gardens

Recent books and articles dealing with natural, or semi-wild, gardens show the trend toward a wider use of native plants. A natural garden is informal; it departs from strictly mathematical beds and borders. Such a garden should not be unrestrained, but should follow a pattern, even if not a formal design. A natural garden could be a shady plot under an old oak tree with native woodland plants, or it could be a series of gravelly mounds on which species and cultivars of *Ceanothus* will find sun and well-drained soil to their liking. For most gardeners a feeling of naturalness comes from curving paths, open spaces alternating with thickets of evergreen and deciduous shrubs, and firm-leaved, native ground covers in place of grass or ivy. It is easier to develop a natural garden around remnants of the native flora, but one can be completely planned by a thoughtful choice from among the native materials suggested in the coming chapters.

Descriptions of a few gardens with a minimum of development, except for a certain amount of clearing and replanting, may inspire similar, natural-type gardens. In the Tahoe area along the Truckee River, there was a summer home which I visited often. The garden was simple in design with a clover lawn dipping toward the river, and with several clumps of Quaking Aspen *(Populus tremuloides),* which had been retained when the property was first cleared. Against a boulder was a spreading currant *(Ribes* sp.), whose round, scalloped leaves became a delicate golden yellow in autumn. Each summer the owners brought flats of exotic plants, including brilliant blue delphiniums, yellow and orange Iceland poppies, and assorted pansies, and concentrated them in a wide border. These plants flowered all summer, providing a dazzling splash of color in an otherwise quiet setting.

In a chaparral-like area near Santa Barbara, a large garden was developed from a wilderness of stunted live oaks *(Quercus agrifolia).* After some removal and thinning of the oaks, beds and borders of various sizes were carved out. They were connected by curving paths to bring new vistas and sometimes surprising plant combinations at each turn. A near-complete collection of species and cultivars of California lilacs was used along with other kinds of shrubs, hardy perennials, bulbs, annuals, and native succulents, resulting in a delightful, all-California garden.

Another kind of natural garden was developed in the San Bernardino Mountains, where a minimum of brush was removed to encourage other existing plants. Large colonies of Southern Hartweg's Iris *(Iris hartwegii* ssp. *australis)* bloom abundantly among the shrubs in spring. In autumn large patches of California Fuchsia *(Zauschneria californica* ssp. *latifolia)* produce a long succession of fiery red trumpets. Other plants which provide beautiful and often spectacular flowers include Rocky Mountain Iris *(Iris missouriensis),* tall stalks of Bloomer's Tiger Lily *(Lilium humboldtii* var. *bloomerianum),* and the fragrant Lemon Lily *(L. parryi),* all set off by Giant Red Paintbrush *(Castilleja miniata).* Many other local native plants provide interesting flowers and foliage with only a little encouragement from the owners.

In practically every region of California similar gardens can be made with local natives enhanced by further selections to suit the situation and garden design. Suggested plantings for some areas not already described here will be found in the listings, such as for deserts, seashore, etc. However, this book does not encompass all of the regions of California, each with its special soil, growing conditions, microclimates, and other factors. The methods in this book can be applied anywhere, from the arid Modoc Plateau to the perpetually moist redwood forest, using the radically different kinds of local native plants. A tremendous accumulation of garden records would be necessary to predict which plants would be adaptable to all regions. Where there are no records of garden experiences, only general directions for growing natives can be given.

3. PROPAGATION OF NATIVE PLANTS

Native plants can be propagated by seeds, cuttings, offsets, division of roots, layering, and grafting. Some native plants have become rare or even close to extinction, and propagating materials must be used to best advantage to obtain the maximum number of new plants. Digging wild plants from their natural habitat is against the law, and it is often needlessly destructive. Digging can deprive both would-be growers and nature of the seed that would have been produced. Many people think that native plants are hard to grow from seed, but this is true of only a few whose seeds have been conditioned by nature to withstand easy germination. For most native plants, reproduction from seed is the easiest way, but other methods will also be discussed.

PROPAGATION BY SEED

For several reasons, growing plants from seed is the most important method of reproduction. It is often the only way to obtain a desirable native plant. From seed, plants can be produced in quantity, and there is always the possibility of obtaining superior forms from crosses. Each seed holds the miraculous possibility for a new flower color, for a new leaf type, texture, or color, and even for a new plant size or shape.

Seed Collecting

Learning to recognize garden-worthy natives by their seed vessels, and to collect seed at the best time, can be an adventure and not just a practical necessity. Seeds of many native plants are available from specialists, and sometimes from general seed catalogs. But a wealth of fine and useful trees, shrubs, perennials, annuals, and bulbs can be obtained only by collecting their seeds in the wild. Mark well the plant from which seed is to be collected because when out of flower it seems to disappear completely. It is hard to believe that the extensive colonies of silky pink Grand Linanthus *(Linanthus grandiflorus),* so conspicuous in April, can leave hardly a trace by July. Mark the plant with strips of colored cloth and with wooden stakes. To avoid losing particularly precious seeds, tie cheesecloth or paper bags over the seed vessel. Many seeds can be collected directly into paper bags, and these should be labeled immediately. The serious collector will always carry a notebook to record the location of plants for later seed collecting. Shrubs with bright berries are easily seen but birds and small animals may find them first, so they too should be protected with bags, or collected promptly.

Each seed vessel has its own manner of opening and of seed dispersal. Most annuals ripen their seed quickly when temperatures rise. Others with larger vessels may take longer, but are apt to burst or explode when the seeds are ripe, and a few have silky tails that carry the seeds far and wide. Determining the time of seed ripening requires close attention. Vessels should be plump and the seed well formed before they are gathered. Seed does not have to be completely ripe. If it is not, cut the vessel with a few inches of stem and allow it to complete ripening in a paper bag. For a few immature vessels, immerse the stems in 6 oz. of water to which a teaspoon of sugar has been added to complete the ripening process.

Handling and Storing Seed

Collected seed should be thoroughly dried, put into containers, labeled, and dated. To dry small quantities of seed, spread the vessels on papers, out of the wind until the vessels have opened. Remove leaves, stems, or bits of the seed vessel by shaking in a coarse sieve, allowing the seed to fall on fresh papers. Seed can then be put in a clean container. For large pods or large quantities of seed, place them in paper bags until the vessel opens, sort, and place in containers. For fleshy fruits, such as berries or drupes, soak for an hour or so, and then work in a sieve under running water to remove the pulp.

This frees the seed which may be planted immediately, or dried and stored. Inspect the bags in which seed vessels are being dried; some pods may contain insects who will devour the contents. A pinch of dry captan will discourage insects and fungus if these are present in the seed vessels. Always be certain that the seed is thoroughly dry before storing. If it must be held for more than one season, store it in polyethylene bags in the refrigerator. Containers for storage may be small paper bags, pill bottles, boxes, covered cans, or coin envelopes.

Seed Germination

Growing any plant from seed begins with its germination, and the gardener will soon discover that the time required varies among the species. Germination of seed depends upon several factors: whether the seed remains viable over a long period or must be used fresh; whether it germinates readily or with difficulty; and what pretreatment is required for seeds that resist germination. Observation of how seed germinates in the wild will give you clues on procedure. Alternate freezing and thawing, wetting and drying, buffeting of seed by wind and rain, and fire are some of the ways that seed coats are penetrated. To these can be added cold stratification, hot water, and chemicals. In some cases a combination of two methods may be necessary.

General Guidelines

A large proportion of native plants germinate readily without pretreatment of seed, including practically all annuals, many perennials and biennials, most of the bulb plants, and some of the shrubs and trees. These can be planted by direct seeding where wanted in the garden, or in prepared outdoor beds. Best results come from planting in autumn during the rainy season when a high percent of seed germination can be expected. Volunteer plants often appear from established plants, indicating that the species has accepted the conditions of cultivation. The reader is urged to consult the manuals and leaflets on propagation for further details, and for germination tables.

Seed Scarification

This method is used to break the seed coat of some members of the legume family. It consists of rubbing small amounts of seed between two pieces of coarse sandpaper. Seed may also be mixed with coarse sand and shaken vigorously in a jar, and then planted directly into the garden. Large seed may be perforated with a file or knife, but be careful not to injure the embryo.

Hot-Water Treatment

In this method water is heated to 180°F., the seed is dropped in, and allowed to cool and soak for 12 to 24 hours. Following this the seed must be planted immediately. Seed of redbud generally responds to this treatment with good germination.

Burning Treatment

Plant the seed in a flat as usual, and over it spread pine needles or excelsior, set it afire, and allow to burn down. Water well after the flat has cooled somewhat. This method is used for manzanita seed and others with very hard coats, but is not entirely dependable.

Mulching

This is a new method in which the planted flat is covered with a thick mulch of wood shavings (not redwood or cedar), to which compost starter has been added. The flat can either be kept moist, or allowed to dry out in the summer and then watered again in the autumn. Seed of certain of the manzanitas are said to respond to this treatment. For other seed which may be slow to germinate, allowing the flat to remain open to the elements and seasonal changes can aid in its germination.

Cold Stratification

Internal dormancy is a problem with seed of certain species and cold stratification often helps to overcome this. Mix the seed with moist sand, peat moss, or sphagnum moss, place in plastic bags or foil, close, and date. Check for moisture of the medium and for swelling of the seed, which indicates that it is ready to germinate. Once this has happened, plant immediately in flats or pots.

Acid Treatment

Seed with exceptionally tough coats may have to be treated with an acid before the coat can be penetrated and germination can begin. This is a method for professional propagators only, and complete directions are given in *Collecting and Handling Seeds of Wild Plants,* by Mirov and Kraebel, 1939.

Soil Mixtures

Most of the wild plants of California tolerate wide variations in soil, so special mixes are seldom required. A standard mixture of equal parts of loam, sand, and peat is suitable for the majority of seed. Well-composted organic materials or leaf mold may be used in place of the peat. They should be worked through a ½-inch screen, and thoroughly mixed with the other ingredients. Near planting time, fill flats or pots according to the amount of seed to be planted, and scald them with boiling water to kill insects and start the germination of weed seeds. Allow the soil to drain and work it with a hand fork or trowel, repeating the scalding if it seems necessary. This wetting and working of the soil helps to refine it, as well as to destroy the germinating weed seed. To plant seed reputed to be difficult or subject to damping-off, sterilization of the soil may be necessary. Put the soil in shallow pans and then in the oven set at 180°F. and allow to remain for thirty minutes. Chemical sterilizing agents may also be used, and directions should be followed carefully. Pots, flats, and garden tools should also be sterilized ideally; a common household bleach may be used. Certain of the natives may require additions to the standard soil mix, such as a trowel of coarse sand to a pot of soil for chaparral plants, and extra leaf mold for woodland plants. Native ferns, orchids, and a few alpine plants benefit from a mixture of peat or screened sphagnum moss mixed with medium fine sand.

Seed Planting

The soil should be moist but not sticky or gummy for seed planting. Smooth and firm the soil; make it evenly distributed in the flat, and about one inch below the rim of the flat or pot. Scatter the seed thinly or sow in rows. Cover it with the soil mixture, very lightly for fine seed, more for large ones, so that

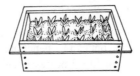

Figure 1 Flat of seedlings

the seed is no longer visible. A light covering of milled sphagnum moss is often recommended for very fine seed. To water, immerse the container allowing the water to be drawn up through the soil with no disturbance of the seed. Cover the container with glass and then newspaper, and check frequently. As soon as the seed begins to germinate, remove the paper and raise the glass slightly. As growth continues, the glass should gradually be raised higher and finally removed. As soon as green leaves show, put the flats where they get morning sun; afternoon sun may scald the young foliage. If the container cannot be moved, shade it with a lath frame or old window screens. Sow seed of plants that resent transplanting in fiber pots, and plunge them in a large box filled with damp sawdust. When plants are of the correct size and roots are showing through the pot, they can be planted in their permanent quarters. It may be necessary to remove the bottom of the fiber pot because it sometimes prevents free drainage of water. Shrubs and strong-growing perennials that make long tap roots should not be grown in fiber pots, but rather in deep clay pots or cans.

Transplanting

When seedlings have a second or third pair of leaves, they are transplanted to individual clay or fiber pots, to another flat, or for shrubs and trees, into gallon cans. Use the standard soil mix recommended for the first seeding. Have the containers and soil ready, and transplant young seedlings quickly, removing only a few at a time to prevent drying of the tender rootlets. Water thoroughly after transplanting, and keep shaded for a few days or until danger of wilt has passed. Although fertilizer is seldom necessary for natives, a little bone meal may be used for strong-growing shrubs and perennials after they are established.

Most perennials seeded in early autumn will be of proper size to go into the garden border in eight to ten months. Do not allow trees and large shrubs to remain in containers until the roots curl around the bottom; this greatly inhibits their growth when planted out. Any special directions are given with the description of individual plants in the following chapters.

Cold Frame

Sheltered places, such as a covered bench or cold frame, are needed to propagate plants from seed or cuttings. The most useful is the cold frame which can be placed against a fence or the wall of a building. It should have plenty of light but not direct sunlight. My frame was built against the garden house wall. It was about 10 feet long, 2½ feet wide, and 18 inches deep. Old window frames covered with plastic were hinged to the wall and lowered during cold weather, or for added protection of young plants. One side was partially filled with well-moistened sawdust, into which pots of young seedlings were plunged. The other half contained potting soil, and enough room for about ten short rows of seedlings. Into this I put seed of wild bulbs, lilies, wild irises, or any plant which required extra care and attention. Such sheltered places can be of any size to suit the gardener. A small bench roofed with lath is enough for most home gardening. For small quantities of seedlings or cuttings, cover the flat with a frame of equal size to which plastic has been attached, raising the cover as needed for light and air. This is one way to shelter fern spores until they germinate.

Figure 2 Small cold frame

Figure 3 Frame with lath cover

Outdoor Propagating Bed

A long, narrow bed is best for growing large quantities of seed. The bed can be of almost any size, mine is 4 feet long, 2½ feet wide, and 18 inches deep. Redwood side boards extend about two inches above the ground level, and ½-inch wire screen is placed on the bottom to keep out gophers. To protect young seedlings from being scratched out by birds, use a light frame covered with wire mesh. Such a frame is easily removed for weeding, thinning seedlings and watering. A standard, friable soil mixture is used, and my bed takes three to four wheelbarrows full. In this outdoor bed I have grown several species of *Calochortus, Brodiaea, Fritillaria,* and *Lilium.* The great advantage of this bed is that young plants can remain undisturbed until a mature bulb of flowering size has formed.

Damping-Off

Seedlings of many plants are subject to damping-off fungi. Keeping all tools, the work bench, and containers clean will reduce this danger; a solution of one part clorox to five of water can be used. Damping-off fungi attack the young seedling stem at ground level, and cause wilting and eventual death. Excessive water, lack of air circulation, or a sudden rise in temperature contributes to this condition. Plants should be watered in the morning, and horticulturists recommend putting a layer of washed sand over the soil. As a further precaution professional growers recommend using one of several fungicides now on the market: Benlate, Truban, or Banrot, used carefully according to directions on the package. The planting medium should be sterilized according to directions already given, or with a chemical sterilant, such as Vapam or Panodrench.

PROPAGATION BY CUTTINGS

Plants propagated by rooting cuttings reach maturity faster than they do from seed. Rooting is also the only way to increase stocks of plants which might not reproduce their desirable qualities from seed. Many kinds of woody, semi-woody, and even herbaceous plants can be induced to root under the right conditions. These include taking cuttings at the correct time and using hormones, a sterile rooting medium, and bottom heat and misting for some that are difficult to root.

The correct time of year for taking cuttings varies with each plant. It is important to make cuttings from unflowered, vigorous, healthy tips. Take tip pieces of three inches, removing the leaves from the lower portion. A rooting hormone may be used; follow directions on the label carefully. Various combinations may be used for the rooting medium, but a mixture of equal parts of clean, sharp sand and peat moss is the most universally favored. Vermiculite or perlite is sometimes used in place of sand with peat or sphagnum moss. Pure sand or sandy loam is also sometimes used.

Place the medium in shallow pots, boxes, or any container to suit the number of cuttings, and place in a glass house or closed frame, or cover with polyethylene. A good method for the home gardener who has only a few cuttings is to use a shallow, five- or six-inch pot, covered with a wide-mouth glass jar. An electric seed bed heater, available in several sizes, can be obtained when bottom heat is required. Some cuttings will not root without bottom heat, in others the rooting will be very slow. Cuttings should always have good light, but not direct sunlight.

Figure 4 Pot of cuttings, plastic cover

Figure 5 Cuttings in pot with inverted glass jar

As soon as sturdy roots have formed, transplant cuttings into containers of standard soil mix. In a few cases, where a good root system has already formed, transplant directly into the garden. Water thoroughly and protect the young plants with a tent of shingles until danger of wilt has passed. Keep newly potted plants in a cool place for a few days, then gradually bring to the light. When new roots show through the bottom hole, the plant is ready to set into a permanent garden spot. The complete process of rooting, transplanting, and final planting may take up to a year for woody plants, or possibly more if the cutting was slow to root.

Semi-Woody Cuttings

Rooting of semi-woody or herbaceous materials is usually faster and more successful than for woody plants. The procedures are the same. Several popular garden perennials are in this category, including species of *Penstemon, Monardella, Potentilla, Salvia,* and *Mimulus.* Cuttings taken from the thick, woody caudex of *Heuchera* species will root and provide a new plant within a year's time. A long list of native shrubs, both evergreen and deciduous, will root from tip cuttings, some requiring bottom heat and misting, others rooting readily with only the minimum of protection.

Rooting Conifers

Many coniferous trees may be propagated from cuttings, although most are slow to root and require the most favorable conditions. Port-Orford Cedar roots readily from three-inch pieces placed in a cold frame. Conifers which will root with

Figure 6 Cutting in pot with plastic cover

bottom heat include Macnab Cypress, Incense Cedar, Monterey Pine, and junipers. Even under ideal conditions these conifer cuttings will take four months or longer to root.

PROPAGATION BY DIVISIONS OR OFF-SETS

Any plant that forms rooted off-sets or natural divisions may be separated and replanted at the proper time, generally in early spring. Examples of natives in this category include aster, evening primrose, iris, phlox, strawberry, violet, and others. A polemonium separates naturally into fleshy, rooted pieces. Pacific Bleeding Heart *(Dicentra formosa)* and Northern Inside-Out Flower *(Vancouveria hexandra)* are two which quickly form extensive mats of rooted divisions. Several well-flowered kinds of rock cresses (*Arabis* spp.) form semi-woody crowns that may be detached for new plants. Snowberry *(Symphoricarpos rivularis)* and Oso-Berry *(Osmaronia cerasiformis)* are native shrubs that form removable, rooted sections.

PROPAGATION BY LAYERING

Layering is a method of increasing plants by pegging a branch firmly to the ground until roots form. Rooted pieces are then detached from the main plant, and replanted where wanted. Layering should be used for plants that are known to root in this manner, and that produce branches at or near the ground level. One of the joys of gardening is to discover a layered piece which often occurs naturally in moist, semi-shaded areas and especially where there is a build-up of leaf mold. Trailing manzanitas, California lilacs, and the Evergreen Currant *(Ribes viburnifolium)* frequently provide increase of plants in this manner.

GRAFTING

Experiments have been conducted in grafting certain natives that have sensitive root systems. There has been some success in grafting the beautiful Mountain Dogwood *(Cornus nuttallii)* onto roots of the Asian Dogwood *(Cornus capitata)*. Efforts to cultivate the native dogwood have often failed because of its touchy root system and sensitivity to lack of drainage and to fungus attacks of the lower trunk and roots. The Toyon is sometimes grafted onto roots of the quince for the same reason, although it is not nearly as sensitive as the dogwood.

CONCLUSION

Professional growers use greenhouses, propagating beds with bottom heat, and misting devices to insure good seed germination and rooting of cuttings. The suggestions and directions given here for propagating native plants are geared particularly to the home gardener. Most gardeners can provide some measure of protection by light-weight frames, lath shelters, or plastic covers, and a few may even construct their own misting devices.

4. CULTURE OF NATIVE PLANTS

The native plants of California are tremendously diverse. Because they evolved in a wide variety of soils and climates, they cannot all be given the same cultural treatment. But many of these plants, even those native to dry hills and chaparral, show a surprising tolerance to average garden conditions. The varied responses of native plants to cultivation are a challenge to gardeners and horticulturists. Each unfamiliar plant must be tested for its individual merits and its adaptability.

PRELIMINARY CONSIDERATIONS

Bringing a wild plant into cultivation usually takes many years of careful work, beginning with observation of its natural habitat, preference for sun or shade, and other vital factors. When selecting a wild plant to work on, attention should be given to all-season appearance, to the best time to collect seed, and to germination tests and other methods of propagation. If the plant has been judged worthy of these efforts, then its ornamental and useful qualities can be further tested. Plants with superior qualities for gardens have often been produced by crossing with other species, or by back-crossing with a natural hybrid or with a chance seedling which has already exhibited some desirable trait. Twenty years or more of breeding experiments may be needed to explore the full potential of a wild plant. Home gardeners can contribute to the development of better garden uses of native plants by keeping records of their own experiments.

STEPS IN CULTURE

When trying to grow any relatively unknown plant, you must consider many aspects of its culture. These include water and drainage, drought resistance, soil, dormancy, exposure, root system, pruning and training, disease, cold tolerance, situation, rate of growth, longevity, and adaptability.

Water and Drainage

Water and soil drainage must be considered together since too much water and poorly drained soils are the most frequent causes of failure in the culture of native plants. Most natives may be watered freely during their periods of most active growth, provided that there is no danger of standing water. A large proportion of natives are tolerant or resistant to drought because most of California has long, rainless summers. Any plant that is being transplanted, or moved from one place to another, must have water and attention until the danger of wilt has passed. Thereafter, water is necessary only to ensure that the plant is growing properly. As a rule, for trees, shrubs, and the tough perennials, a deep watering once or twice a month for the first two years is sufficient. Of course, the type of soil, the amount of organic materials that have been added, and the rate of growth are all factors to be considered. Sandy or gravelly, fast-draining soils require more frequent watering than clay soils. If moving or transplanting is done during the rainy months, much less watering will be necessary.

Setting out trees and shrubs known to resent wet soil or mud against their trunks may present another problem in watering. If the newly worked soil has not had time to settle, the plant is pulled down below the soil line after it is planted, allowing water-borne molds, or other types of disease, to attack the trunk, and the plant will not survive. To avoid this prepare the planting hole a few days ahead, fill it with water, and allow the water to seep in and settle the soil. To water newly set out plants, construct a shallow basin and allow water to flow in slowly, but open the basin during the winter so that there is no danger of standing water. These measures tend to induce deep rooting and prepare the plant to become drought-resistant. Light sprinkling may cause surface rooting and is never recommended. Plants which are native to wet meadows, bogs, streambanks, or foggy regions may be watered throughout the year. For some natives, unaccustomed amounts of water tend to cause leggy growth and too much foliage at the expense of flowers.

Drought Tolerance

A drought-resistant plant is one accustomed to no water beyond that provided by the rains. However, if it is available, some summer water should be given to ensure flowering and seed setting, and to keep the plant and its foliage attractive during the dry season. The importance of practicing water economy in gardening was recognized during the dry periods of the 1970s. There are several ways to save water and still keep plants alive. One is to mulch plants during the dry periods, making certain that the ground is well watered before applying the mulching material. Another measure is to hand water any plants in critical need, rather than a whole area. Applying water by slow irrigation, or by the drip method, are other methods of getting water directly where it is needed.

Observation of plants in the wilds during this dry period showed that most dry land species accepted unaccustomed drought without permanent damage, although in some cases there was wilting, early drop of foliage, or an early dormant period. Until native plants which are thought to be resistant to dryness are thoroughly tested, they should be watched carefully in the garden and given water if there is severe wilting.

Soil

The soils in California are diverse and complex. They include silts, sandy loams, stiff clays, adobe, and conglomerates. Most California soils are neutral to alkaline, and are often low in organic content. Some are rocky and infertile, while those of woodlands and forests may be mildly acid and more friable. Practically all soils will benefit from incorporating organic materials, as discussed above, on page 38. The addition of such materials makes the soil easier to work, adds beneficial nutrients, aids in water retention, and helps to promote bacterial action in the soil. Clay and adobe soils have a high water-holding capacity, but poor drainage and aeration. These soils should be worked when slightly moist, and the addition of organic materials and gypsum will help to improve their workability. Most native plants do not seem to have an absolute soil preference, except for those which grow in bogs, in serpentine areas, in decomposed volcanic rock, or in decomposed granite. The lovely Sagebrush Mariposa *(Calochortus macrocarpus)* appears to prefer volcanic soil because it seldom persists elsewhere.

Dormancy

Dormancy is a ripening and hardening process during which the plant shows little activity while its vital processes are renewed for the next growing season. Dormancy is an exacting requirement of many bulbs, corms, and deep-rooted plants. If water is given during the dormant period, the underground parts are apt to rot.

Dormancy of plants in the wilds need not always be a guide to their garden performance. Occasional watering up to the rainy season may suit some of the adaptable natives. In its native habitat the Foothill Penstemon *(Penstemon heterophyllus)* may partially die back during the heat of summer, but in gardens, with water and the removal of dead flowers, plants will retain a crisp appearance and often produce a second crop of flowers. Keeping in mind the long, rainless periods under which most plants evolved, it is a seeming miracle that so many accommodate themselves to garden conditions.

Exposure

To obtain satisfactory growth it is essential to know the requirements of each native for sun or shade. Natives that prefer shade are generally water tolerant and should be grown together, while those that prefer sun and dryness should be grown in another section of the garden. Refer to the chapter on listings by situation for where each native will perform best.

For a few natives, exposure includes direction as well as the amount of sun. In east-facing locations the plants are accustomed to morning light, and may be burned by afternoon sun. There is little recorded information on this subject, although rock gardeners are aware of the problem and sometimes place plants in front of boulders, in warm pockets, or on artificial ledges. Another aspect of exposure is microclimate, particularly small areas where shelter moderates the prevailing climate. Unfavorable microclimates, such as frost pockets or small drafty areas, should be avoided.

Root System

California native plants provide examples of almost every kind of root system, including bulbs, corms, rhizomes, tubers, thickened root stocks, thin, often straggly systems, and some with fibrous roots. Many natives which grow in arid places have deep, often thick, storage roots, that can range widely in search of moisture. Knowledge of a plant's root system is especially necessary for transplanting because the root system may be extensive even though the top growth is only a few inches high. This is usually the case with seedling trees, shrubs, and certain perennials whose roots may be three times more extensive than the top growth. When transplanting young seedling trees and shrubs, the tip of the tap root should be pinched off to discourage coiling of the root while in containers. A few natives, such as poppies, lupines, and others, resent root disturbance, and their seed should be planted directly where wanted. Acquaintance with root systems comes with experience in handling plants, although description of the type of root for each plant can usually be obtained from botany books.

Pruning and Training

Pruning and training has been a somewhat neglected aspect of native plant culture, but records of experiments are now being accumulated. A few native plants resent severe pruning. For most plants, training begins during the first year with pinching of tip growth, or the removal of inner or crossing limbs. Certain evergreen shrubs, especially species of *Ceanothus,* are known to suffer die-back following removal of large limbs of ½–1 inch or more. Such removal should be done in dry rather than wet weather as the chance of infection seems less.

A new and interesting practice is to train large evergreen shrubs into slender trees for use in small gardens. This is accomplished by gradual removal of limbs from the lower trunk, and a few inner ones if an open effect is desired.

Most deciduous shrubs are apt to have vigorous and often ungainly growth and require considerable pruning and sometimes thinning. I was able, by removal of lower limbs and some trimming of the top growth, to train a Smooth Dogwood *(Cornus glabrata)* into a small tree with an umbrella-like crown. For large, old trees such as live oaks, it is best to have professional tree surgery where old limbs or decayed wood must be cut out. In my experience most native plants can be pruned with no harm.

Disease

Native plants are subject to the same sorts of diseases, blights, insects, and pests which affect all plants. The idea persists that natives are more disease prone when brought into gardens, but in my experience a healthy plant, grown with respect for its requirements, is seldom susceptible. Of course chewing and sucking insects are likely to be present on any tasty plant, and scale insects fasten onto woody limbs. For these a regular spray program should suffice. For natives accustomed to dry, moving air, the muggy conditions brought on by too much water, or by crowding, may result in mildew or rust. Native lilaceous plants can be subject to lily diseases, but if their special requirements for well-drained soil, a minimum of water, and a dormant period for some are met, the diseases are not likely to be fatal. Conifers have their own particular pests, ranging from bark beetles to porcupines which chew the bark. If they girdle the tree it will die.

In addition to disease, air pollution affects the growth and health of plants. Most pines are moderately sensitive to certain of the pollutants, and stands of Ponderosa Pine *(Pinus ponderosa)* in southern California have been killed by them. White Fir *(Abies concolor)* and Douglas Fir *(Pseudotsuga menziesii)* are reported to be resistant to air pollution.

Cold Tolerance

Few plants can accept the cold of prolonged frost and snow in regions above that of their native habitat. With some exceptions, natives of mild coastal regions, warm valleys, and foothills will seldom persist in the cold winters of mountains. Elevation is not always the important factor, since plants growing at 4,000 feet on the west-facing slopes of the Sierra may not persist in a cold, shaded, frost-prone gulch at 3,000 feet. Low temperatures do not necessarily kill the plant, but frosts in late spring may damage emerging foliage and flower buds, or the plant may be weakened and fail to make any progress.

I discovered that Toyon, Buckeye, and Hollyleaf Cherry did not tolerate the cold of my mountain garden at 3,000 feet elevation. Nor did *Ceanothus papillosus* var. *roweanus* × *impressus* 'Concha', which has been damaged several times by late spring frosts, and after six years remains at about two feet instead of the six feet or more it would attain in a milder climate. Some native plants seem to have a built-in cold tolerance, such as Huckleberry Manzanita (*Arctostaphylos glandulosa* var. *cushingiana*), which has flourished in my mountain garden. Some protective devices can be used for tender plants, such as growing them on warm protected walls, surrounding them with lath or burlap shelters, or using thick mulches over the crown of the plant.

Situation

The most advantageous use for any plant is to place it in an appropriate setting, and with compatible companions. Plants have their limitations as well as advantages. Creeping Sage *(Salvia sonomensis)* and California Fuchsia *(Zauschneria californica)* are both excellent ground covers that can quickly cover hot slopes, but they are much too rampant for a small, watered garden. Other natives, like the Fuchsia Flowering Gooseberry *(Ribes speciosum),* have outstanding seasonal features, but it must be used where its early leaf drop will not be too apparent.

In my mountain garden I have a tall Chokecherry (*Prunus virginiana* var. *demissa*) that I admire for its many interesting features, beginning with leaf emergence in spring, followed by plumes of ivory white flowers, and bright garnet fruits in summer. Several kinds of birds, including scolding jays, quickly dispose of the berries. The suckers are a nuisance, but I dig them out of the border as part of the regular garden chores, and the ones in the lawn are kept down by the mower, giving off their distinctive almond odor in the process. This rapid-growing deciduous tree can only be recommended to those who would enjoy its advantages and not mind its untidy habits. On the other hand California Huckleberry *(Vaccinium ovatum)*, with its shiny foliage, edible berries, and a uniform growth habit, is a refined plant and quite suitable to a formal or small city garden.

Rate of Growth and Longevity

It is important to know the growth rate of a plant especially when it is to be used near a building, for hedges, or in places where space is restricted. Hybrids and natives of natural refinement can be expected to have a moderate to fast, but generally uniform growth rate. The ultimate height of trees and shrubs should be known, and may be obtained from botanical descriptions, although the figures may vary for plants under cultivation. Fortunately, forest conifers in the garden seldom attain heights that are normal for them in the wilds. First-hand information can be had by observing native plants in botanic gardens and parks, where many have been grown for fifty years or more. Longevity is a closely related factor since many natives have the undeserved reputation for being short-lived. Where known cultural methods are practiced, even the naturally short-lived California lilacs may persist for twenty years. There are published records of several that lived to thirty years or beyond.

Adaptability

An adaptable plant is able to accept conditions which vary from those of its habitat, such as more or less water, more or less sun, etc. Adaptable plants are among the easiest to grow, and seem content with almost any garden situation. Some which accept extremes of moisture and dryness include Rocky Mountain Iris *(Iris missouriensis)* and camas lilies *(Camassia* spp.). These inhabit wet meadows or stream banks, but can tolerate the dryness that frequently occurs by late summer in their natural habitat.

Some gardeners assume that all native plants are easy to

grow. But when, for various reasons, they fail to perform as expected, gardeners often become discouraged and give up trying to grow them. The reasons for failure may be incorrect planting methods, overwatering, casual treatment, and other practices which do not always suit the needs of a newly introduced plant. The gardener is likelier to be successful if the cultural methods described here are followed, since these are the accumulated experiences of horticulturists and home gardeners. This kind of gardening is quite different from traditional methods, and there is less need for water, fertilizer, and working of the soil. A well-balanced choice of native plants, with suitable companions from among old garden favorites, will produce a nearly self-sufficient, western garden.

5. GROWING WILDFLOWERS: ANNUALS

The wild annuals of California, which often occurred in spectacular displays, were once a glorious feature of the countryside. Vast unbroken flowery plains covered many areas of the state, but especially around the great Central Valley where small, but free-flowering species formed Persian carpets. Many such floral mosaics still remain, but most of them are greatly reduced. Mesas, deserts, grassy swards, seemingly bald hills, open woodlands, and sections of the coastal plains all support their particular combinations of native annuals, mostly blooming in the early spring season. Sweeping masses of poppies, lupines, and others may still be seen in some regions, such as Antelope Valley and parts of Kern County where once photographers flocked for colorful vistas. In many sections of the Coast Ranges, gold-fields and Tidy-Tips *(Layia platyglossa)* still enliven the open hills, and eastward from the north Central Valley a rich yellow carpet stretches toward the base of Mt. Lassen. Although most of these annuals require full sun, oak dells are sometimes decorated with such aristocrats as Red Ribbons Clarkia *(Clarkia concinna),* tangerine Wind Poppy *(Stylomecon heterophylla),* silken-petalled wild phlox, and the delicate spires of a collinsia.

TYPICAL COMBINATIONS

California annuals form various combinations, each typical of a particular habitat. One of my favorite oak dells was like a spread of calico in March from the flowers of an annual lupine and a gilia, each of an intense blue, punctuated with the white balls of a popcorn flower. Several kinds of owl's clovers *(Orthocarpus* spp.) fill many fields and slopes with the rose-purple of their solidly packed flower spikes. Several kinds of blue downingias and bright purple or crimson monkey flowers provide color around vernal pools and then disappear completely when the moisture is gone. The matchless turquoise cups of Baby Blue-Eyes *(Nemophila menziesii)* enhance many groupings. A classic, repeating combination of California is blue lupines with orange or yellow poppies.

IN GARDENS

Even though extensive carpets of wild annuals cannot be duplicated on nature's grand scale, it is possible to have them in groups or small colonies in gardens. Drifts of power blue Blue-Headed Gilia *(Gilia capitata)* can complement many other flower choices; Purple Chinese Houses *(Collinsia heterophylla)* makes a delicate splash of color in filtered shade; and a colony of deep blue-purple Parry's Phacelia *(Phacelia parryi)* is a choice plant for a warm pocket in the rock garden. Red Ribbons Clarkia can be used in an azalea bed to provide late season color. These and other native annuals may be used for masses of a single color, in mixtures to broadcast in open areas, for special purposes as border edgings or rock gardens, or for color among other natives.

CULTURE

Wild annuals grow readily from seed with the correct combination of sun and moisture, and few require any special treatment. Seed may be broadcast in autumn, just before the soaking rains if possible since the natural moisture seems to aid in their germination. Some experts suggest that seed be scuffed into the soil as soon as it is ripe to simulate nature's buffeting winds and pounding rain. Areas to be planted should be dug over, raked, or lightly cultivated, and as free of invasive weeds as possible. After planting the seed, rake in and make sure it is in firm contact with the soil. If there is danger of birds or animals disturbing the seeded area, it may be covered with leaves or twiggy branches or any material that does not pack into a solid cover.

Although fall seeding of native annuals is best, seed may be sown at other times of the year depending upon the garden requirements. Species of both *Phacelia* and *Collinsia* have been planted in late spring for autumn color, or to enhance or prolong some special color scheme. In high-mountain areas or where heavy frost prevails, seed of most annuals should be sown about April, except for those known to be hardy. Most wild annuals prefer lean soil and moderate amounts of water unless they are native to areas of abundant moisture. Beds may be watered during the height of the flowering period, or to prolong blooming. But too much water, especially with rich soil, causes leafiness and straggly growth at the expense of flowers. Seed of wild annuals, which are free-flowering and adaptable to cultivation, is available from several specialists.

SPECIES DESCRIPTIONS

Some of the most easily grown annuals are described below. They are arranged alphabetically by generic name.

GENUS *ABRONIA:* SAND VERBENAS
(Family Nyctaginaceae: Four O'Clock)

Ten species of *Abronia* are native to California, five of which are annuals. They are carpeting plants, mostly of deserts and coastal regions.

Abronia villosa
Desert Sand Verbena

HABIT: Branched, with stout, procumbent to ascending stems, 1–5 dm, 4–20 in. Sticky throughout. FOLIAGE: Rhombic-ovate to almost round, dark green, fleshy, and viscid. FLOWERS: Small, purplish rose, in capitate, rounded clusters. FRUIT: Conspicuous, top-shaped, winged capsule. DISTRIBUTION: Common in sandy soils, Mojave and Colorado deserts to Nevada and Arizona.

Culture: Desert Sand Verbena may be grown from seed, sown directly into sandy loam in autumn or early spring. When happily situated it is said to volunteer seedlings. Plants grow rapidly and extend to ten feet or more by flowering time. Requires full sun and will tolerate moderate amounts of water.

Estimate of Garden Value: Although this colorful ground cover has not been extensively tested away from its natural habitat, it should have the opportunity to be used for home gardens and large-scale landscaping, especially for desert and coastal gardens. Records from the Santa Ana Botanic Garden show that it has flowered for a two-month period.

GENUS *CLARKIA:* CLARKIAS
(Family Onagraceae: Evening Primrose)

There are thirty-one species of *Clarkia,* all annuals, and with two flower forms. Some with campanulate or cup-shaped flowers were formerly known as godetias, but are now included in the genus *Clarkia.* Those commonly called clarkias have wheel-shaped flowers with the petals variously slashed and lobed in a unique and attractive design. Flowers are in a wide range of warm colors, further enhanced in some by blotches or freckling of darker colors. Flower buds are pendulous in some, upright in others, while the fruits are generally upright, cylinder-shaped, and containing ample seed. (See Chart 1.)

Garden History: The free-flowering and ornamental qualities of clarkias were recognized early and many quickly became popular garden plants. Horticultural activity began as early as 1840, from seed sent to England by David Douglas and by other explorers. Selected strains of Elegant Clarkia *(C. unguiculata)* soon appeared in seed catalogs, and it continues to be a favorite bedding annual. Among the godetia group most garden forms have been derived from Herald-of-Summer *(C. amoena)* (see Fig. 7) and Ruby Chalice Clarkia *(C. rubicunda).* Horticultural selections from other species have produced the wide assortment of colors and plant sizes now available. These adaptable, free-flowering, and beautifully marked and colored annuals still remain popular garden plants. They bloom over long periods from late spring into summer, and are dependable for special color schemes.

Culture: Clarkias may be grown from seed broadcast in autumn, and again in early spring to extend the season of bloom. They may also be grown in flats, and the seedlings transplanted while young to develop a good root system. Species and selected types are adaptable, and may be used in full sun with moderate amounts of water. They are effective in

CHART 1 *Clarkia*: Clarkias

Plant	Height	Flowers	Culture	Remarks	Distribution
C. *unguiculata* Elegant Clarkia	3–10 dm (12–40 in)	Circular, lobed petals, in lavender-pink, red-purple, salmon, white. May–June.	Sun, water. Mixed plantings, borders, massed.	Selected colors and double flowers available.	Dry shade, Mendocino and San Diego to Butte and Kern cos.
C. *concinna* Red Ribbons Clarkia (see Fig. 8 and Pl. 1F)	1–3 dm (4–12 in)	4 petals slashed and lobed, bright rose-purple. May–July.	High shade, moisture, leaf mold in soil.	Shaded beds and borders, unique for lively color.	Loose soil, Siskiyou to Santa Clara and to Butte and Yuba cos.
C. *deflexa* Punchbowl Clarkia	3–9 dm (12–36 in)	Cup-shaped, delicate pink to lavender-pink, red flecks. April–June.	Sun, moderate water. Mixed flower borders, with others of genus.	Both drought and water tolerant.	Dry slopes, Monterey, Orange, and Riverside cos.
C. *purpurea* ssp. *viminea* Purple Clarkia	1–5 dm (4–19 in)	Bowl-shaped, intense rose-purple. May–July.	Sun, semi-dry. In borders, massed, and with other species.	With bulbs, annuals, perennials having same requirements.	Dry slopes, cismontane Calif.

C. amoena Herald-of-Summer	3-10 dm (12-36 in)	Cup-shaped, lavender-pink, cherry-red center. June-Aug.	Sun, moderate amounts of moisture.	Flower borders, among other species or perennials.	Bluffs on coast, Humboldt to Marin cos.
C. amoena ssp. *whitneyi* Large-Flowered Clarkia	2-5 dm (8-19 in)	Large cup, lavender-red splotch in center. June-Aug.	Sun, moderate amounts of water.	For summer color in mixed borders; massed with others of genus.	Coastal bluffs, Humboldt and Mendocino cos.
C. dudleyana Dudley's Clarkia	3-7 dm (12-29 in)	Open cup, lavender-pink, red-flecked. May-July.	Sun, water tolerant. Best seeded thickly.	Pretty with Mariposa Tulips, Elegant Clarkia.	Open hills, Tuolumne to Kern cos. and Los Angeles to Riverside cos.

Figure 7 *Clarkia amoena,* Herald-of-Summer

a flower border, or in masses, either of a single color or in mixtures. Plants flower over a long period, but seed capsules should be removed for neatness. At high elevations, or where frost continues into spring, seed should be planted about April or later. Innumerable garden combinations are possible by using clarkias with either similar or contrasting colors. The powder blue flowers of Blue-Headed Gilia *(Gilia capitata)* make a sparkling combination with one of the delicate pink or lavender godetias. Few plants have more luminous flowers than those of Red Ribbons Clarkia *(C. concinna,* see Fig. 8), which is unexcelled for shade and to interplant with azaleas.

GENUS *COLLINSIA:* COLLINSIAS
(Family Scrophulariaceae: Figwort)

There are sixteen species of *Collinsia,* all annuals, and at least one has long been a garden favorite. Some are incon-

Figure 8 *Clarkia concinna,* Red Ribbons

spicuous individually, such as Few-Flowered Collinsia *(C. sparsiflora),* but effective in masses on warm, rolling hills. All plants tend to be erect, sometimes branched, quite leafy with oblong, entire, and opposite leaves. Flowers are in whorls around the stem, or in a few cases, scattered. The blossoms have two lips, like those of snapdragons; the upper lip is cleft, and the lower is three-lobed, often jutting conspicuously.

Collinsia heterophylla
Purple Chinese Houses

HABIT: Erect, branched, 2–5 dm, 8–20 in. FOLIAGE: Lance-oblong, serrate on margins, bright green. FLOWERS: In whorls on upper stem; like small snapdragon, the upper lip white to pale lilac, the lower violet to rose-purple. (See Pl. 1D.) FRUIT: Rounded capsule, abundant seed. DISTRIBUTION: Common in shady woods, many plant communities of cismontane California.

Culture: Purple Chinese Houses can be easily grown from seed broadcast in autumn, and again in early spring to extend the season of bloom. It may also be grown in flats, transplanting seedlings to fiber pots, and set in permanent quarters in early spring. Where well established and allowed to seed, it will volunteer plants and form permanent colonies. Its requirements include high, broken shade, regular amounts of moisture, and a little humus in the soil. Plants are exceptionally free-flowering and distinctive for the "pagoda-like" inflorescence.

Estimate of Garden Value: This popular annual has a delicate charm, and may be used in a cool border, massed among trees or shrubs, in a shaded rock garden, or mixed flower border. It blooms in April and May, and when plants are robust, I have sheared them back for a second flowering. Seeded in late spring, this collinsia will provide more flowers about September.

Collinsia grandiflora
Blue Lips

HABIT: Simple to branched, 1–4 dm, 4–15 in. FOLIAGE: Oblong to obtuse, entire to crenulate. FLOWERS: In small whorls, upper lip white with pale purple tint, lower vivid violet-blue. FRUIT: Capsule. DISTRIBUTION: Open grassy or rocky places, Coastal Prairie, Mendocino and Siskiyou counties, northward.

Culture: The same as for *C. heterophylla.*

Estimate of Garden Value: A very attractive species for its well-colored flowers on low plants. May be used as a ground cover, in pockets in a cool rock garden, or as a border edging. It is water tolerant, and prefers morning sun, and high or broken shade in the afternoon.

GENUS *COREOPSIS:* TICKSEEDS
(Family Compositae: Sunflower)

Eleven species of *Coreopsis* are native to California, of which six are annuals. All have gay, bright yellow, daisy-like flowers, usually borne singly on long stems, and in generous quantities.

Coreopsis douglasii
Douglas's Coreopsis

HABIT: Erect, 5–25 cm, 2–10 in. (See Fig. 9.) FOLIAGE: Narrow, light green, basal. FLOWERS: Large, single, bright yellow, solid centers. FRUIT: Achene. DISTRIBUTION:

Figure 9 *Coreopsis douglasii,* Douglas's Coreopsis

Gravelly or rocky slopes, inner south Coast Ranges, Santa Clara to Santa Barbara counties.

Culture: Douglas's Coreopsis may be seeded thickly for an edging, or ribbon effect of bright yellow, or in patches in open areas. This species is also colorful when used with other native annuals, such as Birds-Eye Gilia *(Gilia tricolor),* tidy tips, or Cream Cups *(Platystemon californicus).* Plants bloom in March and April, but will flower earlier if seeded in autumn in sheltered places.

Estimate of Garden Value: Useful for early flowers of brilliant color and to complement other annuals of similar requirements.

Coreopsis stillmanii
Stillman's Coreopsis

HABIT: Delicate, erect annual, 10–15 cm, 4–6 in. FOLIAGE: Basal, divided into linear-spatulate lobes. FLOWERS: Orange-yellow daisies on long stems. FRUIT: Achene.

DISTRIBUTION: Grassy slopes, foothill woodland surrounding Central Valley, Butte to Tulare, and Contra Costa to Stanislaus counties.

Culture and Estimate of Garden Value: The same as for *C. douglasii.*

Coreopsis Calliopsidea
Leafystem Coreopsis

HABIT: Stout, with several stems from base, 1–5 dm, 4–20 in. FOLIAGE: Pinnately divided and redivided into linear lobes, light green. FLOWERS: Single daisies, several wide, golden yellow rays form a 2 in. flower. FRUIT: Achene. DISTRIBUTION: Dry, open, and gravelly places. Southern foothills and to desert, Alameda to San Bernardino counties.

Culture: Leafystem Coreopsis may be grown from seed, broadcast in November or December for flowers in March. Open, sunny areas and sandy loam are preferable.

Estimate of Garden Value: This bright native *coreopsis* is very effective in masses, but does not always persist in gardens.

GENUS *DOWNINGIA:* DOWNINGIAS
(Family Campanulaceae: Bellflower)

There are twelve species of *Downingia,* all annual, and they usually occur around vernal pools, marshes, and hog wallows. Downingias are famous for the masses of flowers, resembling those of lobelia, which they provide in spring. Although seldom considered as garden materials, most species have dainty flowers in good shades of blue, frequently marked in contrasting colors. Experience in growing the downingias is limited mostly to botanical gardens. Under simulated vernal pool conditions some species germinate well, but fail to reseed and die out after a few years. There is practically no record of their use in garden borders, but their flowers of quaint appearance, in nice shades of blue and purple, should make them candidates for gardens.

Downingia concolor
Fringed Downingia

HABIT: Branched from base, 5–20 cm, 2–8 in. FOLIAGE: Small, lance-shaped. FLOWERS: Tubular with two lobes, short upper ones of blue, the lower three notched, spreading, and of velvety purple. FRUIT: Capsule. DISTRIBUTION: Vernal pools, Coast Ranges, Trinity and Lake to Monterey counties, plains of Sacramento Valley.

Culture: Fringed Downingia may be sown from seed, planted thickly, in sun and with ample moisture. Recommended as border edging for spring color. Might also be tried as a pot plant.

Estimate of Garden Value: Too little is known of its response to garden conditions, but it should be used where it will not have too much competition from garden plants.

Downingia cuspidata
Toothed Downingia

HABIT: Slender, 5–25 cm, 5–9 in. FOLIAGE: Small, lanceolate. FLOWERS: Bright to pale blue or lavender, spreading lower lip with yellow spots on white inner section. May–June. FRUIT: Capsule. DISTRIBUTION: Wet and drying clay soil, Coast Ranges from Humboldt and Shasta counties to San Luis Obispo County, and Sierran foothills, Calaveras to San Diego counties.

Culture and Estimate of Garden Value: The same as for *D. concolor.*

GENUS *ESCHSCHOLZIA:* CALIFORNIA POPPIES
(Family Papaveraceae: Poppy)

Eight species of *Eschscholzia* are native to California, all annuals or short-lived perennials treated as annuals. Foremost is the California Poppy *(E. californica)* chosen as the state floral emblem in 1903 for the following attributes: wide distribution, long flowering period, and brilliant color and satiny texture of the flowers. All the species have shallow to deep, cup-shaped flowers of orange, yellow, and occasionally white. They grow from carrot-like taproots which may persist for several years. The foliage is composed of three fan-shaped divisions, each one redivided, and these slashed into linear divisions. Plants are branched and become large and often widely spreading by the end of their first season. The California Poppy is distinguished by having two rims below the flowers. The pointed cap, which is formed of the two united sepals, is pushed off from the outer, spreading, and red-edged rim as the petals expand. All of the flowers are further enhanced by prominent clusters of large stamens. These poppies are among the most adaptable of all wildflowers, and once plants are established, they perpetuate themselves by volunteers. All members of this genus are durable and hardy in gardens and require very little in the way of water or cultivation.

Horticultural History: As with many of California's unique wildflowers, horticulturists in England began many years ago to select out special flower and color forms, including both double and semi-double flowers, some with prettily crinkled inner petals. The extended color range includes creamy white, rose, crimson, flame, shades of yellow and orange, and some bicolors. These are useful with other spring wildflowers, or separate colors may be used in some special color scheme.

Eschscholzia californica
California Poppy or Golden Poppy

HABIT: Annual or perennial, 2–6 dm, 9–24 in. Flowers the first year from seed. FOLIAGE: Ternately dissected into narrow segments, smooth, pale green. FLOWERS: Large cup, satiny, deep orange, or copper tinted, to straw yellow. On single stems held above plants. (See cover photo.) FRUIT: Long, slender, erect capsule with many round seeds. DISTRIBUTION: Common in grassy slopes, fields, foothills throughout California, mostly west of main Sierran crest.

Culture: California Poppy is easily grown from seed, broadcast where wanted from late summer into the winter months. Depending on climate and exposure, plants may flower from February all through the summer. All species prefer lean soil, full sun, and will tolerate water during their periods of active growth. Well-established plants will continue to come up each year from the deep root and to provide a wealth of seedlings. Old plants which have become straggly may be cut to near ground level in autumn.

Estimate of Garden Value: The California Poppy is apt to seed abundantly in the garden and may intrude where it is not wanted. It is, however, invaluable for dry, sunny areas, and to mix with other native plants. Some combinations which I have found to be especially lively include: Blue Dicks *(Brodiaea pulchella)*, Triplet Lily *(B. laxa)*, California Blue-Eyed Grass *(Sisyrinchium bellum)*, Birds-Eye Gilia *(Gilia tricolor)*, and other annuals. Much variation within the species has long been recognized, and several varieties have been described.

Eschscholzia caespitosa
Tufted Poppy

HABIT: Many stems from tuft of basal leaves, 1–4 dm, 4–16 in. FOLIAGE: Dissected into many narrow divisions, pale blue-green, glaucous, and glabrous. FLOWERS: Large, shallow cups of pure, bright yellow. FRUIT: Typical, long, slender capsule. DISTRIBUTION: Flats, slopes, valley grasslands around Central Valley, up to 5,000 feet.

Culture and Estimate of Garden Value: The same as for *E. californica.*

Eschscholzia lobbii
Lobb's Poppy

HABIT: Tufted annual, slender, 1–3 dm, 4–12 in. FOLIAGE: Basal, dissected into few linear segments. FLOWERS: Flat, clear yellow, cluster of yellow stamens in center. FRUIT: Slender capsule with burr-like seeds. DISTRIBUTION: Gravelly or clay soil, foothills, rolling valley plains, Sierra foothills to Tulare County, inner north Coast Ranges.

Culture and Estimate of Garden Value: The same as for *E. californica.* A small poppy for full sun, among other annuals, and effective with plants having blue flowers.

GENUS *GILIA:* GILIAS
(Family Polemoniaceae: Phlox)

Twenty species of *Gilia* are native to California, almost all of them annuals. Plants are usually small, often slender and delicate in appearance. Some species, by their great numbers, provide vast masses of color on the wild landscape. Flowers are funnelform to salverform, in open heads, or small clusters, or borne singly. Colors are yellow, white, vivid rose, and range through several shades of blue, sometimes of intense quality.

Garden History: Only a few species have had much history

in gardens, and the three described here are available from seed specialists. Gilias are useful in mixed flower borders, or in open areas which have been lightly cultivated. They may be used in mixtures of native annuals, or in masses of a solid color. These are among the most dependable of wildflowers and will provide color from April into early summer.

Culture: Gilias may be planted from seed broadcast in late autumn to early spring, but they germinate more freely when planted with the early autumn rains. If allowed to go to seed, they will usually provide volunteers the following season. All prefer sun, soil on the lean side, and will tolerate moderate amounts of water. For special purposes seed may be planted in mid-spring, such as small groups of Birds-Eye Gilia among *Brodiaea elegans,* or the Blue-Headed Gilia among the soft pinks and lavenders of summer-flowering godetias. The vivid blue-violet of California Gilia *(G. achilleaefolia)* combines well with many colors, and is especially striking with the large, bright yellow daisies of Sea Dahlia *(Coreopsis maritima).* *G. capitata,* with seven subspecies, has wide distribution throughout the state.

Estimate of Garden Value: All species known in cultivation have good flower color, a relatively long flowering period, perpetuate themselves by volunteers, and require very little attention.

Gilia capitata
Blue-Headed Gilia

HABIT: Slender, 2–8 dm, 8–31 in, branched above. FOLIAGE: Bipinnately dissected into linear lobes, reduced upwards. FLOWERS: Small, dense, terminal heads of powder blue, exserted stamens. FRUIT: Ovate capsule. DISTRIBUTION: Open slopes, Mixed Evergreen Forests, Coast Ranges from Marin County north.

Culture and Estimate of Garden Value: See generic description above.

Gilia tricolor
Birds-Eye Gilia

HABIT: Slender, erect, 1–4 dm, 4–16 in. (See Fig. 10.) FOLIAGE: Leaves dissected into narrow segments. FLOWERS: Funnelform, lobes light blue or violet, throat yellow

with dark purple ring at top. FRUIT: Capsule. DISTRIBU-
TION: Grassy plains, slopes, valley grasslands, Coast Ranges
from San Benito to Humboldt counties, Central Valley from
Tulare to Tehama counties, Sierra foothills from Plumas and
Lassen to Shasta counties.

Culture and Estimate of Garden Value: See generic description above.

Gilia achilleaefolia
California Gilia

HABIT: Erect, branched above, 1–7 dm, 4–24 in.
FOLIAGE: Bipinnate, ultimate segments sickle-shaped.
FLOWERS: Funnelform, blue-violet in one to several dense
heads. FRUIT: Ovoid capsule. DISTRIBUTION: Loose soil of
open places, Foothill Woodlands, Mixed Evergreen Forests,

Figure 10 *Gilia tricolor,* Birds-Eye Gilia

Chaparral, Coastal Strand, etc., Santa Barbara and Contra Costa to Marin counties.

Culture and Estimate of Garden Value: See generic description above.

GENUS *LAYIA:* TIDY TIPS
(Family Compositae: Sunflower)

Fifteen species of *Layia* are native to California, all annuals, and mostly found in masses in open places. (See Pl. 1B.) With other small, quick-flowering native annuals they form the colorful carpets, still to be found in many parts of the state. Leaves are narrow, toothed to pinnatifid, some with a strong, pungent odor although one is said to have the odor of apples. Both ray and disk flowers are fertile so that ample seed can be expected. Many flower as early as January, and continue into April. Their constant companions include goldfields, Johnny-Tuck *(Orthocarpus erianthus),* and several other kinds of owl clover, along with many brodiaeas, and other typical field flowers. (See Chart 2.)

Culture: Several species have long been grown at botanic gardens, usually in field rows. Seed takes about two weeks to germinate. If seed were available, at least four species would be excellent garden materials, as border edgings, or to seed in open, sunny places. Their requirements include semi-dry soil and sun with moderate amounts of water during their period of active growth.

Estimate of Garden Value: Species of *Layia* must have sun and quite lean soil or the plants become leggy and produce fewer flowers. They are excellent in combination with some of the blue gilias, Baby Blue-Eyes *(Nemophila menziesii),* or one of the small, annual blue lupines. At the end of summer, birds are apt to devour all of the seed unless it is protected.

GENUS *LINANTHUS:* LINANTHUS
(Family Polemoniaceae: Phlox)

There are thirty-four species of *Linanthus,* and all but one are annuals. The plants are mostly slender and dainty, like gilias except that linanthus foliage is cleft to the base. Many are very attractive for their open clusters of phlox-like flowers

CALIFORNIA NATIVE PLANTS
INTRODUCED OCT/NOV 1987

Latin Name	Common Name
Aquilegia eximia	Van Houtte's Columbine
Archtostaphylos stanfordiana	Louis Edmonds Manzanita
Artemisia pycnocephala	Sand Hill Sage
Ceanothus impressus (cultivar)	Julia Phelps Ceanothus
Dyplacus vinity	Yellow Monkeyflower Hybrid
Eriogonum crocatum	Saffron Buckwheat
Eriogonum grande rubescens	Red Buckwheat
Fremontodendron mexicanum	Flannel Bush
Lupinus albifrons	Silver Circle Lupine
Lupinus arboreus	Tree Lupine
Myrica californica	California Wax Myrtle
Penstemon (cultivar)	Midnight Beard-tongue
Polystichum munitum	Western Sword Fern
Rhamnus californica	California Coffeeberry
Ribes viburnifolium	Evergreen Currant
Romneya coulteri	Matilija Poppy
Salvia leucophylla	Purple Sage
Zauchneria californica	Hummingbird Fuschia 'Gray Form'
Zauchneria cana	Hoary California Fuschia

CHART 2 *Layia*: Tidy Tips

Plant	Height	Flowers	Culture	Remarks	Distribution
L. platyglossa Coastal Tidy Tips	1-3 dm (4-12 in)	Large, yellow, white-tipped daisies. March–June.	Sun, lean soil. With Baby Blue-Eyes, Cream Cups, etc.	Stout plant. Leaves dentate to pinnatified.	Flats on coast, Mendocino Co. to Santa Cruz Id.
L. glandulosa White Layia	1-10 dm (4-36 in)	Glistening white, mustard yellow center. March–June.	Sun, lean soil. Border edging, with annual lupines.	Branched plant. Leaves dentate to lobed.	Deserts and West Sierra Nevada, Contra Costa to San Diego cos.
L. chrysanthemoides Smooth Layia	1-4 dm (4-16 in)	Large, bright yellow daisies. March–May.	Sun, moist soil. Borders, or in masses.	Plant erect, branched. Leaves pinnately cleft.	Woods, grasslands, Mendocino to Monterey cos.
L. pentachaeta Sierra Tidy Tips	2-8 dm (8-30 in)	Large daisies, yellow, white, deep centers. March–May.	Sun, moderate amounts of water. With Gold Fields, etc.	Leaves pinnate to bipinnate, acrid odor.	Woods, Chaparral, Placer to Kern cos.

in delicate shades of pink, rose, yellow, or in white, variously enhanced with dark spots or a contrasting ring within the flower. Of the four species described, Grand Linanthus (*L. grandiflorus*) is the most popular, and often planted thickly for its carpet of soft pink. The various species usually occur in drifts or masses, from coastal regions to deserts, on dry foothill slopes, and into higher elevations. (See Chart 3.)

Culture: Seeds may be sown directly where wanted, broadcasting in autumn and covering the beds with twiggy branches to prevent disturbance. Certain birds seem to be especially fond of sprouting seeds, and I have lost several plantings of the lovely Ground Linanthus to them. Cultural requirements include sun, lean soil, and moderate amounts of water after the

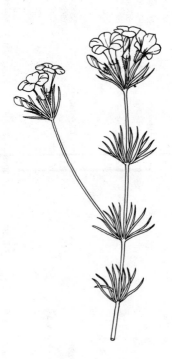

Figure 11 *Linanthus androsaceus,* False Baby Stars

CHART 3 *Linanthus:* Linanthus

Plant	Height	Flowers	Culture	Remarks	Distribution
L. grandiflorus Grand Linanthus	1-5 dm (4-20 in)	Funnelform, in large heads, white, lilac pink, silken texture. April-July.	Light shade, moderate water.	Persistent in cultivation. Blooms into summer.	Woods, Sonoma, Santa Barbara to Merced cos.
L. androsaceus False Baby Stars (See Fig. 11)	.5-3 dm (2-14 in)	Salverform in dense heads, rose, lilac, white, dark spots. April-June.	Open areas to high shade, water.	5 subspecies, widely distributed.	Woods, grasslands, Monterey to Shasta cos.
L. dianthiflorus Ground Linanthus (See Pl. 1C)	5-12 dm (2-6 in)	Funnelform in clusters, lilac to bright pink, fringed. Feb.-April.	Sun, lean soil. Edge of shrubs, rock garden.	May not persist, but highly attractive.	Sandy, open, Santa Barbara and San Diego cos.
L. montanus Mustang Linanthus	1-6 dm (4-22 in)	Salverform in crowded heads, white, pink, dark spots. May-Aug.	Sun, open areas. Mix with other natives.	Flower heads bristly from bracts.	Dry, mountains, Nevada to Kern cos.

rains have stopped. The various species may be used as border edgings, massed in open areas or dry slopes, or in small colonies in a rock garden.

Estimate of Garden Value: Although only two or three kinds of linanthus have any garden history, they should be more widely used for their dainty aspect and clear, pastel colors. Grand Linanthus has been the most persistent under cultivation, and will flower into the summer if watered.

GENUS *LUPINUS:* LUPINES
(Family Leguminosae: Pea)

Lupinus is a large genus with thirty species that are annuals. These attractive plants are a prominent feature of many types of terrain, including open, grassy fields, rolling hills, and coastal plains. Sometimes they are the dominant plant and cast a blue haze over the landscape, but in most places they mingle with other typical spring wildflowers. In my experience, White Whorl Lupine *(L. densiflorus)* and its several varieties and the early-flowering Succulent Lupine *(L. succulentus)* were among the most adaptable to garden culture. (See Chart 4.)

Culture: Seeds of most annual lupines germinate readily. Where pretreatment is needed, follow the suggestions on propagation given above, on page 28. Seeds should be broadcast where wanted, raked in, and covered lightly with twiggy branches. As a rule lupines resent handling, but may be started in flats if shifted while still small and transplanted with no delay. Seeds may also be planted in fiber pots and the plants can be set intact into the beds, after first removing the bottom section of the pot. All lupines prefer full sun, lean soil, and water to supplement the spring rains. Too much water and lack of air circulation can cause mildew of stems and foliage. Annual lupines are excellent in mixtures of other annuals, with native bulbs, and among perennials having the same requirements. Seed is sometimes available from specialty nurseries, or can be collected from the wilds.

Estimate of Garden Value: There is very little information on the persistence and reseeding of annual lupines. In my experience a sunny, semi-dry border among other natives has been the best situation, but even then fresh seed must be

CHART 4 *Lupinus:* Annual Lupines

Plant	Height	Flowers	Culture	Remarks	Distribution
L. nanus Douglas's Lupine	1-5 dm (4-20 in)	Rich blue, in separate whorls. April-May.	Sun, lean soil, moderate water. With poppies.	Massed planting in open areas. Free-flowering.	Grassy hills, fields, slopes, Coast Range, Santa Cruz to Santa Barbara cos.
L. bicolor Miniature Lupine (See Fig. 12)	1-4 dm (4-16 in)	Blue and white, in dense spikes. March-May.	Sun, semi-dry. Mixed borders, or solid planting.	Variable, with 6 ssp. and 2 varieties. Widely distributed.	Grasslands, foothills, coastal regions.
L. densiflorus Whitewhorl Lupine	2-4 dm (8-16 in)	In whorls, white, lilac, rose, tinted blue or violet. April-June.	Sun, semi-dry. Massed, with other natives.	Good color selection from varieties.	Fields, hills, Santa Clara, Humboldt to Butte cos.
L. subvexus Valley Lupine	1.5-4 dm (5-20 in)	In whorls, violet-purple, lilac, rose. April-May.	Sun, moderate water. With mix of other natives.	Leaves soft, hairy. Plants reseed.	Fields, slopes, Lake, Tulare, and Tehama cos., Ventura to Kern cos.

Figure 12 *Lupinus bicolor,* Miniature Lupine

planted every few years. In this border the Valley Lupine *(L. subvexus)* and the pretty dwarf Douglas's Lupine *(L. nanus)* were both satisfactory but reseeded only sparingly. Experiences with lupines at botanic gardens have been similar to mine.

GENUS *MENTZELIA:* BLAZING STARS
(Family Loasaceae: Loasa)

There are nineteen species of *Mentzelia,* most of them coarse-appearing perennials or biennials, but the annual Blazing Star here described is one of California's classic plants. It has long been used in gardens, and was formerly known as *Bartonia aurea.* A frequent companion is the blue-flowered Chia *(Salvia columbariae)* whose seed was so valuable to the Indian diet.

Mentzelia lindleyi
Blazing Star

HABIT: Erect, generally branched above, 1–6 dm, 4–24 in.
FOLIAGE: Lanceolate to ovate with narrow divisions, like a

stiff fern. FLOWERS: Solitary, or in loose terminal clusters, saucer-shaped, bright yellow, red-orange, or vermillion center, conspicuous stamens. (See Pl. IE.) FRUIT: Capsule, linear-clavate, numerous-angled seed. DISTRIBUTION: Sunny, rocky slopes, Alameda to Santa Clara counties, to south Coast Ranges; west of Fresno to Stanislaus counties.

Culture: Blazing Star may be grown from seed broadcast in autumn, in lean, well-drained soil. It will tolerate water during period of active growth.

Estimate of Garden Value: When properly used, Blazing Star can provide bright color and is especially valuable with plants having blue flowers. Several penstemons, phacelias, or small lupines make suitable companions.

GENUS *MIMULUS:* MONKEY FLOWERS
(Family Scrophulariceae: Figwort)

More than half of the seventy-seven species in the large genus *Mimulus* are annual plants. Most are diminutive in stature and frequently have disproportionately large flowers. Flowers are highly colored and marked with contrasting lines and spots giving the monkey face, or sometimes pansy-like appearance. Each flower is tubular with the two upper lobes erect, or turned back, and the three lower lobes larger, spreading, and often rounded. Several have pointed upper lobes which give the flower a horn-like appearance. Flower color is most often rich shades of crimson, purple, rose-purple, red, and yellow. Several are typical of vernal pools, such as Tricolor Monkey Flower *(M. tricolor)* with flowers in purple, yellow, and white. Some grow in places which are damp for most of the year, while the remainder are mostly of arid slopes and flats in gravelly or sandy soils. (See Chart 5.)

Culture: There is practically no garden history of the pert little monkey flowers, and seed is seldom available. Seed can be collected but the plants have to be observed frequently because they dry and disappear by late spring. My only experience has been with Layne's Monkey Flower *(M. layneae),* a species of my mountain area which grows in gravelly soil. It did not persist beyond two or three years, possibly because of encroaching shade or the lack of sharply drained soil. When

Figure 13 *Mimulus douglasii,* Purple Mouse-Ears

seed is available these richly colored annuals should be planted in full sun, in lean soil, and given moderate amounts of water only during their period of active growth. They would be superb in a sunny rock garden, as ground covers in exposed places or to mix with other plants having similar requirements.

Estimate of Garden Value: For all of their wide distribution and great number of species, some annual monkey flowers are seldom cultivated. Experiences at botanic gardens show them to be generally unsatisfactory as garden plants, and even when freshly grown from seed, they seldom perpetuate themselves with volunteers. All who are acquainted with these bold-colored, diminutive plants hope that they may eventually be adapted to garden use.

GENUS *MONARDELLA:* MONARDELLAS
(Family Labiatae: Mint)

Eight species of the twenty in the genus *Monardella* are annuals. Leaves of this genus have a characteristic, pleasant,

CHART 5 *Mimulus*: Annual Monkey Flowers

Plant	Height	Flowers	Culture	Remarks	Distribution
M. layneae Layne's Monkey Flower	1-2 dm (4-8 in)	Tubular, spreading, rose to red-purple. May-Aug.	Sun, lean soil. Dry slopes, rock garden.	May be branched above.	Dry, sandy, Napa Co. north, to Fresno Co. north.
M. douglasii Purple Mouse-Ears (see Fig. 13)	3-4 cm (8-10 in)	Funnelform, glowing, purple, ear-like lobes. March-May.	Sun, lean soil. Edging, massed planting.	Leaves and flowers in low tufts.	Wet places, San Benito Co. north and Tulare Co. north
M. kelloggii Kellogg's Monkey Flower	.3-3 dm (1-11 in)	Long tube, erect upper lobe, bright purple. March-June.	Sun, lean soil. With brodiaeas, grass iris, other annuals, etc.	Leaves viscid, purplish on reverse.	Pine, oak, Napa to Trinity cos. and Kern to Shasta cos.
M. bicolor Yellow and White Monkey Flower	1-2.4 dm (4-10 in)	Open tube, upper lobes white, lower yellow. April-June.	Sunny border, mixed annuals and perennials, and blue lupines.	Narrow, oblong foliage.	Open places Sierra foothills, Shasta to Tulare cos.

minty fragrance. They are mostly plants of dry, open hills, and of deserts from central to southern California. In most cases the flowers are in dense heads, each one a narrow tube, and surrounded by firm bracts, these sometimes purplish tinted. Flower colors include lavender, rose, rose-purple, and one in white with purple dots. In the wilds I have encountered Fenestra Monardella *(M. douglasii)* growing with White Mariposa Lily *(Calochortus venustus),* a rare and lovely combination.

Culture: Although these annual mints are handsome and seem worthy of a place in gardens, there are scant records of their cultivation. Experiences at botanic gardens show that seed sown in November germinated readily, and plants flowered the following May. Judging from their native habitat, these colorful mints should have a semi-dry, sunny situation, and be used with native bulbs, such perennials as penstemons and buckwheats, or with some of the shrubby mints. Five species have been recommended for gardens in southern California, including Brewer's Monardella *(M. breweri),* Fenestra Monardella *(M. douglassi),* Desert Penny Royal *(M. exilis),* Mustang Mint *(M. lanceolata),* and Merced Monardella *(M. leucocephala).*

Monardella douglasii
Fenestra Monardella

HABIT: Erect, branched above, 1–3 dm, 4–12 in. (See Fig. 14.) FOLIAGE: Lanceolate to narrow-oblong, dark green. FLOWERS: Tubular, in heads, reddish purple, surrounded by lanceolate bracts with the intervening spaces translucent. FRUIT: Nutlets. DISTRIBUTION: Foothill slopes, inner Coast Ranges, Contra Costa to Monterey counties.

Culture: Semi-dry borders, full sun, well-drained soil. Could be used with perennial species of *Monardella,* with several of the brodiaeas and species of *Calochortus,* and with penstemons and buckwheats.

Estimate of Garden Value: Should have wide use as a drought-tolerant plant for low-maintenance, western gardens.

Figure 14 *Monardella douglasii,* Fenestra Monardella

Monardella lanceolata
Mustang Mint

HABIT: Erect, simple or branched, 2–5 dm, 8–19 in. FOLIAGE: Oblong-lanceolate to lanceolate. FLOWERS: Tubular, in dense heads, rose-purple, stamens exserted. FRUIT: Brownish nutlets. DISTRIBUTION: Hill slopes, valleys, Sierra foothills from Shasta to Mariposa counties; Monterey County to San Bernardino and San Jacinto mountains to San Diego County.

Culture and Estimate of Garden Value: The same as for *M. douglasii.*

Monardella breweri
Brewer's Monardella

HABIT: Erect, branched, 1.5–3 dm, 5–12 in. FOLIAGE: Oblong to narrowly ovate. FLOWERS: Tubular, rose, surrounded by purplish bracts. FRUIT: Nutlets. DISTRIBUTION: Sandy flats, Foothill Woodland, inner Coast Ranges, Alameda to north Los Angeles County.

Culture and Estimate of Garden Value: The same as for *M. douglasii.*

GENUS *NEMOPHILA:* NEMOPHILAS
(Family Hydrophyllaceae: Waterleaf)

The eight species of *Nemophila* native to California are all annuals. Baby Blue-Eyes has long been a favorite garden plant, both here and abroad. Flowers are solitary, rotate to campanulate, like shallow saucers, of several shades of blue, and in white sometimes with contrasting spots.

Culture: Species of *Nemophila* are easily grown from seed broadcast in autumn, and may be sown again in early spring for late bloom. Plants are water tolerant, grow in sun to a little high, broken shade, and seem not particular as to soil. They may be used in many garden situations, especially in mixtures with other annuals, or in colonies among other plants. Most will volunteer abundantly once a planting is allowed to go to seed. In the wilds it is a typical and admirable feature of many half-shaded oak dells and north-facing slopes, forming a sparkling combination when it occurs with the yellow Johnny-Jump-Up *(Viola pedunculata).*

Nemophila menziesii
Baby Blue-Eyes

HABIT: Widely spreading, 1–3 dm, 4–12 in. FOLIAGE: Oval to oblong, pinnately divided into oval or oblong divisions. FLOWERS: Bowl-to-wheel-shaped, turquoise with white center. (See. Pl. 1A.) FRUIT: Round to ovoid capsule. DISTRIBUTION: Moist flats and slopes; inner north Coast Ranges from Tehama County south, and Sierra foothills from Butte County south.

Culture: Baby Blue-Eyes are propagated from seed broadcast where wanted. In a warm, sunny site they may begin to bloom in early March, and with some moisture will continue for several weeks. They have long been used as ground covers in bulb beds, border edgings, slopes, and with other annuals, or in little groups among native bulbs and perennials. This species is especially handsome with Tufted Poppy *(Eschscholzia caespitosa)* for the contrast of its clear, primrose-yellow flowers.

Estimate of Garden Value: Dependable spring annuals of good flower color and nicely proportioned.

Nemophila maculata
Fivespot

HABIT: Stems several, decumbent, forming close, mounding plant, 1–3 dm, 4–12 in. (See Fig. 15.) FOLIAGE: Oblong to oval, deeply pinnately parted, pale green. FLOWERS: Bowl-shaped, white, dark-veined, with large, purple spot at tip of each petal. April–July. FRUIT: Capsules. DISTRIBUTION: Moist places, west base and slopes of Sierra Nevada, Plumus to Kern counties.

Culture and Estimate of Garden Value: The same as for *N. menziesii.* Fivespot makes a pleasing combination with

Figure 15 *Nemophila maculata,* Fivespot

grass iris, early-flowering brodiaeas, and I once had a mat of it at the base of the Long-Petaled Iris *(Iris longipetala)*.

GENUS *OENOTHERA:* EVENING-PRIMROSES
(Family Onagraceae: Evening-Primrose)

About half of the forty-two species of *Oenothera* are annuals. Most are stout, sometimes coarse plants, of easy culture, but some are of doubtful garden value. Many kinds decorate deserts and coastal regions, while others inhabit foothills and grow in meadows. Saucer-shaped flowers are often large, with conspicuous four-parted stigma, and in several shades of yellow as well as white and rose. Seed capsules are large, sometimes woody, and may be straight, curved, or coiled. Several kinds bloom in the evening and into mid-morning, and these attract certain moths. Others have a delicate, fruity fragrance which is seldom mentioned in descriptions.

Culture: Some of the evening-primroses have long been used in gardens, grow readily from seed, and generally provide many volunteers. They prefer a sunny situation, with well-drained soil, and may be watered during their flowering and seed-setting seasons. Most may be used in sunny, watered, flower borders, and a few are valuable for a long flowering period that extends from mid-winter into late spring.

Oenothera deltoides ssp. cognata (Oe. trichocalyx)
Fragrant Evening-Primrose

HABIT: Erect, branched above, 2–4 dm, 8–15 in. FOLIAGE: Somewhat diamond-shaped, coarsely toothed, dark green. FLOWERS: Large, saucer-shaped, white, bright yellow stamens, day-blooming, fragrant. March–May. FRUIT: Woody, cylindric capsule. DISTRIBUTION: Sandy plains, grasslands, San Joaquin Valley to Antelope Valley.

Culture: Fragrant Evening-Primrose is adaptable to gardens and grows well from seed. Plants seem more robust when seeded in flats, transplanted to three-inch pots, and then to permanent quarters in early spring. The large, pure white flowers bloom from long, greenish ivory buds, and continue to bloom over a long period. Plants perform well in coarse or sandy soil, full sun, and moderate amounts of water.

Estimate of Garden Value: An adaptable, long-flowering, and easily handled plant. I have used it in semi-dry borders with other natives, such as buckwheats, Sea Dahlia *(Coreopsis maritima),* blue gilias, lupines, and others. Seed is sometimes available from specialty catalogs.

Oenothera bistorta
Southern Sun Cups

HABIT: Prostrate to ascending stems, 0.5–8 dm, 1–31 in. (See Fig. 16.) FOLIAGE: Linear-oblanceolate with irregular teeth, to clasping on upper stem. FLOWERS: Open, lemon yellow, brown spot at base, from red buds. FRUIT: Woody, curved or contorted capsule. DISTRIBUTION: Coastal Strand, Los Angeles County southward.

Culture and Estimate of Garden Value: The same as for *Oe. deltoides* ssp. *cognata.*

Figure 16 *Oenothera bistorta,* Southern Sun Cups

GENUS *PHACELIA:* PHACELIAS
(Family Hydrophyllaceae: Waterleaf)

Phacelia is a large genus of eighty-seven species, about sixty of which are annuals. At least six or eight species have long been popular garden plants, and no doubt there are others equally attractive. Flowers are campanulate or bell-shaped and occur in cymes which may be curved or scorpioid. In several species the stems, and sometimes the foliage, have rough, prickly hairs; a few have juice which makes a brown stain. The range of flower color includes many shades of blue, some of dark and intense hue such as violet, purple, salvia-blue, and lavender. Most of these richly colored forms are native to mesas and deserts of southern California, but they are generally adaptable to cultivation.

Culture: As with practically all members of the waterleaf family, phacelias are easily grown from seed, generally broadcast in autumn. Seed may also be grown in flats, transplanting the seedlings to fiber pots, and setting in borders when a sturdy plant has formed. Several have a very long blooming period, beginning some time in March and continuing for a month or more. (See Fig. 17.) These phacelias prefer sun and are water

Figure 17 *Phacelia campanularia,* Desert Bluebells

tolerant, but overhead watering should not be practiced because it can cause mildew.

Estimate of Garden Value: Phacelias are valuable for their rich flower colors, their usefulness in many garden situations, and combinations with other plants. They make a striking combination with Birds-Eye Gilia *(Gilia tricolor)* and the violet-purple bells of Elegant Brodiaea *(Brodiaea elegans)* in a semi-dry border. *P. ciliata* and *P. distans* have flowers in more delicate shades of blue and are excellent in mixed borders to blend with almost any flower color. The tall Tansy Phacelia *(P. tanacetifolia)* is generally considered to be too coarse for flower borders, but can be used as a background plant, or in a mixture of hardy natives for uncultivated sections. Four or five species are available from specialty seed catalogs.

Phacelia minor
California Bells

HABIT: Erect, simple or branched from base, 2–6 dm, 6–24 in. FOLIAGE: Ovate to oblong, coarsely serrate, dark green. FLOWERS: Tubular-campanulate, purple, in cymes. March–June. FRUIT: Oblong-ovoid capsules. DISTRIBUTION: Common in dry and disturbed places, cismontane southern California, from Santa Monica Mountains to edge of desert.

Culture: California Bells may be grown from seed, broadcast thinly, or sown in flats, and require sun, lean soil, and only moderate amounts of water. I have used California Bells as a border edging with purple-leaf basil to make a distinctive combination. Small groups of this phacelia make a lively splash of color in a sunny rock garden. This species and some of the others from mild areas are not cold hardy; where spring frosts can be expected, they should not be planted until April or after the heavy frosts.

Estimate of Garden Value: Adaptable, free-flowering over long periods, and in most cases reseed generously.

Phacelia parryi
Parry's Phacelia

HABIT: Simple, or few-branched, 1–4 dm, 4–15 in. FOLIAGE: Ovate-oblong, irregularly dentate. FLOWERS:

Open campanulate, violet to purple, pale center, in many-flowered cymes. March–May. FRUIT: Oblong-ovoid capsule. DISTRIBUTION: Dry slopes, disturbed places, Coast Ranges from Monterey County to lower California, and to edge of Colorado Desert.

Culture and Estimate of Garden Value: The same as for *P. minor.*

Phacelia viscida
Sticky Phacelia

HABIT: Erect, simple to few-branched, hairy and glandular throughout, 1–7 dm, 4–27 in. FOLIAGE: Oblong-ovate, doubly serrate on margins. FLOWERS: Rotate-campanulate, vivid blue with white center, in many-flowered cymes. March–June. FRUIT: Oblong-ovoid capsule. DISTRIBUTION: Sandy and disturbed places, Coastal Sage Scrub, Monterey to San Diego counties, and Channel Islands.

Culture and Estimate of Garden Value: The same as for *P. minor.*

GENUS *PLATYSTEMON:* CREAM CUPS
(Family Papaveraceae: Poppy)

There is only one species of *Platystemon,* which varies considerably from place to place, and five varieties are recognized.

Platystemon californicus
Cream Cups

HABIT: Many stems from base, softly hairy, 1–3 dm, 3–10 in. FOLIAGE: Mostly on lower plant, lance-linear, pale green, hairy. FLOWERS: Shallow, cream white to pale yellow, from pendant buds. March–May. FRUIT: Slender, jointed capsule, separating into one-seeded sections when ripe. DISTRIBUTION: Common on open, grassy fields, slopes, Oak Woodlands, over most of cismontane California to the edge of deserts.

Culture: Cream Cups may be grown from seed, broadcast and raked in before the winter rains begin. It will perform best in full sun, but will tolerate light afternoon shade, and moderate amounts of water. Plants are known to seed abundantly in burn areas, and to enter cultivated grain fields. The entire plant is very attractive with its open flowers centered with creamy stamens, blooming from the drooping, downy buds. Several native annuals make suitable companions, including Baby Blue-Eyes *(Nemophila menziesii),* small, bright blue lupines, and various kinds of collinsia and gilia.

Estimate of Garden Value: All who love small plants are intrigued by this native annual which resembles a diminutive Iceland poppy. It should be placed with companions of similar proportions, away from large or aggressive plants.

GENUS *SALVIA:* SAGES
(Family Labiatae: Mint)

There are nineteen species of *Salvia* in California, two of them annuals. All are noted for aromatic foliage and vigorous, robust habit.

Salvia columbariae
Chia

HABIT: Erect, simple or branched, with ash-colored hairs, 1–5 dm, 4–20 in. FOLIAGE: Mostly basal, oblong in outline, pinnatifid into toothed divisions, rugose and finely pubescent on the upper surface. Upper leaves reduced along the stem. FLOWERS: Interrupted, capitate whorls, dense, with bright blue flowers protruding from purplish calyx, amid pointed, wine-colored bracts. March–June. FRUIT: Smooth nutlets, abundantly produced. DISTRIBUTION: Common in dry, often disturbed places, below 4,000 feet elevation; Coastal Sage Scrub, Chaparral, etc., inner Coast Ranges, from Mendocino County, and throughout southern California to Baja California.

Culture: Chia requires full sun and dryness, although it is tolerant of water during its period of active growth. Its normal habitat is gravelly slopes or sandy washes in lean soil and full sun. It may be seeded where wanted by raking in during the autumn months, or seeds may be planted in flats in early spring. It is excellent with other sun-loving annuals, brodiaeas, or among drought-tolerant perennials.

Estimate of Garden Value: Used correctly, this handsome annual is satisfactory in open, sunny places. In botanic gardens, plants flower in about three months, often attaining two feet in height, and branching freely. It is particularly valuable for its foliage, which looks like a thick, gray-green fern. Chia is also well known for its nutritious seeds which were a staple of the Indian diet. The seeds were often roasted, ground into a meal, and mixed with water to make a soothing and nutritious gruel.

GENUS *STYLOMECON:* WIND POPPY
(Family Papaveraceae: Poppy)

There is only one species of *Stylomencon,* universally admired for its brilliant flower color and delicate petal texture.

Stylomecon heterophylla
Wind Poppy

HABIT: Slender, erect, many stems, 3–6 dm, 1–2 ft. FOLIAGE: Pinnatifid, the lobes entire or in turn dissected, pale green, thin texture. FLOWERS: Flat, poppy-like of four orange-red silken petals, with basal purplish spot, opening from nodding buds. Petals fall soon after flowering. April–May. FRUIT: Upright capsule, clavate-ovoid, with abundance of minute seed. DISTRIBUTION: Grassy, brushy slopes, Coast Ranges from Lake County south, San Joaquin Valley, foothills of southern Sierra to Baja California and Channel Islands.

Culture: The Wind Poppy may be grown from seed scattered in autumn where wanted. It requires open, sunny exposure to high or broken shade, but not deep shade. Use with other natives, either a mixture of annuals, or in groups among shrubs or large perennials. Records from a botanic garden show that the Wind Poppy may be seeded in flats and then transplanted to protected beds.

Estimate of Garden Value: Even though the Wind Poppy is fleeting, and not entirely dependable as a garden plant, it is worth growing for its brilliantly colored flowers.

6. GROWING WILDFLOWERS: PERENNIALS

The perennials native to California occur in a wide range of sizes and of ornamental qualities. I have boundless enthusiasm and admiration for them and for their ability to fill many garden situations. The beautifully veined leaves of Hartweg's Ginger *(Asarum hartwegii)* and the superb Matilija Poppy *(Romneya coulteri)* are just two of the contrasting types from among the wealth of perennial plants. In this book, a perennial plant is considered to be one of three kinds: herbaceous with a persistent root system, but with the top foliage dying in winter; evergreen with firm, to slightly woody, lower stems; or evergreen without a woody base. Several species in the genera *Penstemon, Lupinus,* and *Phlox* are included in the last category.

DISTRIBUTION

In the wilds, different kinds of perennials form resplendent seaside gardens or carpet the deserts, or cover valleys and low hills. Other kinds fill moist meadows and stream banks in garden-like array. Some are understory plants of woods and forests, and many from the redwoods have handsome foliage to grace the shade borders. A surprising assortment are restricted to special habitats such as rock ledges, talus slopes, and alpine regions. Most important to western gardens are the tough, sun-loving, and water-saving perennials from chaparral and arid foothills. Each in its own way can contribute a western flavor to gardens and large-scale landscaping.

VITAL QUALIFICATIONS

A great number of plants from this wide range of sizes, types, and habitats should provide satisfactory garden materials, but few have been tested. Some species and selections have been used in gardens over the years, including penstemons, buckwheats, sages, monkey flowers, irises, etc., either because of their adaptability or for some element of refinement. Refined traits include neat appearance through most of the seasons; foliage of good substance, color, and texture; flowers in abundance or excellence of color to make the plant attractive. Some of these provide the delight of fragrance or unusual seed vessels.

Certain characteristics of perennials being considered for garden use should be known. Some perennials of arid places may have deep-seated, thick rootstocks; in other types the root system may be straggly and far ranging. Knowing the type of root system will reduce damage in handling and transplanting. Consideration should also be given to drought tolerance, water requirements, rate of growth, and most suitable garden situation. Properly selected, native perennials can be used in regular flower borders, shaded areas, rock gardens, semi-dry borders, as ground or slope covers, edgings, and a few as house plants.

There is now a deepening interest in exploring native perennials as useful garden materials. It is especially heartening to see a renewed interest in Pacific irises, the shrubby monkey flowers, the lively, blue-flowered penstemons, and in the sculptured appearance of some large buckwheats. Over the years, native plant enthusiasts have urged that these perennials be more widely used, but it has only been recently that drought-tolerant borders of hardy natives have become popular. The exciting trend in modern landscaping is toward self-sufficient and naturalistic gardens.

FERNS

California has a magnificent array of ferns that grow in a wide variety of habitats. Several form the conspicuous and extensive understory in redwood forests. Others occur in moist gulches, wet slopes, and stream banks where they form springy masses in contrast to other vegetation. Several species decorate rock crevices, or grow in dry, desert-like places. Among the fifty-three species of native ferns, some are large and bold, such as the Giant Chain Fern *(Woodwardia fimbriata),* in contrast to the small, lacy Coffee Fern *(Pellaea andromedaefolia).* These and others are becoming increasingly popular as garden plants.

SPECIES DESCRIPTIONS

Following are some of the hardy and adaptable perennials, many of proven garden value. Perennials to suit many situations are included, especially those that are self-sufficient.

GENUS *ABRONIA:* SAND VERBENAS
(Family Nyctaginaceae: Four O'Clock)

Ten species of *Abronia* are native to California, mostly of coastal, desert or desert-like, sandy areas. About half of the species are perennial, and the two described here are well known for their spreading habit and free-flowering tendencies.

Abronia latifolia
Yellow Sand Verbena

HABIT: Creeping, evergreen, fleshy stems, form leafy mats, spreading 3–10 dm, 12 in–3 ft. (See Fig. 18.) FOLIAGE: Broad-oval, thick, succulent, sticky. FLOWERS: Small, in rounded clusters, bright yellow, fragrant. FRUIT: Turbinate anthocarp, seeds united to walls of ovary. DISTRIBUTION: Coastal Strand, San Miguel Island, and from Santa Barbara County north.

Culture: Yellow Sand Verbena may be grown from seed, but germination is irregular and often slow. It has been recommended that seed be sown directly where wanted in autumn so that rain can aid germination. Seeds may also be planted in pots or flats, but losses are high, because of rot or because seedlings resent being disturbed. The Yellow Sand Verbena appears to dislike clay soil. Plant in sun and in sandy, friable soil where it is tolerant of moderate amounts of water.

Estimate of Garden Value: A useful ground cover plant in its home area, but probably needs much more testing away from its native habitat.

Figure 18 *Abronia latifolia,* Yellow Sand Verbena

Abronia umbellata
Pink Sand Verbena

HABIT: Spreading, mat-forming evergreen, fleshy, reddish stems, 2–10 dm, 8–36 in. FOLIAGE: Lance-oblong, irregular in outline, sticky. FLOWERS: Small, in broad heads, rosy lavender to white, fragrant. Blooms off and on for most of the year. FRUIT: Anthocarp. DISTRIBUTION: Coastal Strand, San Miguel Id., Los Angeles north to B.C.

Culture: Seeds of the Pink Sand Verbena are reported to germinate in about four weeks. If planted in October or November, plants will flower the first year. Some losses have been noted from disturbance by moles, or from rabbits eating the foliage.

Estimate of Garden Value: As with other species of *Abronia,* this is a valuable ground cover for coastal regions. It has also been used away from the coast in sandy soil, full sun, and with moderate amounts of water. This species is variable in nature with four subspecies.

GENUS *ACTAEA:* BANEBERRY
(Family Ranunculaceae: Crowfoot)

There is one species in *Actaea*. It is adaptable and has interesting features through the seasons, including emergence of leaves in spring that unfurl like a coarse fern.

Actaea rubra ssp. arguta
Baneberry

HABIT: Herbaceous, robust, with several stems from a short rootstock, 2–6–8 dm, 8–36 in. FOLIAGE: Large, compound, tri-ternately divided, leaflets serrate on margins. Spray-like, up to a foot or more both ways. FLOWERS: Congested, terminal racemes, tiny cream white flowers. February–April. FRUIT: Upright spike of oval, bright red berries contains lenz-shaped seed, considered to be poisonous. Late summer. DISTRIBUTION: Widely distributed in brushy, wooded places, generally in thicket-like growth. Native throughout the Coast Ranges, and in the Sierra Nevada from Tulare County southward, up to 8,000 feet, and in the San Bernardino Mountains.

Culture: Baneberry is grown from seed planted in friable soil containing some wood humus or peat. Remove seed from pulp and plant in autumn. Allow pots to remain in a frame or sheltered place during the winter, and seedlings will appear the following spring. Stratification in a very moist seeding mixture can be used if seed fail to germinate. Plants remain small with one or two sets of typical leaves for the first two years, and begin to flower by the third year. Foliage begins to turn a pale yellow-amber color by late summer and then dies back, at which time it may be cut to the ground.

Estimate of Garden Value: Few native perennials are more valuable for a shady situation than the Baneberry. In my Los Gatos garden a large clump persisted for many years, appearing regularly every February. Plants seem even more vigorous and robust in my mountain garden although the foliage does not emerge until early April. Here they grow in a section shaded by the house, accompanied by columbines and peachleaf campanula, with native irises and border campanulas in front. The glossy, brilliant red berries are ripe by late July, and remain colorful for several weeks. Volunteer plants occur frequently around the established ones. In warm, dry climates, Baneberry may require extra water, shade for most of the day, and humus in the soil.

GENUS *ADIANTUM:* MAIDENHAIR FERNS
(Family Pteridaceae: Fern)

Three species of *Adiantum,* a genus of popular and delicate ferns, are native to California. It has wide occurrence elsewhere, and there are many selected forms.

Propagation: Maidenhair ferns are propagated either from spores or by careful division of the roots. (The methods described here may be used for practically all fern species.) Growing ferns from spores is a long process, although maidenhair ferns of about two inches in height may be expected in one year. The growing medium must be sterilized, and may be a friable mix of at least half leaf mold with sand and loam, a packaged potting soil containing a large proportion of humus, or sphagnum moss with fine sand. The medium is pressed into shallow pots or flats, watered until thoroughly soaked and then allowed to drain. The spores are scattered thinly and evenly over the top and pressed in for firm contact with the medium. The container is covered with glass or it can be entirely enveloped with plastic. It is put in a greenhouse or a sheltered place ideally where a temperature of 65 to 70°F can be maintained. As the spores develop they appear to be a mass of green and are known as prothallus at this stage. The first true fronds form in eight to twelve weeks. The glass or plastic can be raised to allow for air circulation, but the containers must never be allowed to dry out. After the tiny fronds have formed, they may be transplanted by taking small clumps, and when the plants are about one-inch high, they can then be planted individually. Plants should be kept in a sheltered place, and evenly and constantly moist. Propagation by division of roots may be done in late winter to early spring. Dig the plants carefully, wash off the soil, and cut the woody root into sections. Some experts recommend that the fronds be removed at this time to encourage rapid new growth. For some ferns, the new sections can be planted in pots of damp sand and kept moist and sheltered until a vigorous new root system has formed.

Culture: Once established, ferns are apt to be long lived, and they add a different pattern to most other plants. Those which come from moist and shaded areas can be watered throughout the year, and leaf mold or peat can be incorporated in the soil to encourage vigorous growth. Light application of organic base fertilizer, such as fish emulsion, can be given during the growing season. Most rock ferns require some sun, or high, filtered shade, and will tolerate dry conditions and porous soil. All ferns should be groomed by removal of old fronds. Ferns are also popular subjects for pots or baskets, although only a few of the available ones are native.

Estimate of Garden Value: Ferns provide an interesting texture and pattern to other plants, and most are unexcelled for the shade garden. They may be grown among shrubs or perennials of firm foliage, such as species of *Heuchera, Boykinia,* and *Iris,* or among other sturdy, shade-loving plants. Under trees and large shrubs, ferns impart a woodsy feeling, and the maidenhair ferns are especially handsome among low, evergreen shrubs. The Five-Finger Fern is effective when brought forward from among other plants, where its delicate leafiness can show to advantage. Ferns that grow on boulders and relatively dry places are sometimes more difficult to cultivate, but often respond to pot culture. The adaptable ones are excellent in rock gardens and greatly enhance rock walls and dry slopes in filtered shade.

Adiantum pedatum var. aleuticum
Five-Finger Fern

HABIT: Erect fronds from short, thick rhizome, 2–8 dm, 8–30 in. Several wiry stems of finger-like fronds, sometimes drooping, pinnules short-stalked and oblong. (See Fig. 19.) HABITAT: Moist, shaded cliffs, rock crevices, swampy woods, and canyon walls. DISTRIBUTION: Redwood Forests, Mixed Evergreen, Montane Coniferous Forests, and

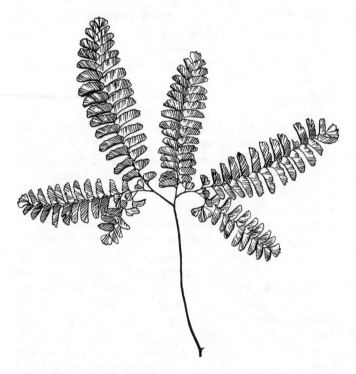

Figure 19 *Adiantum pedatum* var. *aleuticum,* Five-Finger Fern

Chaparral, throughout both mountain ranges, from sea level to 11,000 feet elevation.

Culture and Estimate of Garden Value: See generic description above.

Adiantum jordani
California Maidenhair

HABIT: From slender, creeping rhizome, many close fronds with pinnules fan-shaped, 2–5 dm, 8–19 in. long. Stems black and shiny, fronds ascending or slightly drooping. HABITAT: Damp, shaded banks, at base of rocks and trees. DISTRIBUTION: Several plant communities throughout the Coast Ranges, occasional in Sierra foothills, and islands off the southern California coast, mostly below 3,500 feet elevation.

Culture and Estimate of Garden Value: See generic description above.

GENUS *AQUILEGIA:* COLUMBINES
(Family Ranunculaceae: Crowfoot)

There are four native species of *Aquilegia,* a plant well known for its sprightly, spurred flowers.

Aquilegia formosa
Red Columbine

HABIT: Herbaceous to almost evergreen, thick rootstock, robust, 5–10 dm, 19–36 in. FOLIAGE: Large spray formation, biternately divided, divisions variously lobed, thin, light green, lacy, attractive. FLOWERS: Pendant, spurred, of five alike petals produced backward into hollow spurs, bright red, yellow stamens. May to late summer. (See Pls. 3F and 8A.) FRUIT: Upright, dry follicle, abundant black seed. DISTRIBUTION: Moist woods, streams, Mono and Fresno to Modoc counties, Siskiyou and Del Norte, northward.

Culture: Red Columbine grows readily from fresh seed, and once a few plants are established, volunteers will soon appear. Plants form several sets of small, but typical leaves the first year. By the second year a large, leafy plant has formed and is ready to bloom. Morning sun and high tree shade in the afternoon is ideal, but they will flourish in almost full sun if ample water is given. They will also grow satisfactorily in shade, but will not flower so freely, and may become rangy in habit. Columbine is adaptable to regular flower borders, and may be used with lilies, wild iris, Clustered Bellflower *(Campanula glomerata),* or among shrubs in a shade border.

Estimate of Garden Value: The Red Columbine is one of the most adaptable and dependable of native perennials, and especially useful in a partially shaded flower border. Its flowering period lasts much longer than that of most garden forms, and hummingbirds are constant visitors. It tends to cross with any other columbine that grows in the vicinity. The resulting flower colors are apt to be a bit queer, such as dark orange, terracotta, and some pink shades with overtones of orange. Among shrubs or large perennials in a semi-wild garden, these colors are not unattractive, and continue to feed insects and hummingbirds.

Aquilegia eximia
Van Houtte's Columbine

HABIT: Stout, herbaceous, glandular-pubescent from thick root. 5–10 dm, 2–3½ ft. FOLIAGE: Large sprays, ternately divided, medium dark green. FLOWERS: Large, scarlet, yellow in orifice of spurs, on widely branched stems. FRUIT: Erect follicle. DISTRIBUTION: Springy places, often on serpentine, Coast Ranges Mendocino to Ventura counties.

Culture: The same as for *A. formosa.*

Estimate of Garden Value: In my experience this species did not provide many volunteer plants. It is especially desirable however for its wide, candelabrum-like, branching, and large flowers. It blooms all during the summer, and hummingbirds find it just as attractive as the common Red Columbine.

GENUS *ARABIS:* ROCK CRESSES
(Family Cruciferae: Mustard)

Thirty-five species of this widely distributed genus are native to California, most of them perennials or biennials. There are both ornamental and weedy members. Several whose habitat is rocky ledges or gravelly slopes have distinct possibilities in rock gardens.

Arabis blepharophylla
Rose Rock Cress

HABIT: Low, with several stems, 0.5–2 dm, 1–12 in. FOLIAGE: Basal rosette, obovate to oblanceolate, with forked hairs, deep green. FLOWERS: Typical mustard flowers, in vibrant rose-pink to rose-purple, fragrant. February–April. (See Pl. 3C.) FRUIT: Narrow capsule. DISTRIBUTION: Rocky places of Coastal Scrub, Santa Cruz to Sonoma counties.

Culture: Rose Rock Cress may be grown from seed, planted in early autumn and shifted to three-inch pots after the second pair of leaves have formed. If kept growing vigorously, plants may be set out and will bloom the first spring. In the garden it should have morning sun with high shade in the afternoon, ample water the year around, and well-drained soil. Where there are hot, drying winds, it should have filtered shade and a mulch of peat or leaf mold in summer.

Estimate of Garden Value: This is an elegant plant with bright color and endearing charms which remains neat through the seasons. It is especially satisfactory with nonrampant plants of similar requirements as a border edging, in a rock garden, or on a half-shaded slope. Rose Rock Cress is not cold tolerant, and may be killed by late spring frosts of high elevations.

GENUS *ASARUM:* WILD GINGERS
(Family Aristolochiaceae: Birthwort)

There are three species of *Asarum,* all trailing, evergreen plants with the delightful, typical ginger scent. They are essentially foliage plants because the flowers are usually hidden among the leaves. All inhabit shady, and often moist, forested areas, and *A. caudatum* is especially well known as the common ground cover of the redwood forests.

Asarum caudatum
Long-Tailed Ginger

HABIT: Creeping, evergreen, from elongated, branching rootstocks. (See Fig. 20.) FOLIAGE: Cordate, reniform at base, thick, dark green, petioles with long, woolly hairs. Early foliage paler and pubescent. FLOWERS: Almost stemless, hidden among leaves, dark maroon, three-parted, long-tailed calyx. April. FRUIT: Globular capsule, large seed. DISTRIBUTION: Deep shade, redwood to Yellow Pine Forests, Coast Ranges, Santa Cruz County north.

Culture: Long-Tailed Ginger grows readily from seed which produces quite a large, bright green seed leaf, and from between these the first true leaf eventually appears. Plants are also easily increased by taking rooted sections which are freely produced on vigorously growing plants. They may be grown in deep to high, filtered shade, and are water tolerant although will grow in semi-dry conditions where their growth rate is slower. They will enjoy a covering of leaf mold in autumn.

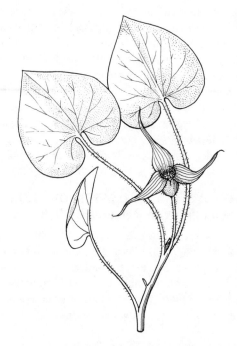

Figure 20 *Asarum caudatum,* Long-Tailed Ginger

Estimate of Garden Value: Long-Tailed Ginger may be too rampant for most gardens, but should be considered for deep shade where walks, fences or buildings can somewhat restrict its increase. This leafy plant can hardly be excelled as an extensive cover on shaded flats, slopes, steep banks or a large rock garden.

Asarum hartwegii
Hartweg's Ginger or Marble-Leaf Ginger

HABIT: Trailing, evergreen from stout rootstock, aromatic. FOLIAGE: Ovate, cordate at base, rich, deep green with pale mottling, on long, hairy petioles. FLOWERS: Dark purple, appearing grayish from soft hairs, with extended calyx lobes. Almost stemless and hidden by foliage. FRUIT: Globular capsule, large seed. DISTRIBUTION: Yellow Pine, Red Fir Forests, Sierra Nevada from Tulare County north, and in Trinity and Siskiyou counties.

Culture: The same as for *A. caudatum.*

Estimate of Garden Value: Hartweg's Ginger is a very handsome plant, the marbled foliage striking in its woodland setting. In nature the plants form a close mat, and appear to be not quite so rampant in habit as *A. caudatum.* It would be suitable as a ground cover on a shaded slope or large rock garden. In the wilds it usually grows with a north or eastern exposure, among shrubs and trees, and is often accompanied by Rattlesnake Orchid *(Goodyera oblongifolia)* and ferns. As a pot plant it seems content for a few years at least, but there is little information on whether this ginger would accept such culture over the years.

GENUS *ASCLEPIAS:* MILKWEEDS
(Family Asclepidaceae: Milkweed)

Milkweeds are mostly herbaceous perennials, with fourteen species of *Asclepias* native to California. The large clusters of fragrant flowers attract butterflies and other insects. Almost no milkweeds have any garden history, although the two described here are adaptable to a minimum of cultivation.

Asclepias cordifolia
Purple Milkweed

HABIT: Stout, herbaceous, from thick, deep-seated root, many stems, 3–8 dm, 12–31 in. FOLIAGE: Opposite, oval, cordate and clasping at base, smooth, bluish green with purplish tints. FLOWERS: Crimson, with pale or pinkish hoods to give a checkered effect, in terminal clusters, slightly fragrant. FRUIT: Large, oblong, pointed follicle, tightly packed with flat, circular seed, each with a silky appendage. DISTRIBUTION: Open, wooded slopes, Chaparral to flats of Mixed Evergreen Forests. Coast Ranges, Siskiyou to Solano counties, Sierra Nevada from Kern to Modoc counties.

Culture: Seed of Purple Milkweed germinates with no pretreatment. Young plants produce a wiry stem strung with three or four sets of round, pale green leaves, which have a coin-like appearance. Plants may be set in their permanent place by the end of the first year, but will not flower until after the second or even third full year of growth. At this time one or more stout stems will emerge in early April with flower buds of deep crimson-purple already formed. Purple Milkweed requires sun and porous soil, and will tolerate moderate amounts of water during its active growing period.

Estimate of Garden Value: From my observation, Purple Milkweed seems to be long lived, and has persisted on an east slope for six years. It has recently been seeded in a semi-dry border in full sun, companioned by lupines, species of *Penstemon,* Coyote Mint *(Monardella rillosa),* and Creeping Sage *(Salvia senomensis).* Although it has an air of refinement, it seems to me very suitable to semi-wild or natural type gardens, where it would give a distinct western flavor. A hardy, drought-tolerant perennial, it is unique for its flowers, foliage, and conspicuous seed vessels.

Asclepias speciosa
Butterfly Weed

HABIT: Stout, herbaceous, soft-tomentose throughout, 5–12 dm, 2–4½ ft. FOLIAGE: Oval to oblong, thick, pale green, 8–15 cm, 4–6 in. FLOWERS: Terminal umbels, corolla lobes rose-purple, hoods pinkish, round flower buds velvety, fragrant. FRUIT: Large follicle, woolly and soft spiny, oblong. DISTRIBUTION: Gravelly places, Yellow Pine and Mixed Evergreen Forests, Coast Ranges from Solano to Siskiyou counties, and west base of Sierra Nevada from Fresno to Inyo counties.

Culture: The same as for *A. cordifolia.*

Estimate of Garden Value: While Butterfly Weed is a handsome and obliging plant, it increases by underground shoots and would become a nuisance in a highly cultivated border. It is ideal for a country garden, or in semi-dry places where its rampant tendencies would be somewhat curbed. Along with its interesting features of very fragrant flowers and conspicuous follicles, this species is one of the host plants for the Monarch butterfly which lays eggs on its stems and leaves.

GENUS *CLEMATIS:* CLEMATIS
(Family Ranunculaceae: Crowfoot)

Three species of *Clematis* are native to California. They are half-woody vines that climb by means of clasping or twining petioles and inhabit wooded regions of foothills and mountains. The large, fluffy seed heads are almost more decorative than the flowers.

Clematis lasiantha
Pipestem Clematis

HABIT: Woody, deciduous, 4–5 m, 15–18 ft. Climbs through shrubs and trees, the tips often curving back to the ground. FOLIAGE: Trifoliate, leaflets lobed and coarsely toothed. FLOWERS: Small, cream white, in open clusters, with numerous stamens. April–May. (See Pl. 8B.) FRUIT: Achene, numerous, mostly long-tailed, silky, in conspicuous heads of pale green. DISTRIBUTION: Chaparral and other communities, Coast Ranges and Sierra foothills, Trinity and Shasta counties to Baja California.

Culture: No special treatment is required to germinate the seed of any species of *Clematis*. But it is usually propagated by taking half-woody shoots from the base of the plant and rooting them in sandy loam. Plants require full sun, and are water tolerant. Pipestem Clematis is quite showy trained on fences and outbuildings, or allowed to climb into trees. Once a year, in early spring, some of the long vines may be pruned out, and a few shortened for good flower production.

Estimate of Garden Value: If it were not deciduous, the Pipestem Clematis might be a more popular garden subject. The sinuous, ropy vines are bare until April, but are effective on a section of fence in my mountain garden, producing a wealth of creamy flower clusters every May. Plants remain green until about October. In my experience this is a persistent plant with some dying back of vines each year, but with many new ones to replace them each spring. Pruning can be done in spring by shortening long shoots, or by eliminating vines as required to suit the space.

GENUS *CLINTONIA:* CLINTONIAS
(Family Liliaceae: Lily)

Two species of *Clintonia* are native to California, both indigenous to shaded, and usually damp woodlands. Both are highly desirable as garden plants, but seem to resist conditions away from their natural habitat.

Clintonia andrewsiana
Andrew's Clintonia

HABIT: Perennial herb from slender rootstock, with stout peduncle, 2.5–5 dm, 10–20 in. FOLIAGE: Basal, broadly elliptic, smooth, glossy, bright green, 15–25 cm, 6–9 in. FLOWERS: Terminal umbel, small, bell-shaped, intense rose-crimson. FRUIT: Dark blue, ovoid berry, showy. DISTRIBUTION: Damp, shaded woods, Redwood Forests, Del Norte to Monterey counties.

Culture: Andrew's Clintonia may be grown from seed, although it is reported to be slow to germinate. Seed leaves are typical of the lily family, gradually enlarging until a mature plant is formed in about five years. Leaf mold, acid soil, ample water, and shade for most of the day are its requirements. Andrew's Clintonia may be used in combination with other shade lovers, such as azaleas, rhododendrons, wild irises, and ferns for contrast in foliage. In a warm, dry climate this clintonia can be used as a pot plant; it needs an acid, humus soil mixture and should be kept in a cool, shaded place.

Estimate of Garden Value: Although a few gardeners have reported success with this lovely plant, others have found it difficult to propagate and to transplant. In my opinion a more intensive study of its requirements and careful handling with attention to soil and exposure could give better results.

GENUS *COREOPSIS:* COREOPSIS, TICKSEEDS
(Family Compositae: Sunflower)

Two perennial and six annual *Coreopsis* are native to California. There are many garden forms from other areas, and some of these have become naturalized. All have attractive, daisy-flowers and make excellent garden plants.

Coreopsis maritima
Sea Dahlia or Coast Coreopsis

HABIT: Stout, branched, from a tuberous taproot, 3–8 dm, 1–2½ ft. FOLIAGE: Divided into narrow lobes, somewhat succulent, yellow-green, like coarse fern. FLOWERS: Large daisies, glistening canary yellow, long stems. Long blooming period, early spring into summer. FRUIT: Oblong achene. DISTRIBUTION: Sea cliffs, coastal dunes and strand, San Luis Obispo to Los Angeles counties, and Channel Islands.

Culture: Sea Dahlia is easily grown from seed planted in autumn, setting the seedlings out in early spring. For blooms the first year, start seed in mid-July, and set the young plants out in October or November. Sea Dahlia requires full sun, moderate amounts of water, and flower stems should be clipped. It is recommended for sandy or shallow soils, is wind tolerant, and should be more widely used for seashore and interior gardens.

Estimate of Garden Value: Although the Sea Dahlia is short lived, it provides an extended season of long-stemmed daisies. In my Los Gatos garden it was especially attractive with the deep blue of California Gilia *(Gilia achilleaefolia),* as well as Whitewhorl Lupine *(Lupinus densiflorus)* and several perennial lupines. In mild coastal areas plants may begin to bloom in January, and continue off and on until summer. Sea Dahlia is not tolerant of cold or of late spring frosts.

GENUS *CYNOGLOSSUM:* HOUND'S TONGUES
(Family Boraginaceae: Borage)

Two species of *Cynoglossum* are native to California, both having conspicuous seed vessels covered with barbed prickles. The one described here has attractive, lively blue flowers, while the other has coils of dull, pinkish brown blossoms.

Cynoglossum grande
Grand Hound's Tongue

HABIT: Erect, robust, herbaceous, from a thick, deep root, 2–4 dm, 8–15 in. FOLIAGE: Large, ovate, long-petioled basal leaves; stem leaves smaller, bright, dark green. Infurled and purplish tinted as they unfold. FLOWERS: Open panicle of bright blue, centered with fine beading of white, from hairy buds. March–June. FRUIT: Barbed nutlets. DISTRIBU-TION: Dry, shaded slopes and woodlands, Coast Ranges from San Luis Obispo County north, and in the Sierra Nevada from Tulare and Butte to Siskiyou counties.

Culture: Grand Hound's Tongue is easily grown from seed, the seedlings producing one or two pairs of typical leaves the first year. Plants may take two or more years to reach flowering size, but appear regularly each spring thereafter. The tightly furled leaves push up in February or March. Grand Hound's Tongue requires high or broken shade, leaf mold in the soil, and moderate amounts of water.

Estimate of Garden Value: This perennial is one of the earliest of spring flowers and is dependable and long lived in my experience. Plants may be cut to the ground in late summer when the foliage dies down. Several clumps are companions for lilies, wild iris, and other shade plants.

GENUS *DELPHINIUM:* LARKSPURS
(Family Ranunculaceae: Crowfoot)

Thirty-one species of *Delphinium* are native to California; all perennials, growing from dry-appearing, fibrous or tuber-like roots. (See Pl. 3D.) Almost all are very attractive because of their handsome, lobed or cleft foliage and luminous flower colors of red, shades of blue and purple, and one in yellow. A few are used in gardens, but some do not respond well to cultivation, and many have never been tested for their adaptability.

Delphinium cardinale
Scarlet Larkspur

HABIT: Erect, simple or branched, deep, thickened, woody roots, 1–2 m, 3–6 ft. (See Fig. 21.) FOLIAGE: Large, round, five-parted, the divisions shallowly lobed. FLOWERS: Typical, spurred, bright red, in open raceme or panicles. May–July. FRUIT: Small, erect follicles. DISTRIBUTION: Dry openings in brush and woods, Monterey to San Diego counties, and Baja California.

Culture: Scarlet Larkspur may be grown from seed and

Figure 21 *Delphinium cardinale,* Scarlet Larkspur

usually germinates well with no pretreatment. Plants produce several sets of leaves the first year, and form their typical, tuber-like roots. Plants should have sun to very light afternoon shade, well-drained, coarse soil, and water only during their period of active growth. One method of handling the brittle roots is to plant them intact in chunks of soil from the flat. Bare roots may also be transplanted while dormant into warm, well-drained soil. In my experience plants go dormant in mid- to late summer, and should not be watered thereafter. Scarlet Larkspur has the distinction of having been used in the development of pink garden delphiniums.

Estimate of Garden Value: There is very little record of larkspurs as garden plants. Experiences at Rancho Santa Ana Botanic Garden show that seed germinated well but that plants failed to live for more than two or three years. Root rot, attacks by rodents, and heavy soil all contributed to losses of the plants. Nor has there been much consideration for species of stream sides and marshy places, such as Tower Delphinium

(*D. glaucum*), so tall and free-flowering as to rival garden delphiniums. In most cases the native delphiniums have a distinct charm of their own, and should not be used in competition with the garden forms. From my own limited experiences I believe that, with attention to their requirements, especially those of porous soil and a dormant period, the wild larkspurs may one day grace the semi-dry garden.

GENUS *DICENTRA:* BLEEDING HEARTS
(Family Fumariaceae: Fumitory)

Five species of *Dicentra* are native to California. This genus has characteristic heart-shaped flowers. Two species that grow in subalpine regions are quite rare and have flowers which resemble a steer's head. Another species from southern California is equally interesting for its white or cream-colored flowers and purple-tipped petals.

Dicentra formosa
Pacific Bleeding Heart or Dutchman's Breeches

HABIT: Herbaceous, with slender stems, from fleshy, pinkish, spreading roots, 2–4.5 dm, 8–18 in. (See Fig. 22.) FOLIAGE: Basal, long-petioled, biternately compound, pale green. FLOWERS: Pendant, heart-shaped, dark or purplish rose, held above foliage, on graceful stems. FRUIT: Two-valved capsule, shining black seed. DISTRIBUTION: Damp, shaded places, Redwood Forest, Northern Oak Woodland, coniferous forests up to 7,000 feet. Coast Ranges, Santa Cruz County north and Sierra Nevada, Tulare to Siskiyou counties.

Culture: Pacific Bleeding Heart may be grown from seed or from sections of the fleshy roots. Plants require humus soil, ample moisture, and high shade, although they will grow in considerable sun if given enough water. Root rot can be a problem in clay or badly drained soil.

Estimate of Garden Value: In a normal, shaded and watered border, Pacific Bleeding Heart will increase at a rapid rate, and it is sometimes considered to be a pest. It has few equals as a lacy ground cover under trees, in heavy shade of buildings or fences. Its ferny foilage affords a pleasing contrast in almost any combination of shade-loving plants.

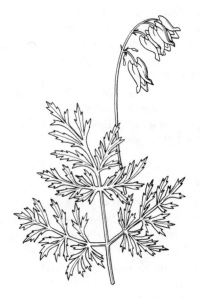

Figure 22 *Dicentra formosa,* Pacific Bleeding Heart

Dicentra chrysantha
Golden Ear-Drops

HABIT: Erect, with several stems from stout root, 5–15 dm, 19 in–6 ft. FOLIAGE: Basal, in large spray, bipinnate and further divided into narrow lobes, glaucous, pale green. FLOWERS: Heart-shaped, golden yellow, many in loose panicle. FRUIT: Oval capsule. DISTRIBUTION: Dry slopes, frequent on burns and disturbed places. Inner Coast Ranges, Mendocino County south, and in Sierra, Calaveras County to Baja California.

Culture: The seed of Golden Ear-Drops resists germination, and the best method is pretreatment by burning straw over the planted flat, and then watering it thoroughly. Even then germination of the seed is spotty. Young plants may be transferred to fiber pots, and eventually into dry, sunny borders, watering only until the plants are established. Soil should be porous, well drained, and kept on the dry side. According to experiences at botanic gardens, plants are short lived unless in full sun and lean soil. This large, attractive perennial should be used with other natives having similar requirements, such as buckwheats, penstemons, shrubby salvias, or Woolly Blue-Curls *(Trichostema lanatum)*.

Estimate of Garden Value: When it can be successfully cultivated, Golden Ear-Drops is valuable for its pale green, divided foliage as well as for its yellow hearts. There is probably much more to learn about growing and handling this species.

GENUS *DODECATHEON:* SHOOTING STARS
(Family Primulaceae: Primrose)

Nine species of *Dodecatheon* are native to California, well known for their spring flowers of reflexed segments and their sprightly bearing. The wide assortment of common names attests to the popularity of this genus, which includes Sailor Caps, Bird-Bills, Mosquito-Bills, Wild Cyclamen, and Rooster Combs.

Culture: Species of *Dodecatheon* may be grown from seed, sown in autumn or early spring, but seedlings go dormant in early summer and no amount of water and attention will change this tendency. Plants do not flower for the first two or three years, but produce a small whorl of leaves and a typical, slender, tuber-like root system. Allow the seedlings to go dormant and withhold water until the following spring. Tubers may be allowed to remain in the flat for another year, following the same pattern of withholding water during the dormant period, or they may be put into a border. My system was to break the firm soil with the roots intact, and plant these chunks in a prepared place. Plants prefer some shade, especially from the afternoon sun, and are tolerant of moderate amounts of moisture in well-drained soil. Although shooting stars accept dryness following seed setting, some gardeners continue to give water and, where the soil is porous, they flourish and make abundant natural increase. Species of *Dodecatheon* are not recommended for a highly cultivated border, but rather a rock garden, raised area, or north or east slope. Some authorities suggest that roots of well-established plants be divided in early spring but, as with seedlings, these will not flower for a year or more following division.

Estimate of Garden Value: Shooting stars are graceful and charming when given the proper care and situation. Rock gardeners have made the greatest contribution to the culture of these woodlanders. Several pleasing garden combinations can be considered, such as with white crocus or among Sapphire Anemone. A choice combination, typical of California's grassy hills, is their use under the native Redbud, since their blooming period coincides and flower color is similar. The shooting star has been chosen as the symbol of the American Rock Garden Society because of its jaunty bearing and because most species belong to North America.

Dodecatheon hendersonii
Henderson's Shooting Star

HABIT: Herbaceous, short, thick rootstock, erect flowering stems, 1.2–4.8 dm, 5–16 in. FOLIAGE: Elliptic to spatulate, light, bright green, forming a whorl at ground level. FLOWERS: Five corolla segments swept back, dark beak set off by yellow band; nodding or outward facing in open umbel at top of smooth scape; rose-pink, rose-crimson, lilac, and occasionally white. FRUIT: Upright, reddish brown capsules, with abundant seed, ripe by mid-summer. DISTRIBUTION: Shaded woods and slopes, many plant communities; Coast Ranges, San Benito County north, and in Sierra, Tulare County north, and in San Bernardino Mountains.

Culture and Estimate of Garden Value: See generic description above.

Dodecatheon clevelandii
Cleveland's Shooting Star

HABIT: Erect, from rootstock, with scapes 1.8–4 dm, 1–2 ft. FOLIAGE: Basal, oblanceolate to spatulate, light green, crisped on margins. FLOWERS: Typical, bright purple to white, maroon beak set off by yellow band. FRUIT: Erect capsules. DISTRIBUTION: Grassy flats and slopes, Los Angeles County south.

Culture: See generic description above.

Estimate of Garden Value: D. clevelandii is somewhat more robust than *D. hendersonii* and is reported to be long lived under semi-dry conditions. Several flowering stems may be produced by each mature plant. Three subspecies have some variations in leaves and flowers, and together occur in several plant communities from central to southern California. Most species have a faint scent which is difficult to define, but which to my nose is the essence of all the spring flowers and grasses.

GENUS *DUDLEYA:* LIVE-FOREVERS
(Family Crassulaceae: Stonecrop)

Twenty-one species of *Dudleya* are native to California, many being spectacular rock plants with thick, succulent leaves. A number of the species are variable and said to hybridize freely, both in nature and when growing together in gardens.

Culture: Most succulents can and should be grown from seed, because of too much digging of wild plants. Seed is fine and should be dusted thinly over the soil on top of a layer of sphagnum moss, watered, and covered with glass until the seed sprouts. Remove the glass and keep flats in a well-lighted place until the plants are large enough to move to another flat or to individual containers. Plants may be put in their permanent quarters after about one year of growth. Succulents are especially adaptable to rock gardens, and may also be used on slopes, terraces, raised borders, or as edgings with other plants of similar requirements. They require coarse, well-drained soil, sun, and very little water. Water should be given as slow irrigation because overhead watering can cause rot of the root crown. Moles that nibble at the root crown also have been a problem at some botanic gardens.

Estimate of Garden Value: Most of the native succulent plants with any garden history seem amenable to cultivation when their requirements are met. They are picturesque and satisfactory pot plants, and are easier to grow and care for in containers. Most are pest free except for an occasional attack of mealybug. Practically all increase by the formation of new rosettes, and most live for many years with very little attention.

Dudleya pulverulenta
Chalk Dudleya

HABIT: Rosette of succulent leaves from a thick caudex, plant covered with a white, mealy powder. (See Fig. 23.) FOLIAGE: Thick, obovate-spatulate, wide at the base and coming to a point; stem leaves smaller and clasping. FLOWERS: Campanulate, red, many on an erect, stout stem. May–July. FRUIT: Follicle, with slender, brown seed. DISTRIBUTION: Rocky cliffs and canyons, Coastal Sage Scrub, Chaparral, etc., near coast from San Luis Obispo County to Baja California.

Culture and Estimate of Garden Value: See generic description above.

Figure 23 *Dudleya pulverulenta,* Chalk Dudleya

GENUS *ERIOGONUM:* WILD BUCKWHEATS
(Family Polygonaceae: Buckwheat)

California has seventy-six species in the genus *Eriogonum*, related to *Pagopyrum* from which buckwheat flour is made. The wild buckwheats are generally sturdy plants, evergreen and drought tolerant. They occupy various types of terrain at practically all elevations, from coastal cliffs to alpine heights and on rocky ridges, serpentine soils, chaparral, exposed foothill slopes, and deserts. The ubiquitous *E. nudum* and its varieties are common and well-known for natural seeding on new road cuts, and for flowers all through the summer heat. From central to southern California, the California Buckwheat *(E. fasciculatum)* forms extensive colonies on coast, mesa, and

Figure 24 *Eriogonum umbellatum* var. *polyanthum,* Sulphur Eriogonum

into the foothills; it is important as a ground cover as well as a bee plant. (See Chart 6.)

Description: Members of the genus *Eriogonum* include some annuals, a great number of perennials, and a few which are considered to be shrubs. Some species are more curious than beautiful, and many are more weedy than ornamental. Others supply hardy and enduring plants that give a western flavor to gardens and large-scale landscaping. Within the genus plants range in size from mat-forming kinds to the four- or five-foot St. Catherine's Lace *(E. giganteum)*. Wild buckwheats grow from a thick, often woody, and far-ranging root system which makes it impossible to dig mature plants. The leaves in most species are basal and frequently appear felted from closely matted hairs, especially on the reverse side. Upper surfaces may be smooth or hairy, often textured, and in many they are thick and leathery. Flowers are small, of petaloid sepals arranged in various types of inflorescences, including tight flower balls, loose clusters, large and open sprays, or in a few may be solitary. Colors include several degrees of white, mostly dull or off-white, cream, yellow, rose, and pink. Fruit is a hard, dry, generally one-seeded achene.

Culture: Species of *Eriogonum* may be grown from seed which germinates well without any pretreatment. Plant seed in autumn using a coarse soil mix, and cover with sphagnum moss to help prevent damping-off. Seedlings may be transplanted to three-inch pots the following spring, and the shrubby varieties in gallon cans, until of proper size to set in their permanent place. These are among the most drought tolerant of all natives and should be planted in full sun, lean soil, and watered moderately until well established. Occasional deep irrigation may be given several times during the dry season, but most resent overhead watering. Many of the buckwheats will provide volunteer seedlings once plants are well established. They can be used with other natives having similar requirements, such as species of *Penstemon, Salvia, Monardella, Eriophyllum, Trichostema,* etc. Although considered to be common, I like to use Naked Eriogonum *(E. nudum)* in a mixed border where it provides an airy effect of

CHART 6 *Eriogonum*: Wild Buckwheats

Plant	Height	Flowers	Culture	Remarks	Distribution
E. crocatum Conejo Buckwheat	1-2 or 3 dm (4-8 or 12 in)	Flat heads, sulphur yellow. April-July.	Sun, dry, well-drained soil. Raised border, rock garden.	Leaves broad-ovate, densely white, felted.	Rocky slopes, Ventura Co.
E. grande var. *rubescens* Red Buckwheat	8-15 dm (31-72 in)	Spherical heads, red to crimson-rose. June-Oct.	Sun, semi-dry soil. Terrace, raised border, rock garden.	Leaves undulate on margin, green above, woolly beneath.	Bluffs, Channel Ids.
E. lobbii Lobb's Eriogonum	.5-2 dm (2-7 in)	Large capitate umbels, white to rose. June-Aug.	Sun, semi-dry border. With drought-tolerant plants, rock garden.	Leaves in rosette, silvery-white.	Slopes, Lake to Siskiyou, Inyo, and Plumus cos.
E. proliferum ssp. *strictum* Proliferous Eriogonum	1.5-2.5 dm (6-12 in)	Terminal, rounded heads, yellow or white, aging rose. June-Aug.	Sun, moderate water. Rock garden, raised border.	Leaves basal, white, felted, thick.	Dry forest, Trinity to Modoc cos.

Species	Size	Flowers	Culture	Plant/Leaves	Habitat
E. arborescens Island Buckwheat	6-15 dm (24-72 in)	Dense terminal cymes, whitish to pinkish. April-Sept.	Sun, water-tolerant with porous soil. Edging, curbing, ground cover.	Dense bushlet with linear leaves.	Rocky canyon, Channel Ids.
E. giganteum St. Catherine's Lace	3-20 or 30 dm (12-40 or 120 in)	Large, forked cymes, tiny, oyster-white flowers, lacy. May-Aug.	Sun, water-tolerant. With shrubs, native perennials.	Thick, ovate leaves, pale above, felted beneath.	Coast Scrub, Santa Catalina Id.
E. cinereum Ashy-Leaf Buckwheat	6-15 dm (24-72 in)	Pinkish heads on elongate branches. June-Dec.	With other buckwheats, or Woolly-Blue-Curls.	Leaves ovate, ashy, green, white beneath.	Coast, Santa Barbara and Santa Rosa ids.
E. nudum Naked Eriogonum	3-10 dm (12-36 in)	Terminal capitate heads, white, pink, yellow. July-Aug.	Sun, semi-dry, tolerates moderate amounts of water. Mixer, dry borders.	Erect plant. Basal, long-stemmed leaves. 7 varieties.	Dry, rocky, Coast Ranges, San Francisco north, Sierra Nevada, Tulare Co. north.
E. umbellatum var. *polyanthum* Sulphur Eriogonum (See Fig. 24)	3-10 dm (12-36 in)	Large umbel, bright yellow, bracts below inflorescence. June-Aug.	Sun, sandy to porous soil. Dry border, rock garden.	Pale green, ovate leaves, white beneath.	Dry soil, Placer, Siskiyou, and Modoc cos.

many spherical flower balls. Island Buckwheat *(E. arbores-cens)* and California Buckwheat have been used in massed plantings, sometimes as extensive ground covers in dry areas. The mat-forming species are also suitable for rock gardens, semi-dry borders, dry slopes and terraces, raised borders, rock walls, or in a thin planting of native shrubs.

Estimate of Garden Value: It is difficult to estimate the worth of this large genus when the advantages of the various members are hardly known to gardeners. They are foremost among California's drought-tolerant plants, and their pos-sibilities as enduring, hardy, and accommodating materials seems almost endless. They have a long flowering period be-ginning in June and extending into early autumn, are relatively long lived under proper conditions, and none, to the best of my knowledge, has invasive tendencies. Several of the large ones have a natural shapeliness, often described as sculptured. St. Catherine's Lace is especially handsome with its foot-wide sprays of lacy, oyster white flowers. These interesting plants should enhance California gardens, and provide materials in keeping with our climate, terrain, and western landscaping.

GENUS *ERIOPHYLLUM:*
WOOLLY SUNFLOWERS
(Family Compositae: Sunflower)

Thirteen species of *Eriophyllum* are native to California, stout in habit, and often woody based. They are considered too coarse for the refined garden, but are useful in the background of a native plant border, and valuable for long flowering period in summer. Variable in compactness and in size and cut of foliage.

Eriophyllum confertiflorum
Yellow Yarrow

HABIT: Erect, branched, herbaceous stems from woody base, stems white-felted, 2–6 dm, to 2 ft. FOLIAGE: Cuneate to obovate in outline, lobed into oblong or linear divisions, pale green above, woolly beneath. FLOWERS: Small, bright yellow daisies, arranged in solid heads. FRUIT: Achene with pappus. DISTRIBUTION: Common on brushy slopes, many plant communities, sea level to mountains. Coast Ranges Mendocino and Tehama to San Diego counties, and in Sierra foothills, Calaveras to Inyo counties.

Culture: Yellow Yarrow may be grown from seed, but botanic gardens have recorded loss of seedlings following transplanting. Since this species was native to the Los Gatos area, I moved some small seedlings to my semi-dry border where they flourished among a thin planting of native shrubs. Plants should have sun for most of the day, well-drained soil, and will tolerate some moisture in porous soil.

Estimate of Garden Value: Yellow Yarrow is valuable for summer flowers, and might be used with the brilliant blue Royal Penstemon *(Penstemon spectabilis)* and other natives that need similar conditions. In my experience it is enduring if not over-watered. For neatness, plants may be cut to within a few inches of the ground in late autumn.

Eriophyllum lanatum ssp. arachnoideum
Dwarf Woolly Sunflower

HABIT: Herbaceous from semi-woody base, spreading to decumbent, most parts with soft, woolly hair, 3–6 dm, 1–2 ft. (See Fig. 25.) FOLIAGE: Broad in outline, lobed, margins revolute, pale green, thinly hairy beneath. FLOWERS: Dark yellow daisies, single on each stem. (See Pl. 2C.) FRUIT: Achene. DISTRIBUTION: Coastal bluffs, shady banks, Monterey to Del Norte counties.

Culture: Dwarf Woolly Sunflower may be grown from seed, planted in autumn, transplanted to pots when the second leaf has formed, and into permanent quarters in early spring. It requires full sun and only moderate amounts of moisture. With too much water, plants tend to become straggly with small flowers. Blooming begins about April, and continues into mid-summer if the old flower heads are removed. This is not an invasive plant, forms close mats, and could be used with Bowl-Tubed Iris *(Iris macrosiphon),* Elegant Brodiaea *(Brodiaea elegans),* and pockets of California Bells *(Phacelia minor).* For many years in Los Gatos I grew this engaging

Figure 25 *Eriophyllum lanatum* ssp. *arachnoideum,*
Dwarf Woolly Sunflower

plant with Foothill Penstemon *(Penstemon heterophyllus)*
where they bloomed together providing contrasting flower and
foliage color.

Estimate of Garden Value: In mild climates Dwarf Woolly
Yarrow is evergreen, forming a pleasant cover of closely
spaced, pale green leaves. Plants tend to become woody after
several years, but volunteers appear frequently, or new plants
may be raised from seed. It is not entirely cold hardy in my
mountain garden, merely surviving, but not spreading or
blooming in its accustomed manner.

GENUS *ERYSIMUM:* WALLFLOWERS
(Family Cruciferae: Mustard)

There are thirteen native species of *Erysimum* in California;
most are free-flowering and worthy of garden culture.

Erysimum capitatum
Douglas's Wallflower

HABIT: Erect, stout biennial, branched above, 2–8 dm,
8–31 in. FOLIAGE: Basal leaves long, slender, dentate on the

margins, and somewhat reduced on upper stem. FLOWERS: In terminal heads, of yellow, orange, and sometimes brick red or a purplish maroon, fragrant. March–July. FRUIT: Long, slender, somewhat flattened pod, light brown seeds. DISTRIBUTION: Frequent on dry, stony places of hills and low mountains in many plant communities. Away from coast in cismontane and montane California.

Culture: Douglas's Wallflower requires sun for most of the day, is drought tolerant but accepts moderate amounts of water with well-drained soil. As with most of the genus, it grows readily from seed, best planted in late summer. Young plants may be shifted from the flat to three-inch fiber pots, and set out in winter or early spring. Most will bloom after the first full year of growth. Although a biennial, Douglas's Wallflower is inclined to persist for several years, and provides a few volunteer seedlings. In the semi-dry border of my Los Gatos garden the flowering period extended from spring into early summer. My plants had flowers in rich yellow, and companion plants included California Poppies, several species of *Lupinus* and of *Brodiaea,* and the tall, blue-flowered Tansy Phacelia *(Phacelia tanacetifolia).* It may also be used among shrubs, or to the rear of the brilliant, blue-flowered Foothill Penstemon *(Penstemon heterophyllus).*

Estimate of Garden Value: Douglas's Wallflower has been in cultivation for many years, but still has not attained its deserved popularity. This species and several others are adaptable, long-flowering, and have performed well in a semi-dry, sunny situation with other native plants.

Other Species:

Erysimum concinnum, Pt. Reyes Wallflower, is one of the outstanding natives of the coastal strand at the Point Reyes National Seashore, and has recently become a popular garden plant. Large heads of soft yellow to creamy flowers begin to bloom in February, and continue into mid-spring. It is a low plant with oblong, dark green leaves, a biennial or short-lived perennial which grows from a deep taproot. Flowers have a delicate fragrance typical of the genus.

Erysimum menziesii, Menzies' Wallflower, is similar, but not cultivated to my knowledge. It is a delightful plant of sand dunes from Monterey County northward. Only a few inches high, it has dense heads of soft yellow flowers that appear to be sitting on a circular pad of long-stemmed, spatulate leaves. Flowers have a pronounced, sweet fragrance.

GENUS *HEUCHERA:* ALUM-ROOTS
(Family Saxifragaceae: Saxifrage)

Heuchera is an entirely American genus of plants, of which sixteen are native to California. Compact plants have rich green leaves, variously notched, lobed, or toothed, and are valuable in the shade garden.

Heuchera micrantha
Crevice Heuchera

HABIT: Compact evergreen, from thick caudex, with flower stems rising above, 3–7 dm, 12–30 in. FOLIAGE: Basal, roundish cordate, five- to seven-lobed, sparingly hairy, dark green. FLOWERS: Tiny, on slender panicle, white, airy in appearance in contrast to dark foliage. May–June. (See Pl. 3B.) FRUIT: Small capsule. DISTRIBUTION: Moist, rocky banks, near coast from San Luis Obispo to Del Norte counties.

Culture: Crevice Heuchera may be grown from seed, requiring about two years to reach flowering size. It is also simple to take cuttings from the thick neck section, rooting these in sand, and planting out after an ample root system has formed. Authorities report that alum-roots cross readily when several species are grown together, and interesting hybrids can be expected. They are unexcelled for shaded areas, such as a large rock garden, terraces or slopes, or border edging. Crevice Heuchera also makes a fine pot plant, persisting for several years before needing repotting.

Estimate of Garden Value: Even without flowers this is an excellent plant for the shade border because the foliage remains neat through the seasons. Overwatering or poor drainage can cause root rot.

Heuchera maxima × H. sanguinea
'Santa Ana Cardinal' cultivar

HABIT: Evergreen, clumping, 6–9 dm, 2–3 ft. FOLIAGE: Round, cordate, scalloped edges, dark green. FLOWERS:

Tiny, urn-shaped, freely borne on tall, wand-like stems, rose-red. May–July, but almost everblooming in mild areas. FRUIT: Capsule. DISTRIBUTION: Island Heuchera *(H. maxima)* is native to canyon walls and cliffs on Santa Cruz, Santa Rosa, and Anacapa islands. *H. sanguinea,* from which the garden Coral Bells was derived, is native to Arizona, New Mexico, and into Mexico.

Culture: The same as for *H. micrantha.*

Estimate of Garden Value: This hybrid is a large and almost ever-blooming perennial which is especially effective for massed plantings among trees and other areas of light shade. Its slender flower spikes and lovely color give an element of grace to borders and wooded places. Hybrids are vigorous and strong growing, and require only moderate amounts of moisture. Selections for pleasing flower color are still being made, and two new ones of this same cross include *H.* 'Susanna' with deep pink flowers on twenty-inch stems, and *H.* 'Genevieve' with soft pink flowers on delicate stems.

GENUS *IRIS:* IRISES, FLEUR-DE-LIS
(Family Iridaceae: Iris)

Thirteen species of *Iris* are native to California, and all are beardless. They occupy various kinds of habitats, including redwood forests, coastal plains, oak woodlands, mixed forests, and mountain meadows. All but two species are low and spreading, some eventually forming huge mats. The natural refinement and sprightly appearance of these irises makes them outstanding garden materials. (See Chart 7.)

Description: The native irises are perennial herbs, usually evergreen and growing from a creeping, tuberous rhizome. Leaves are long and narrow, from pale to dark green, and tough in substance. Threads from these linear leaves were used in Indian basketry. Flower stems are erect, simple in most but branched in a few, and in Bowl-Tubed Iris *(Iris macrosiphon),* there is scarcely any stem. Blossoms vary somewhat in spacing of the parts, width of falls (sepals), and the inner, erect standards (petals). Colors range from pale blue, lavender, and mauve to deeper shades of blue and purple, along with yellows of varying intensity, cream, and white, often with contrasting

CHART 7 *Iris:* Irises, Fleur-De-Lis

Plant	Leaf Height	Flowers	Culture	Remarks	Distribution
I. innominata Golden Iris (See Pl. 2E)	to 3.5 dm (14 in)	Yellow shades, lavender, purple, etc. May-June.	Broken shade, moderate moisture, humus in soil.	Slender. Outstanding hybrid with Douglas's Iris, borders, under trees.	Shade, Del Norte north.
I. munzii Munz' Iris (See Fig. 26)	to 5 dm (19 in)	Large, pale lavender, blue-violet, white. March-April.	Sun or high shade. Water-tolerant borders.	Erect. Distinct from other species.	Woods, dry, Tulare Co.
I. tenuissima Slender Iris	to 4 dm (16 in)	Cream, lavender to red-brown veins, narrow sepals. April-June.	Dry shade, humus in soil. Slow to spread, crosses with *I. macrosiphon.*	Narrow, gray-green leaves, reddish at base. Rock garden.	Dry woods, Butte, Siskiyou, to Humboldt cos.
I. longipetala Long-Petaled Iris	to 7 dm (28 in)	Large, pale blue, dark veining. March-May.	Sun, moisture. Border with native annuals, bulbs, perennials.	Erect. Robust in habit. Endemic to central Calif.	Coast, Monterey to Mendocino cos.

I. douglasiana Douglas's Iris	to 10 dm (36 in)	Typical, in blue, lavender, purple, cream, white. Feb.-May.	Shade, moisture, humus in soil. Vigorous, with spreading clumps.	Rock garden, ground cover, borders.	Coastal forest, Santa Barbara Co. to Ore.
I. macrosiphon Bowl-Tubed Iris	to 3 dm (12 in)	Blue, violet, yellow, apricot, white, rounded falls. April-May.	Sun to broken shade, moderate moisture, porous soil.	Spreading. Cover, edging, rock garden. Variation in flower color.	Open to wooded, Sierra foothills, inner Coast Ranges.
I. hartwegii Hartweg's Iris (See Fig. 27)	to 4.5 dm (20 in)	Cream or yellow with lavender veining. May-June.	Semi-dry, sun to high shade, leaf mold in soil.	Naturalized under trees.	Woods, Butte to Kern cos.
I. hartwegii ssp. *australis*	to 4.5 dm (20 in)	Lavender to purple. May-June.	Semi-dry, sun to broken shade, leaf mold in soil.	Border edging, ground cover.	Dry woods, mts. so. Calif.
I. fernaldii Fernald's Iris	to 4 dm (16 in)	Cream with lavender to red-brown veining. April-May.	Sun to high shade, moderate moisture.	Borders, among shrubs, trees.	Woods, Santa Cruz to Solano cos.

Figure 26 *Iris munzii,* Munz' Iris

veins and color zones on the falls. Seed is generously supplied in conspicuous, oval to oblong, upright capsules.

Culture: Practically all of the native irises are unexcelled for shade situations, even the dense shade of walls and fences. High tree shade is ideal, although they will tolerate sun for most of the day in mild areas, and should have afternoon shade and ample water in the interior regions. Plants may be watered the year around; they will grow in any soil, but the addition of leaf mold will promote vigorous growth and the production of new rhizomes. When allowed to increase freely, plants will naturalize and eventually form extensive ground covers. Unless the seed vessels are removed there will be many volunteer plants, but if inferior flower size or color appears it should be culled immediately. In autumn old leaves should be removed from the center of large clumps, the foliage cut back, and a mulch applied, especially if the irises are being naturalized in a

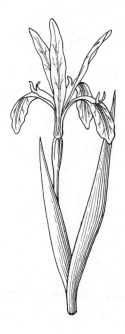

Figure 27 *Iris hartwegii,* Hartweg's Iris

semi-dry area. Among the various species there is a long period of bloom, with Douglas's Iris beginning on the coast in January or February, and the mountain dwellers flowering into June. All species which I have grown in the mountains are cold hardy except for Douglas's Iris, and Long-Petaled Iris *(Iris longipetala).* Hybrids of Douglas's Iris and Golden Iris *(I. innominata),* however, perform well where low winter temperatures prevail.

Propagation by Seed: Iris seed is easily collected from the large capsules. If stored for any length of time, a pinch of Captan should be used to prevent the seed from being devoured. In my experience autumn is the best time for seeding; germination begins in two or three months and often continues beyond that time. A friable seed mixture of sand, loam, and either peat or screened leaf mold is best, covering the seed with sphagnum moss to aid in preventing damping-off of seedlings.

Young plants can be shifted to three-inch pots and held until late summer, and then put into their permanent quarters. Plants will begin to bloom by their second year if growth has been continuous. Direct seeding is possible in places which can be left undisturbed, as among shrubs, or among low perennials where the seedlings can be sheltered.

Propagation by Division: Native irises in the wild tend to produce only a small, dry rhizome with stringy roots which is difficult to dig, in addition to being illegal. Vigorous garden plants produce firm, white, growing roots especially in winter and spring growing seasons, and clumps are easily divided at those times. Remove a new fan with fleshy roots, set in a prepared site, water it, and provide shade for a few days if the place is in full sun. Frequent division appears to keep the plants vigorous, as well as being the best method of increasing the supply of superior forms.

Garden Uses: Since they are adaptable garden plants, the wild irises may be used in a number of garden situations. In my Los Gatos garden they seeded freely and the resulting extensive mats in lightly wooded areas were a constant delight. In the semi-dry border the Long-Petaled Iris with its clear blue flowers began to bloom in February, and was especially striking with an underplanting of Fivespot Nemophila *(Nemophila maculata)*. The late and renowned horticulturist, Sydney B. Mitchell, used the Douglas's Iris as a ground cover on the east slope of his Berkeley garden. Plants were sheared back each autumn following seed gathering until a dense carpet was formed. Few plants give a better performance under trees where the irises contrast to other shade plants. In broken tree shade the clear yellow flowers of the Golden Iris have a luminous quality, and would be superb edging a bed of azalea-mollis hybrids.

Estimate of Garden Value: Native irises are free flowering, most are long lived, require very little attention, and provide an abundance of seed. Because they cross freely in the wilds there has been considerable activity in selecting out superior forms, and a few named hybrids have long been popular garden plants. This interest is now becoming intensified with the realization that the range of flower color and markings is practically unlimited. Flowers in different sizes and with wide, ruffled, or fluted falls, in clear, vibrant colors, along with contrasting veins or large eye-spots are being developed. These lovely flowers are attaining the popularity which they deserve, and exciting possibilities continue to beckon the adventurous.

GENUS *LEWISIA:* LEWISIAS
(Family Portulacaceae: Purslane)

The genus *Lewisia* is confined to the western states; of eighteen species, thirteen are native to California. Members of the genus have a reputation for being difficult to grow, although some have long been grown by botanists and rock gardeners who know their requirements. These aristocrats of the plant world are rare in nature and most have beautiful flowers, often compared to waterlilies.

Lewisia rediviva
Bitterroot

HABIT: Short caudex from a fleshy taproot, with many stems, 1–3 cm, 1–1½ in. FOLIAGE: Basal, linear, fleshy, club-shaped, slightly longer than the stems. FLOWERS: Flat, of petaloid sepals and petals, rose or white, from brownish buds. March–June. FRUIT: Ellipsoid capsule, dark, shining seeds. DISTRIBUTION: Loose, gravelly slopes, rocky places, Santa Lucia Mountains to Siskiyou, Modoc, Mono, and Trinity counties. Widely distributed in the northwest, and state flower of Montana.

Culture: Bitterroot is propagated from seeds, which germinate readily and should be planted the first few months after ripening. Seedlings have tiny, club-shaped leaves the first year, and require several years to form a flowering plant. The soil can be of equal parts crushed rock or coarse sand, and screened leaf mold. This species generally provides ample seed, and volunteer plants are apt to be found around established ones. Bitterroot should be grown in coarse, gravelly soil, watered only during its spring period of growth and flowering, and then allowed to go dormant. If watered constantly, the thick root may rot or the plant may wear itself out trying to remain green and produce flowers. A collar of coarse sand can be put around the plant to aid in keeping the caudex dry. Pot culture is usually the easiest method of growing the lewisias.

Estimate of Garden Value: Bitterroot is exacting in its requirements, but tends to persist for many years when these are satisfied. It should not be used among aggressive plants where it may be crowded, but rather on inclines or in rock gardens, preferably with a north or east exposure. It should have a summer dormant period similar to that required by small bulbs, such as species of *Allium* or *Calochortus,* and by some of the rock garden buckwheats. Bitterroot has been famous as an article of Indian diet.

Other species:

Lewisia cotyledon, Siskiyou Lewisia, is one of the most adaptable species, and has two recognized variants, *L. cotyledon* var. *howellii* and *L. cotyledon* var. *heckneri.* A number of horticultural forms have been developed by American, Scotch, and English horticulturists and have long been popular pot and rock garden plants, along with the natural varieties. All are characterized by thick, fleshy, evergreen leaves, spatulate to oblanceolate, and often with curled or undulate margins. Flowers are produced on branched panicles that are held above the leaves and bear a wealth of blossoms in white with red mid-veins, or in shades of pink, rose, crimson, and cherry red.

Culture: Siskiyou Lewisia and its varieties may be propagated from seeds that require no pretreatment, but may be a bit slow to germinate. The more popular method of propagation is to remove a section, or to take cuttings from the thick caudex in spring or early summer. If the section has a few roots, it can be potted immediately and kept watered and shaded until thoroughly established. A cut piece with no roots can be dipped into a rooting hormone, and put into clean, sharp sand until a root system has formed. The new plant may flower the following year, or take up to two years. A potting mixture of equal parts of coarse sand and screened leaf mold will provide food and good drainage. Lewisias are not for the ordinary garden border, but should be used on rock walls, rock gardens, sharply drained slopes with morning sun, or in containers. This species and its forms remain evergreen throughout the year.

GENUS *LOBELIA:* LOBELIAS
(Family Campanulaceae: Bellflower)

Two species of *Lobelia* are native to California. This widely distributed genus is valuable for bright summer color.

Lobelia cardinalis ssp. **graminae**
Scarlet Lobelia or Cardinal Flower

HABIT: Erect, increases by offsets, 3–10 dm, 1–3 ft. (See Fig. 28.) FOLIAGE: Lanceolate to linear-lanceolate, mostly basal, those on stem reduced, serrate on margins. FLOWERS: Tubular, corolla two-lipped and lower deeply divided, intense red, in racemes. July–October. FRUIT: Two-sectioned capsule. DISTRIBUTION: Boggy places of hills and mountains to 6,000 feet elevation, Los Angeles to San Bernardino and San Diego counties.

Culture: Scarlet Lobelia may be grown from seed. It should be sown thinly because the tiny plants may become entangled

Figure 28 *Lobelia cardinalis,* Scarlet Lobelia

and difficult to separate for transplanting. Propagation can also be by division of old plants which produce offsets. Plants are subject to crown rot; they tolerate regular watering, but the soil must be well drained. Where the weather is mild, this lobelia may be grown in full sun, otherwise partial shade and ample water are necessary. The brilliant flower color is especially effective in high tree shade, and gives color in summer when few other plants are in bloom.

Estimate of Garden Value: Botanic gardens have cultivated this lobelia with success for many years. It is considered to be most valuable for its summer color in borders or woodsy places. It may be used in masses, or singly among shrubs and perennials. Scarlet Lobelia has long been a popular garden plant in eastern and southern states and this subspecies is its western form.

GENUS *LUPINUS:* LUPINES
(Family Leguminosae: Pea)

Eighty-two species of *Lupinus* are native to California, and about fifty are perennial. Members are easily recognized for their palmately compound leaves with each segment coming from a common center like a cartwheel. The pea-shaped flowers along upright stems are equally distinctive and occur in a wide range of blue, purple, and yellow shades, and occasionally in white. Although the basic pattern of flowers and leaves is the same, there is a great variation in size, from the semi-prostrate Lyall's Lupine *(Lupinus lyallii)* to the five-foot, shrubby Silver Bush Lupine *(L. albifrons).* Most of the species are erect, many-stemmed plants of one to three or more feet. Frequently they occur in sweeping and colorful masses, and are a common and widespread feature of fields and hilly slopes, with a few species occurring in moist fields and meadows. (See Chart 8.)

Culture: In spite of their presence in almost every type of terrain, lupines are seldom thought of as garden materials. A few have been cultivated in botanic gardens, and no doubt some in home gardens also, but there are few records of these experiences. The several which I have grown over the years have all proven adaptable to open, sunny areas, tolerating moderate amounts of water with well-drained soil. Particularly adaptable is Broadleaf Lupine *(L. latifolius)*, whose flowering period extends over four or five weeks. It is a herbaceous type whose foliage should be cut to the ground when it turns brown. For the many evergreen types, old flower heads and tough stems may be removed for neatness and to encourage the development of a leafy base. Lupines may be combined with an almost endless number of other natives, especially hardy perennials and shrubs. In my semi-dry border several kinds of lupines are accompanied by Creeping Sage *(Salvia sonomensis)*, Coyote Mint *(Monardella villosa)*, Bowl-Tubed Iris *(Iris macrosiphon)*, and an assortment of native bulbs.

Propagation: Lupines generally provide abundant amounts of seed in conspicuous pods, and these may be gathered when ripe, shelled, dried, and stored until planting time. Most will

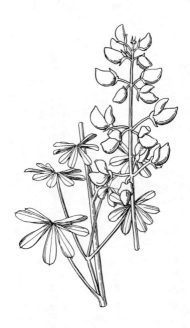

Figure 29 *Lupinus latifolius,* Broadleaf Lupine

CHART 8 *Lupinus*: Perennial Lupines

Plant	Height	Flowers	Culture	Remarks	Distribution
L. latifolius Broadleaf Lupine (See Fig. 29)	3-12 dm (24-48 in)	Dense racemes, blue, pale blue, light purple. April-July.	Sun to high shade, water tolerant. Benefits from leaf mold in soil.	Adaptable, free-flowering. Half-shaded borders.	Woods, Del Norte, Los Angeles cos.
L. latifolius ssp. parishii Canyon Lupine	.5-2 m (2-6 ft)	Dense racemes, rose to lavender. April-July.	Sun, semi-dry. Borders with other natives.	Used in breeding program.	Coast to mts. San Diego to Tulare cos.
L. formosus Summer Lupine	3-8 dm (12-30 in)	Whorled spikes, violet, lilac, white. April-Oct.	Sun, semi-dry, water-tolerant. Borders, edging, slopes.	Pale, silky green leaves. Variable, 2 varieties.	Dry, sandy, Humboldt Co. south.
L. albifrons Silver Bush Lupine	6-15 dm (24-36 in)	Tall, graceful spikes, blue-red-purple. March-June.	Sun, semi-dry. With shrubs, large perennials, background.	Pale green, silky foliage. Spreading habit.	Sandy, rocky, Humboldt to Ventura and Tulare cos.

L. albifrons var. *flumineus* Silver Circle Lupine (See Pl. 2D)	1-2 dm (4-8 in)	Dense spikes, blue-purple. April–May.	Sun, semi-dry, lean soil. Mat-forming, border edging, rock garden.	With Creeping Sage, Coyote Mint, other lupines.	Yellow Pine, Siskiyou, Mendocino cos.
L. arboreus Tree Lupine	1-2m (3-6 ft)	Dense spikes, clear yellow, blue. March–June.	Sun, water-tolerant. Background.	Rapid grower, but subject to root rot.	Coast, Del Norte to Ventura cos.

germinate without pretreatment, but there are several methods to aid germination where required. One is to soak the seeds in either cold or hot water. Another is to shake the seeds in a jar half-filled with coarse sand, broadcast the seeds, and rake in to cover lightly. For seeds which need further treatment, scarify gently between two pieces of sandpaper, then drop into hot water and allow to stand until the water has cooled, and then plant. Since most lupines resent handling, seeds may be sown directly into the border, preferably as the autumn rains begin. Some gardeners have had success starting the seeds in fiber pots, and then planting them intact when roots show through the bottom. A few lupines will flower the first year while others require two years, and most will provide an abundance of volunteer plants. Lupines are seldom available from nurseries, but seeds of a few can be obtained from specialty catalogs.

Estimate of Garden Value: Although cultivated lupines are relatively short lived, about three to five years, they are free flowering and provide volunteers as constant replacement. In clay soils, care must be taken to provide good drainage, otherwise root rot will be a problem. Most will accept moderate amounts of water during the period of rapid growth, but resent overhead sprinkling. With few exceptions, full sun and semi-dry conditions suit them very well. Both herbaceous and ever-green kinds grow in my mountain garden, providing flowers from mid-April through May, with one evergreen type forming an attractive, silky, pale green mat. Members of this genus should be appreciated for their natural shapeliness, soft to vivid flower colors, and fine foliage of the majority of species, and there are vast possibilities for future selections. A beautiful strain of lupine has been developed at Santa Barbara Botanic Garden by crossing Canyon Lupine (*L. latifolius* var. *parishii*) with the Russell lupines, derived partly from the native Blue-Pod Lupine *(L. polyphyllus)*. A long and patient breeding program resulted in beautifully colored flowers in dense spikes on disease-resistant plants which are adaptable to the semi-dry California climate. It has been named *Lupinus* 'Canyon Sunset', and blooms in April to June with dense spikes of flowers in a wide color range including red, rose, coral, pink, yellow, purple, and white.

GENUS *MIMULUS:* MONKEY FLOWERS
(Family Scrophulariaceae: Figwort)

In *Mimulus,* a large and widely distributed genus, there are seventy-seven species and many varieties native to California. Less than half are perennial and of these seven species are shrub-like, and by some botanists considered to be in the genus *Diplacus*. The various species occupy contrasting habitats, from arid and often rocky or gravelly foothills, to drippy slopes, stream banks, or meadows. The flowers are tubular and vary somewhat in size, type of lobe, and in the markings which give them their quaint, face-like appearance, and the common name of monkey flower. Each flower has a pair of ridges on the lower throat. (See Chart 9A and B.)

Figure 30 *Mimulus lewisii,* Lewis's Monkey Flower

Culture: Monkey flowers are easily propagated from seed, and a few can be grown from cuttings, while others make natural increase of rooted stolons. The seed is fine and should be lightly dusted over the soil, pressed in, and covered until germination takes place. After the formation of the second or third pair of leaves, a block of soil can be cut out and the seedlings separated and replanted in small pots. Seed planted in July or August in mild climates will give plants of flowering size by the following summer. The shrubby monkey flowers should have full sun, moderate amounts of water, rather lean soil, and may be used with other drought-tolerant materials. Those accustomed to moisture can be used where they will get ample water, in sun to high or broken shade. Common Monkey Flower *(M. guttatus)* makes a fine pot plant. It is almost everblooming with water and small amounts of fertilizer, and the pot is soon filled with rooted stolons. The shrubby monkey flowers may be propagated from soft wood cuttings taken in spring when they seem to root most readily. When grown as bedding plants, set vigorous seedlings into prepared borders and pinch the tips for bushy growth and a long season of bloom. Otherwise they are cultivated as a hardy perennial, used in a semi-dry border with other compatible plants.

Estimate of Garden Value: The various species of *Mimulus* have much to offer the gardener, being adaptable to cultivation under conditions similar to their natural ones. (See Fig. 31.) They are free flowering over a long period from early to late summer, with blossoms in lively colors and markings. Among shrubby kinds, a program is underway to cross the various species for an extended color range, and possibly for plants of more floriferous habit. Those with desirable traits should be tested for gardens, such as the small, pert Primrose Monkey Flower *(M. primuloides),* a fine candidate for a sunny border with its bright yellow, freckled flowers. Scarlet Monkey Flower *(M. cardinalis)* has an exceptionally long flowering period lasting into autumn, but it may become too large and sprawling for the average garden. In combination with other plants, many monkey flowers can provide new and attractive materials for western gardens.

CHART 9A *Mimulus*: Perennial Monkey Flowers For Moist Situations

Plant	Height	Flowers	Culture	Remarks	Distribution
M. guttatus Common Monkey Flower (See Pl. 2A)	5-10 dm (7-36 in)	Campanulate, throat closed, lobes spread, yellow, brown spots. March-Aug.	Very adaptable, sun with water. May become rampant.	Increase by rooted stolons. Variable in nature.	Common in wet places.
M. primuloides Primrose Monkey Flower	.1-5 dm (1-5 in)	Tubular, bright yellow, freckled brown. June-Aug.	Wet soil, sun to light shade.	Increase from stolons.	Mt. meadows, Sierra Nevada. Tulare Co. north, north Coast Ranges.
M. cardinalis Scarlet Monkey Flower	2.5-6.8 dm (10-24 in)	Large, pouchy, bilabiate, red. April-Oct.	Sun, water. Massed, or mixed borders.	Branched, large and spreading, long-flowering	Streams and seeps, common.
M. lewisii Lewis Monkey Flower (See Fig. 30)	3-8 dm (12-31 in)	Large, tubular, pink, rose, white. June-Sept.	Light shade, water, humus. Summer, long-flowering.	With columbines, lilies, azaleas, etc.	Streams, Sierra Nevada, Tulare to Modoc and Siskiyou cos.

CHART 9B *Mimulus*: Perennial Monkey Flowers For Dry Situations

Plant	Height	Flowers	Culture	Remarks	Distribution
M. longiflorus Southern Monkey Flower	3-12 dm (12-48 in)	Tubular, orange-yellow, buff, white. March-July.	Sun, semi-dry, some summer water.	With mixture of natives, or mass planting.	Dry foothills, San Luis Obispo to San Diego cos.
M. longiflorus var. *calycinus* Lemon Monkey Flower	to 8 dm (36 in)	Large, open tubes, lemon-yellow. April-July.	Sun to light shade, semi-dry, lean soil.	Drought tolerant, borders, mixtures.	Chaparral, Fresno, San Diego cos.
M. longiflorus var. *rutilus* Velvet Red Bush Monkey Flower	6-12 dm (24-48 in)	Large, tubular, deep velvety red. May-July.	Sun, semi-dry border, lean soil.	Natural hybrid, similar to sp.	Ventura, Los Angeles, Riverside cos.
M. aurantiacus Sticky Monkey Flower	6-12 (or 20) dm (24-48 [or 80] in)	Tubular, buff to yellow-orange. March-Aug.	Dry borders, with penstemons, bush salvia, native bulbs.	Much branched, shrubby, long-lived.	Dry hills, Coast Ranges, Del Norte to Santa Barbara, central Sierra foothills.

M. clevelandii Cleveland's Monkey Flower	3-9 dm (12-36 in)	Narrow tube, golden-yellow. May-July.	Sun, light shade, semi-dry.	Freely branched, perennial, background.	Chapparal, Santa Ana Mts. to San Diego Co.
M. bifidus Azalea-Flowered Monkey Flower	4-7 dm (12-28 in)	Trumpet-shaped buff, salmon-orange. April-July.	Sun to high shade, water tolerant but not overhead. Spreading mat.	Shaded slope, rock garden, terrace, wall.	Rocky foothills Plumus, Butte, Placer cos.

Figure 31 *Mimulus puniceus,* Red Bush Monkey Flower

GENUS *MONARDELLA:* MONARDELLAS
(Family Labiatae: Mint)

Twenty species of *Monardella* are native to California, about ten of which are evergreen plants. The ones which I have grown have fragrant foliage, neat and unobtrusive habits, and are long lived under semi-dry conditions.

Monardella villosa
Coyote Mint

HABIT: Low, many stemmed, evergreen, slightly woody based, 1–6 dm, 9–18 in. FOLIAGE: Small, ovate, dark slate green, pungent fragrance. FLOWERS: Small, tubular in congested, flattish heads, lavender, light purple, rose-purple, to whitish. June–August. FRUIT: Nutlet. DISTRIBUTION: Dry, rocky or gravelly places, road cuts, Humboldt to San Luis Obispo counties. Several subspecies recognized.

Culture: Coyote Mint requires no pretreatment to propagate from seed, although it is sometimes slow to germinate. It may also be grown from rooted side shoots, potted in coarse soil, and held until of a size to plant in the garden. Flower color varies widely so select cuttings from plants having the best colors. In the wild, this plant forms mats. It should be used in semi-dry conditions, as border edgings, slope or terrace cover, or in rock gardens, but it should not be used in a well-watered flower border where it is apt to become leggy, and lose its intrinsic qualities.

Estimate of Garden Value: When used in the correct situation, Coyote Mint is one of California's most useful and accommodating perennials. It is usually free flowering, increases at a moderate pace, and is long lived.

Monardella odoratissima
Mountain Monardella

HABIT: Woody based, branched perennial, mat-forming, 1.5–3.5 dm, 5–15 in. FOLIAGE: Small, lanceolate, firm, slate green, fragrant. FLOWERS: Dense heads, fuzzy, white to pale lavender, ruff of bracts, often purplish. FRUIT: Ovoid nutlets. DISTRIBUTION: According to Munz, five subspecies are found in various parts of California, and the species is from Oregon and Washington. Well distributed throughout the mountain ranges, from about 3,000 to 10,000 feet elevation. Gravelly flats, dry slopes, road cuts, and forest floors.

Culture: Mountain Monardella may be grown from seed or cuttings, with culture the same as for *M. villosa*. Three-months stratification for stored seed.

Estimate of Garden Value: This species or one of its forms should eventually become a popular ground cover. Although slow-growing it will form a loose mat, and while drought tolerant, will also accept moderate amounts of water. Plants are especially attractive before flowering when the firm, round, purplish-tinted buds are held above the foliage.

Monardella macrantha
Large-Flowered Monardella

HABIT: Low, branched from woody rootstock, stems 1–3 or 5 dm, 6–24 in. FOLIAGE: Ovate to elliptic, dark green. FLOWERS: Funnelform, scarlet, in terminal heads, surrounded by large bracts. June–August. FRUIT: Straw-colored nutlets. DISTRIBUTION: Dry slopes and ridges, Santa Lucia Mountains, Monterey County to San Gabriel Mountains of San Diego County.

Culture: The same as for *M. villosa.* No treatment for fresh seed; three-months stratification if stored.

Estimate of Garden Value: Recommended for coastal regions, into hills and low mountains, in full sun and lean soil. Excellent for summer flowers and to use with buckwheats and other drought-tolerant plants. May also be used in raised border or mounded area to insure good drainage. Once established it tends to form extensive mats, and is useful as border edgings, on dry slopes, and in rock gardens where the brilliant summer color can show to advantage.

GENUS *NOLINA:* NOLINAS
(Family Agavaceae: Agave)

Three species of *Nolina* are native to deserts and mountains of southern California. They are large plants with sword-like leaves, very similar to the yuccas, and are sometimes used in large-scale landscaping.

Nolina parryi
Parry's Nolina

HABIT: Large, robust, thick, woody base, which is sometimes underground and may be branched. FOLIAGE: Dense rosette, thick, dark gray-green, serrate on the margins, come to a sharp spine at tip, 6–10 dm, 2–3½ ft. FLOWERS: Borne on tall, stout, naked stalk, 6–10 dm, to 6 ft; small, white, cup-shaped flowers in congested, branched panicle. April–June. FRUIT: Capsule with wrinkled, light brown seeds. DISTRIBUTION: On dry slopes below 3,000 ft., Chaparral, Coastal Sage Scrub, San Diego, Orange, Riverside, and Ventura counties. Up to 5,500 ft. in Pinyon-Juniper Woodland, and desert slopes of the Santa Rosa and San Jacinto mountains.

Culture: Parry's Nolina may be propagated from seed with no pretreatment. Seedlings may be shifted to four-inch pots, and set out in about six months. Some plants are lost if set out at an earlier stage. Full sun, with some water and attention the first year are required. Parry's Nolina takes seven to eight years to reach flowering stage and is long lived when its requirements are met. This bold plant may be used in an all-native collection, to edge or provide a hedge for a large garden, and is well suited to a cactus garden. It is frequently available from nurseries.

Estimate of Garden Value: Although this unusual plant may not be suitable for a small home garden, it has a dramatic appearance and may be used as an accent specimen in parks, large estates, or around industrial sites.

GENUS *OENOTHERA:* EVENING PRIMROSES
(Family Onagraceae: Evening Primrose)

Forty-two species of *Oenothera* are native, about half either perennial or biennial. A number are coarse plants but very hardy, and some provide extensive carpets in desert regions. Others grow in moist places and are likely to be rampant in gardens. Unknown kinds should be used with discretion until their value can be determined.

Oenothera cheiranthifolia
Beach Primrose

HABIT: Bushy, stems prostrate to decumbent, from center rosette, 1–6 dm, 4–24 in. FOLIAGE: Oblanceolate from rosette, lower cauline ones lance-oblong, tip leaves short and broad, thick, grayish-pubescent. FLOWERS: Small, cup-shaped, bright yellow, long blooming. FRUIT: Coiled capsules. DISTRIBUTION: Coastal Strand, Santa Barbara north, Santa Rosa and San Miguel islands.

Culture: Beach Primrose is propagated from seed, but this does not always germinate well. Once established in a proper situation of sun, sandy soil, and very little water, plants thrive and produce a few volunteer seedlings.

Estimate of Garden Value: Sturdy plants are dense and flower over a long period in summer. Under less favorable conditions, Beach Primrose is a sparse, open plant but considered to be attractive because of the silvered leaves.

Oenothera caespitosa
Tufted Evening Primrose

HABIT: Tufted, from thick caudex, stems to 2 dm, 8–10 in. (See Fig. 32.) FOLIAGE: Linear-lanceolate, sinuate-pinnatifid, on long petioles, 3–10 cm, 1–3 in. FLOWERS: Large, fragrant, white aging pink, vespertine. April–August. FRUIT: Capsule, linear-cylindric. DISTRIBUTION: Dry or stony slopes, deserts, Santa Rosa Mountains, Riverside County to White Mountains, Inyo County.

Culture: Tufted Evening Primrose is propagated from seed,

Figure 32 *Oenothera caespitosa,* Tufted Evening Primrose

and volunteer plants can be expected. Plants require full sun, sandy soil, and very little water.

Estimate of Garden Value: This is an attractive plant with stems of large, fragrant, white flowers above the long, basal leaves. Although reported to be short lived, it will produce volunteer plants when happily situated.

Oenothera hookeri
Hooker's Evening Primrose

HABIT: Erect, stout, branched, stems red, 4–12 dm, 16–48 in. FOLIAGE: Lanceolate or oblanceolate, cauline leaves lanceolate, numerous, all with soft hairs. FLOWERS: Large saucers, pale yellow, in terminal clusters, from prominent buds. June–September. FRUIT: Woody capsule. DISTRIBUTION: Moist places, coastal strand, Coast Ranges from Lake and Trinity to San Luis Obispo counties.

Culture: Hooker's Evening Primrose is easily grown from broadcast seed. Plants are vigorous and apt to spread and become naturalized in sun with proper moisture.

Estimate of Garden Value: This species should be used carefully because it is coarse in appearance, although the flowers and furry buds are quite handsome. It can be used in a mixed flower border, in country gardens, and naturally moist places.

GENUS *PENSTEMON:* PENSTEMONS OR BEARD-TONGUES
(Family Scrophulariceae: Figwort)

Fifty-eight species and many distinctive varieties of *Penstemon,* a superb genus, are native to California. It is an American genus except for a single species native to Japan. Species of *Penstemon* inhabit many types of terrain, including rocky inclines, ledges, dry slopes and flats of hills and mountains, high ridges, deserts, woodlands, and meadows. (See Chart 10.)

Description: Members of the genus *Penstemon* embrace a wide range of plant sizes, from the low mats which so beautifully decorate boulders and rocky ledges to those which reach shrub sizes. In between is an assortment of sizes, mostly low, branched, and sometimes dense plants of about one to three feet. Foliage is evergreen, in medium green shades to

CHART 10 *Penstemon:* Beard-Tongues

Plant	Height	Flowers	Culture	Remarks	Distribution
P. spectabilis Royal Penstemon	8-12 dm (31-48 in)	Large tubes, vivid blue, open panicle. April-June.	Sun, moderate water to semi-dry.	Stout. Short-lived, cold hardy. Propagated by seed, basal pieces.	Dry places, San Luis Obispo to so. Calif.
P. clevelandii Cleveland's Penstemon	3-7 dm (12-28 in)	Tubular, funnelform, in panicle. Light red to rose-carmine. March-May.	Sun, semi-dry. Propagated by seed and basal shoots.	Erect. With other natives, not cold hardy, background, borders.	Dry slopes, San Diego Co. Baja Calif.
P. palmeri Palmer's Penstemon	5-12 dm (19-48 in)	Expanded tube, pink, rose, white, fragrant. May-July.	Sun, lean, sandy, well-drained soil.	Erect. With other penstemons, natives of similar requirements.	Kern Co. to so. Calif. and deserts.
P. centranthifolius Scarlet Bugler (See Fig. 33)	3-12 dm (12-48 in)	Narrow, tubular, scarlet, tall thyrsus. April-July.	Sun, coarse soil, moderate water.	Erect. With native perrennials, shrubs, etc.	Dry, chaparral, Lake to San Diego cos.

Species	Height	Flowers	Culture	Habit / Use	Distribution
P. heterophyllus Foothill Penstemon (See cover photo and Pl. 2C)	3-5 dm (12-24 in)	Large tubes, rose-violet, with blue or lilac lips. June.	Sun, semi-dry but water tolerant. Free-flowering.	Branched. Mixed planting, rock garden, edging, large clumps.	Dry hills, Humboldt to San Diego cos.
P. heterophyllus ssp. *prudyi* Blue Bedder Penstemon	2.5-7 dm (9-24 in)	Large tubes, bright blue. May-July.	Sun to light shade, water tolerant. Spreading clumps.	Branched. Mass planting, edging, or in mixtures.	San Bernardino and Humboldt to Trinity cos., Butte to Placer cos.
P. heterophyllus ssp. *australis* Violet Penstemon	3-4 dm (12-16 in)	Gaping, tubular, violet-blue. June-Aug.	Sun, well-drained soil, moderate water. Spreading.	Mixed planting, large rock garden, slopes, terraces.	Chaparral, Monterey to San Diego cos.
P. azureus Azure Penstemon (See Fig. 34)	2-5 dm (8-19 in)	Large, gaping, tubular, dark azure to blue-purple. May-Aug.	Sun, lean soil, semi-dry. Vigorous, spreading.	With native shrubs, perennials, bulbs, etc.	Dry slopes, Fresno, Butte, Humboldt cos.
P. gracilentus Slender Penstemon	2-7 dm (10-24 in)	Small, tubular, in interrupted whorls, dark blue-purple. June-Aug.	Shade borders, water tolerant. In mixtures.	Adaptable. Eventually forms clump. Suitable with columbines, etc.	Open forest, Tahoe, north Modoc and Siskiyous cos.

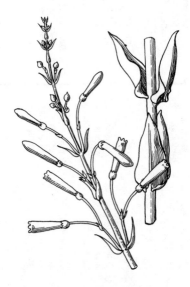

Figure 33 *Penstemon centranthifolius,* Scarlet Bugler

paler tones, often glaucous and in a few cases becoming purplish tinted in winter. Leaves range in shape from small ovals to elliptic, lance to oblanceolate, petioled at the base, and reduced upward along the stem. Flowers are tubular, some very narrow, others slightly inflated, and with the lower lips cleft into shallow lobes or deeply slashed. Brilliant flower color is an outstanding feature, including lively shades of blue, blue-purple, blue-violet, lavender, azure, red, crimson, yellow, and occasionally white. Seed is generously provided in numerous capsules. Since *Penstemon* species range through many elevations, most are cold hardy, except for a few from mild coastal regions. Cleveland's Penstemon *(P. clevelandii)* did not survive in my mountain garden where frosts prevail until mid-spring, but all forms of Foothill Penstemon *(P. heterophyllus)* have done exceedingly well.

Culture: Most penstemons are neat, self-contained, free-flowering, and adaptable to garden culture. A few, particularly those which grow on sheer rock faces, may require special conditions of a rock garden, and attention to soil, exposure,

Figure 34 *Penstemon azureus,* Azure Penstemon

and drainage. Others are suitable to a variety of situations, including semi-dry borders, dry slopes, raised borders, and with a mixture of drought-tolerant natives. As a rule they prefer sun and lean, porous, well-drained soil, and they may be watered during their period of active growth, but too much moisture and crowding by other plants is apt to cause mildew. Die-back of stems is a problem with a few species.

Propagation: Almost all penstemons may be propagated from seed without pretreatment, but in some cases is slow to germinate. Flats containing seed should not be discarded since some of it may germinate a year after planting. Young, vigorous plants should be individually potted and set out after several months. Some experts contend that seedlings that are too small do not survive. Penstemons may also be propagated from stem cuttings, best taken in summer and rooted in sharp sand or a mixture of sand and peat. Cuttings should be taken from young, basal shoots rather than from old, woody portions.

Remove all but three or four pairs of leaves before inserting into the rooting medium.

Estimate of Garden Value: Several factors, in addition to their outstanding flower color, make penstemons desirable garden plants. Their evergreen foliage, of firm substance and well disposed along the stems, gives them a neat appearance through the seasons. They have no rampant tendencies and, while some volunteer seedlings, none in my experience have ever become invasive. Some are not long lived in gardens, but the ease of producing new plants either from the abundance of seed, or from cuttings, makes their replacement simple. Their longevity depends on growing conditions, and rich soil along with too much water tends to shorten life. A few species, if not cut back in autumn, will become woody and fail to produce flowering stems for the next year. Much work is being done in crossing the various species to yield a wide assortment of rich flower colors on free-flowering plants. The challenge remains however to learn how to propagate and cultivate some of the desirable species.

GENUS *POLYSTICHUM:* SWORD FERNS
(Family Aspidaceae: Fern)

Six species of *Polystichum* are native to California. They are large, coarse ferns, mostly of coastal and montane coniferous forests.

Polystichum munitum
Western Sword Fern

HABIT: Coarse, erect, evergreen, from scaly rhizome, in heavy crowns or clumps, 6–14 dm, 2–5½ ft. FOLIAGE: Rigidly upright, blades pinnate, lustrous dark green, ear-shaped at base, and with teeth on margins. Leaf-stalk with red-brown scales, and short, pointed ones. DISTRIBUTION: Damp woods, below 2,500 feet, Redwood, North Coastal Coniferous, and Douglas Fir Forests, near coast, Monterey to Del Norte counties, and Santa Cruz Island.

Culture: Western Sword Fern may be grown from the abundantly produced spores according to the directions for growing

Five-Finger Fern (see page 88). Plants may also be increased by division of the rhizome in early spring, keeping them moist and shaded until new growth begins. The old fronds should be removed at this time. Experts consider that seedlings eventually make a more symmetrical plant. Western Sword Fern is probably the most adaptable of any known native fern, thriving in humus-rich soil, without summer water. It may be used in deep shade as well as with half-day sun, but should have high or filtered shade in warmer climates away from the coast.

Estimate of Garden Value: Western Sword Fern forms a fountain of vigorous, upright fronds, and may be used as a filler or background in a shade border. It is excellent among shrubs having similar requirements, and especially under oak trees because it requires only a minimum of water. The firm fronds are handsome in arrangements, or they can be pressed and used in winter bouquets with dried materials.

Polystichum munitum ssp. **curtum** is a tough plant, typical of the species, but less robust and with shorter fronds. It is native to canyon slopes from Chaparral to montane coniferous forests of Santa Lucia Mountains to the mountains of San Diego County.

GENUS *ROMNEYA:* MATILIJA POPPIES
(Family Papaveraceae: Poppy)

There are only two species in *Romneya,* both quite similar in appearance and inhabiting dry canyons of southern California. The stately Matilija Poppy has been in cultivation since before the turn of the century.

Romneya coulteri
Matilija Poppy

HABIT: Large, stout, herbaceous, from underground rootstock, 1–2.5 m, 4–8 ft. FOLIAGE: Round-ovate, pinnately parted into coarse divisions, firm texture, blue-green. FLOWERS: Large poppy from rounded bud, petals white, crinkled, with column of golden yellow stamens, fragrant. May–July. FRUIT: Conspicuous, erect capsules, ample seed.

DISTRIBUTION: Dry washes and canyons, Coastal Sage Scrub away from immediate coast, Santa Ana Mountains to San Diego County.

Culture: Matilija Poppy is best propagated from cuttings of young lateral roots, taken in November or December. These are cut into small pieces, placed horizontally in a sandy rooting medium, either in flats or in large, shallow pots. Containers should be kept moist and shaded, and rooting can be expected within a month, with the new shoots appearing soon after. The following April, plants can be set into permanent quarters and will begin to flower the second year. Propagation may also be from seeds, but this is not generally recommended. Seed is slow to germinate and requires stratification or burning straw over the flat, but germination is still uneven after pretreatment. This poppy is tolerant of dry conditions, but occasional deep watering may be given during its period of active growth. Full sun and light, well-drained soil are also desirable. Old plants should be cut to within a few inches of the ground in autumn. If unrestrained, large patches will be formed by the creeping, underground rootstocks. The Matilija Poppy is effective in masses where there is space, or with a wide assortment of native perennials and shrubs.

Estimate of Garden Value: This statuesque poppy is universally admired and has been cultivated in England for many years. Its tendency to spread makes it too rampant for small gardens, and it is most useful in large gardens, parks, roadsides, and large-scale landscaping. Although it has been cultivated to some extent in the eastern United States, the Matilija Poppy has yet to be tested at high elevations where spring frosts could damage the foliage, if not the whole plant.

Other Species:

Romneya trichocalyx, Ventura Matilija, is considered to be a separate species, although similar in most respects to *R. coulteri.* Horticulturists prefer it because it has larger flowers and a more compact growth habit.

Romneya coulteri × **R. trichocalyx** 'White Cloud' is an intermediate type, bushy in habit, and bearing eight-inch flowers on stalks of five to six feet.

GENUS *SALVIA:* SAGES
(Family Labiatae: Mint)

Nineteen species of *Salvia* are native to California, of which two are annual. Several species have been introduced and are now common in some areas. All have a typical, delightful pungency, and those described here have special value for their ornamental qualities.

Salvia sonomensis
Creeping Sage

HABIT: Herbaceous to somewhat evergreen, creeping, with ascending flower stems. FOLIAGE: Elliptic-obovate, sage-green, fine network on upper surface, 3–6 cm, about 2 in. FLOWERS: Tubular, with expanded lower lip, exserted stamens, violet-blue, in a spike of whorls. April–June. FRUIT: Smooth nutlet. DISTRIBUTION: Dry slopes, Chaparral, Oak Woodland and Yellow Pine Forests, foothills of Sierra Nevada, Shasta to Calaveras counties; Coast Ranges, San Diego to Siskiyou counties.

Culture: Creeping Sage may be grown from seed which requires three-months stratification for good germination. However, since this species roots frequently along the creeping stems, new plants are easily obtained. If there is no natural increase, tip cuttings may be taken at almost any time of year and rooted in sharp sand. Transplant to pots of friable soil and hold until a mass of roots have formed, and then set in place. Creeping Sage requires full sun, lean soil, and moderate amounts of moisture. For more rapid growth, water can be given the year around as long as the soil is porous.

Estimate of Garden Value: In the early days of interest in the culture of native plants, Creeping Sage was seldom available because it was considered to be too rampant for most gardens. However, for gardens in outlying, foothill or country gardens, or any place where a fast growing, drought-tolerant ground cover is needed, this species is highly useful. The leafy stems make a loose ground cover, and the pale green foliage is compatible in almost any combination of plants. Plants increase at a moderate rate in full sun and semi-dry conditions, and somewhat faster with regular watering. It is an ideal companion for many species of *Brodiaea, Calochortus, Penstemon,* silvery-leaved lupines, and many others. In my opinion, this creeping perennial is one whose usefulness has yet to be realized.

Salvia spathacea
Hummingbird Sage

HABIT: Coarse herb from creeping rhizome, erect, 3–7 or 10 dm, 1½–3 ft. (See Fig. 35.) FOLIAGE: Numerous, oblong, hastate, rugose, green above, ashy beneath. FLOWERS: Tubular, purplish red, in spicate whorls, from purplish, ovate bracts. April–July. FRUIT: Plump, brown nutlet. DISTRIBUTION: Grassy, shaded slopes, Chaparral, Solano County through the Coast Ranges to Orange County.

Culture: No treatment is required for seed of Hummingbird Sage, and volunteers can become too numerous in most gar-

Figure 35 *Salvia spathacea,* Hummingbird Sage

dens. There is also increase from the creeping rhizomes, and large clumps are formed where there is sun and moisture. Highly colored flowers and bracts form a solid mass of crimson red, which is very attractive to hummingbirds.

Estimate of Garden Value: Although a large, coarse plant, this sage may be used in backgrounds, among shrubs or other large perennials. It thrives with constant moisture, but is also relatively drought tolerant. When used in wooded areas, the competition of other plants keeps it within bounds.

Salvia clevelandii
Cleveland's Sage or Fragrant Sage

HABIT: Rounded, shrubby, gray-white, about 1 m, 3 ft. (See Fig. 36.) FOLIAGE: Elliptic-oblong, grayish white from fine hairs, rugose. FLOWERS: Narrow tubes, in compact, capitate whorl, dark blue-violet, fragrant. April–July. FRUIT:

Figure 36 *Salvia clevelandii,* Cleveland's Sage or Fragrant Sage

Nutlet, light yellow. DISTRIBUTION: Dry slopes, Chaparral, San Diego County to Baja California.

Culture: Cleveland's Sage may be propagated from seed which germinates in four to nineteen days. Seedlings are transplanted into small pots and set in place when sturdy plants have formed. Plant in full sun and water only until plants are well established; losses may occur in clay soil if overwatered. Cleveland's Sage is excellent for semi-dry borders among such natives as Woolly-Blue Curls (*Trichostema lanatum*), Matilija Poppy (*Romneya coulteri*), species of *Penstemon,* etc.

Estimate of Garden Value: Cleveland's Sage and others have been used on road cuts for erosion control and for ornamental purposes. Foliage has a distinct aromatic fragrance and is recommended as a seasoning for food.

GENUS *SILENE:* CAMPIONS
(Family Caryophyllaceae: Pink)

Twenty-six species of *Silene,* some rather weedy, but at least three very attractive, are native. Flowers somewhat resemble garden pinks (*Dianthus*), with the petal blades at right angles to the tubular calyx and the petals either entire or cleft into linear segments.

Culture: Most of the campions may be grown from seed, planted while fresh, using deep pots and friable soil. In my experience the seed germinates slowly, sometimes not appearing in my mountain garden until the following spring. Only one or two pairs of leaves are produced the first year, but a slender, four-inch taproot is produced with feeding roots down to the bottom of the pot. Early the following spring, the contents of the pot may be planted intact for the least disturbance of the taproot. Choose a partially shaded place with some shelter from afternoon sun, and well-drained soil in which some leaf mold has been incorporated. Moderate amounts of water may be given, but should be withheld in late summer when the roots go dormant.

Estimate of Garden Value: Most authorities consider the ornamental campions to be prime rock garden plants, and in this situation they are most apt to prosper. They are also adaptable to dry slopes, raised borders, and lightly shaded places. Seed is generally ripe in July, after which the foliage yellows and soon disappears. Well-established plants in the correct growing situation will increase each year and send out many stems, each tipped with an abundance of flowers.

Silene californica
California Indian Pink

HABIT: Herbaceous, from stout taproot, suberect stems; often forms a low, compact plant, with many stems. (See Fig. 37.) FOLIAGE: Ovate to oblanceolate, sticky, dark green. FLOWERS: Lobster red to crimson, petals deeply four-lobed. Late April–July. FRUIT: Ovoid capsule, red-brown seed. DISTRIBUTION: Brushy or wooded places, foothills, Coastal Scrub to Yellow Pine Forests, Los Angeles and Kern counties, north.

Figure 37 *Silene californica,* California Indian Pink

Culture and Estimate of Garden Value: See generic description above.

Other Species:

Silene hookeri, Hooker's Indian Pink or Indian Cartwheels, produces many stems at ground level with large flowers, whose deeply slashed petals of white, pink, or salmon are very effective against gray-green leaves. Bolander's Indian Pink *(S. hookeri* ssp. *bolanderi)* has even larger flowers, with the petals cleft into narrow segments, freely borne on low, compact plants. Flowers may be white or pale pink, all with a glistening quality and lovely to behold.

Silene laciniata, Mexican Pink, has scarlet flowers, but is considered to be too straggly for most garden purposes.

GENUS *SISYRINCHIUM:* GRASS-IRISES
(Family Iridaceae: Iris)

Six species of *Sisyrinchium* are native to California. The plants characteristically form clumps and have flat, grasslike leaves with an abundance of open, silken flowers.

Sisyrinchium bellum
California Blue-Eyed Grass

HABIT: Tufted, many stems, slender to stout, 1–4 or 6 dm, 4-12 in or 2 ft. FOLIAGE: Narrow, grasslike, dark green, slightly shorter than flower stems. FLOWERS: Small, open saucers of six segments, blue-purple, dark violet, lilac, or rarely white, enclosed in a pair of bracts. March–May. (See Pl. 2F.) FRUIT: Globose capsule. DISTRIBUTION: Widely distributed in open, grassy fields or meadows, near coast, Ventura to Humboldt counties. Many plant communities, and several variants.

Culture: California Blue-Eyed Grass may be grown from seed, either in flats or sown directly where wanted. Plants form clumps with many stems and a long succession of flowers from early to late spring. Clumps may be divided in early spring. It thrives in full sun and will tolerate both semi-dry and watered situations. In my Los Gatos garden it was accompanied by several kinds of brodiaea, Long-Petaled Iris, poppies, lupines and an assortment of spring annuals. At one time I had an albino form which bore large, pure white flowers sparked by yellow-tipped stamens. This cherished plant bore a long succession of large flowers.

Estimate of Garden Value: California Blue-Eyed Grass tends to reseed generously, but seldom interferes with other plants because of its slender habit. Use of this species as a ground cover in country gardens has been suggested.

Sisyrinchium californicum
Golden-Eyed Grass

HABIT: Low, tufted, 1.5–4 dm, 4–12 in. FOLIAGE: Grasslike, smooth, light green, rather lax, darkens when dry. FLOWERS: Flat, oblong, pointed segments, bright yellow. FRUIT: Capsule, rounded. DISTRIBUTION: Moist places, freshwater marsh, near coast, Monterey County northward.

Culture: Golden-Eyed Grass requires ample moisture and full sun. It may be used at the edges of lawns or in well-watered borders. It is not cold hardy, but in mild climates is almost ever-blooming.

Estimate of Garden Value: Golden-Eyed Grass does best where there is ample moisture with sun. It should be used with other plants of similar requirements, and would be pretty with Blue-Eyed Grass or Baby Blue-Eyes *(Nemophila menziesii).* As the foliage dies in autumn, the black color is unsightly and should be removed.

GENUS *TOLMIEA:* TOLMIEA
(Family Saxifragaceae: Saxifrage)

There is only a single species in *Tolmiea.* It has long been a popular house plant, with several common names arising from the way the plant produces new ones from the old leaves.

Tolmiea menziesii
Piggyback Plant

HABIT: Clustered stems, scaly rootstock, 3–8 dm, 18–28 in. FOLIAGE: Basal, round-cordate on long stems, shallowly lobed, with stiff hairs; cauline leaves smaller. FLOWERS: Tiny, cylindric-funnelform, greenish white, on stems held above foliage. Summer. FRUIT: Capsule, many seeds. DIS-

TRIBUTION: Redwood Forest, other moist, cool forests, Glenn, Del Norte, and Siskiyou counties, northward.

Culture: Because the popular Piggyback Plant so freely reproduces vegetatively, there is little record of its being grown from seed. Where stem and leaf join on mature plants, the area becomes slightly thickened, and here in miniature a new plant begins to form. These may be removed with the mother leaf, and potted in a soil mix designed for house plants. Tolmiea is primarily a foliage plant, and may be used in shaded areas and as an edging. It tolerates wet soil to which humus has been added.

Estimate of Garden Value: Piggyback Plant is excellent for shade gardens and is cold hardy to temperatures close to zero, but it does poorly in hot, dry climates. In such situations, it can be potted and kept in a shaded patio, or misted to alleviate the drying air.

GENUS *TRILLIUM:* TRILLIUMS
(Family Liliaceae: Lily)

Three species of *Trillium* are native to California. Although highly respected woodland plants, they are not yet much used in gardens. They are distinctive for the whorl of three large leaves at the top of thick stems, setting off the three slender petals. Members of this genus are refined and tidy, except for the short period in late summer when they die down.

Trillium chloropetalum
Giant Trillium

HABIT: Stout, with smooth stem, thick rootstock, 3–5 dm, 12–30 in. FOLIAGE: Three rhombic-ovate, in whorl at top of stem, dark green, mottled with a deeper shade. FLOWERS: Of three sessile petals, erect, pale greenish to creamy white, faintly fragrant. March–May. (See Pl. 3A.) FRUIT: Globose, capsule-like berry, reddish as ages, containing ample seed. DISTRIBUTION: Brushy or wooded slopes, outer Coast Ranges, San Mateo and Napa counties north, Sierra Nevada north of Placer County.

Culture: Giant Trillium may be propagated from seed which requires five to seven years to produce a mature rootstock.

Seed should be planted as soon as ripe, and kept moist and shaded until germination occurs. Alternate freezing and thawing of seed can aid in its germination. Under favorable conditions of shade and moisture, volunteer seedlings may appear; for the first few years these will be bright green, shiny, single leaves. When nearing the flowering stage, three small, but typical leaves will occur at the top of the stalk. Where plants are growing satisfactorily the rootstock may increase naturally, and old clumps may have two or three stems each season. Giant Trillium requires rich, humusy, well-drained soil and will tolerate water all through the year. Filtered shade, especially in the afternoon, and the partial protection of shrubs will keep them flourishing.

Estimate of Garden Value: A natural or man-made woodland is the perfect setting for the Giant Trillium, but I have seen them used at the edge of a shaded lawn amid a mat of white violets. They are also handsome in a shade border with wild irises, snow drops, and Baneberry *(Acteae rubra* ssp. *arguta).*

Trillium ovatum
Western Trillium

HABIT: Fleshy rhizome, smooth stem, 2–5 dm, 8–19 in. FOLIAGE: Rhombic-ovate, stemless, medium bright green, veined. FLOWERS: Of three white, smooth petals, slightly spreading, held on short stem above leaves; flowers age to soft, then to deep rose. FRUIT: Capsule-like berry, somewhat winged; the three styles remain attached. DISTRIBUTION: Moist woods, Redwoods, Mixed Evergreen Forests, Coast Ranges from Monterey to Siskiyou and Shasta counties.

Culture: Similar to that for *T. chloropetalum,* with leaf mold in the soil, and a moderate supply of water through the year. The dark rose flowers are especially attractive in redwood forests where the Western Trillium may be accompanied by huckleberry, Salal *(Gaultheria shallon),* violets, windflowers, and many others.

Estimate of Garden Value: Western Trillium is an elegant plant for the shade garden, and may be used with primroses, garden azaleas, violets, and scillas. Under deciduous trees and accompanied by small ferns, they make a stunning spring picture. Plants are long lived once established, and tend to be evergreen in mild climates. In hot climates with drying winds, trilliums need the protection of trees or shrubs and a constantly moist soil into which leaf mold or peat has been incorporated.

GENUS *VANCOUVERIA*: INSIDE-OUT FLOWERS
(Family Berberidaceae: Barberry)

Three species of *Vancouveria* are native to northwestern California, all with a delicate beauty from the divided foliage. They have few equals for rambling ground covers in shaded areas.

Vancouveria hexandra
Northern Inside-Out Flower

HABIT: From creeping rootstock, spread extensively, 1–4 dm, 4–16 in. FOLIAGE: Bi- to triternately divided on wiry stems, rounded, apple green; dainty, resembling a large Maiden-Hair Fern. FLOWERS: White, of reflexed petals with stamens set in beak effect, nodding. May–July. (See Pl. 8C.) FRUIT: Pointed follicle, two-valved, splitting from base. DISTRIBUTION: Deep shade, Redwood and Douglas Fir Forests, Mendocino and Del Norte to west Siskiyou counties, northward.

Culture: Northern Inside-Out Flower may be grown from seed, but the increase from the creeping rhizomes is so rapid that any other method is unnecessary. Plants require leaf mold in the soil, ample water, and will increase vigorously in both filtered and solid shade. Although plants will tolerate some dryness in summer, increase will not be so rapid and plants may go dormant by late summer. In mild climates this plant is practically evergreen. It is superb as a light, ferny ground cover, to mingle with wild iris, azaleas, or as a cover for lilies.

Estimate of Garden Value: Northern Inside-Out Flower is a dainty ground cover whose only drawback is the brief period of dying foliage in early autumn. Its period of special interest for me is the spring emergence when the furled leaves are truly fernlike. Its attractiveness continues over a long period, and it is apt to hurdle retaining logs, grow into paths, and ignore tree roots which sometimes discourage highly cultivated plants.

Vancouveric planipetala
Redwood Inside-Out Flower

HABIT: Compact, creeping, from rhizome, 1.5–5 dm, 5–20 in. FOLIAGE: Bi- or triternately compound, rounded, cordate at base, apple green. May be persistent in winter. FLOWERS: Of unequal sepals and petals, reflexed for inside-out effect. FRUIT: Follicle. DISTRIBUTION: Shade of coniferous forests, Santa Lucia Mountains, Monterey County, northward.

Culture: The same as for *V. hexandra.*

Estimate of Garden Value: Suitable for shade borders and large, cool rock garden with compatible companions.

Vancouveria chrysantha
Golden Inside-Out Flower

HABIT: Spreading, from creeping rhizome. FOLIAGE: Biternate or three- to five-foliate, leaflets ovate, evergreen, 2–4 dm, 8–16 in. FLOWERS: Typical, bright yellow, in loose panicle. FRUIT: Follicle. DISTRIBUTION: Open woods and thickets, Del Norte and Siskiyou counties to Oregon.

Culture and Estimate of Garden Value: The same as for *V. hexandra.*

GENUS *ZAUSCHNERIA:* WILD FUCHSIAS
(Family Onagraceae: Evening Primrose)

Four species are in *Zauschneria,* all native to California, including the Channel Islands and into Baja California. All form spreading, carpet-like plants, liberally set with scarlet trumpets.

Zauschneria californica
California Fuchsia

HABIT: Low, spreading, branched evergreen, semi-woody, 3–9 dm, 1–3 ft. (See Fig. 38.) FOLIAGE: Lanceolate to oblong, grayish green. FLOWERS: Funnelform tube, petals cleft toward tips, bright red. August–October. FRUIT: Linear

Figure 38 *Zauschneria californica* ssp. *latifolia,* California Fuschia

capsule with tuft of hairs. DISTRIBUTION: Dry, stony or gravelly places, many plant communities, Sonoma and Lake counties to Baja California.

Culture: California Fuchsia may be grown from seed, but it also produces underground runners which may be removed and potted until a good root system has been formed. Although it will thrive with water, it is drought tolerant and best in semi-dry places with lean soil to somewhat curb its rampant tendencies. It is ideal as an edging, or in a large, sunny rock garden where the brilliant red flowers give color from late summer into autumn. The subspecies *latifolia* is considered to be superior for its large and attractive flowers.

Estimate of Garden Value: This is an adaptable species but much too eager and invasive for small gardens. However, because of its evergreen foliage and late, scarlet flowers, it should be more commonly used as a ground cover for arid places. A country gardener has encouraged it to form a natural ground cover in dry places among native shrubs, and even admires the fly-away seeds in autumn.

Zauschneria cana
Hoary California Fuchsia

HABIT: Decumbent, spreading, slightly woody at base, stems 3–6 dm, 1–2 ft. FOLIAGE: Soft hairy, linear-lanceolate in bundles along stem. FLOWERS: Bright red tube. FRUIT: Capsule, curved to almost straight. DISTRIBUTION: Dry slopes, Chaparral, etc., Monterey to Los Angeles counties; Santa Cruz, Anacapa, and Catalina islands.

Culture and Estimate of Garden Value: The same as for *Z. californica.*

7. GROWING NATIVE BULBS

The number and kinds of California bulb plants are one of the most remarkable features of the native flora. They have drawn admiration from the earliest explorers to present-day enthusiasts. Among the several genera of bulbs, mostly the amaryllis and lily families, some are restricted to specific environmental conditions and may be exceedingly rare, while others are more widely distributed over the state. A few appear to have reached an advanced stage of development in certain sections of the state and most have aspects of refinement. Members of the genus *Calochortus* are exquisite in almost every detail; wild onions and brodiaeas often provide extensive masses of color from their flowers; fawn lilies and fritillaries have sprightly and endearing charms, while the true lilies are among the most elegant flowers to be found anywhere.

These bulb plants grow in a variety of habitats including light woodlands, open forested areas, in moist meadows and in dry fields, where some occur in amazing quantities. The abundance of some species, however, may soon be only a memory as land development constantly takes its toll of the native flora. Some of the native bulbs produce offsets, but most increase is from seed only, and where their growing area has been disturbed, seedlings do not have the opportunity to reach maturity. Thus a few of the rare bulbs are in very real danger of becoming extinct. From three to five years, or sometimes longer, are required from seed to maturity. Disturbance during these critical years may cause the young seedlings to die. There is still much to be learned about how to propagate and grow these bulb plants. Their life cycles present many mysteries and their behavior is sometimes puzzling.

Successful cultivation of native bulbs requires knowledge of their native habitat, including the type of soil, exposure, and the amounts of light or shade, and of water. Most species require sharply drained soil, and a few must have a summer dormant period. Others, such as the majority of true lilies, species of *Erythronium* and woodland *Fritillaria,* may be watered throughout the year. Most native bulbs have conspicuous seed capsules and bear an abundance of seeds which usually germinate without pretreatment. Many of the native bulbs and corms can reproduce by offsets, which occur in the sheath of the stem or around the base of the bulb, or as an underground stem at the end of which a new bulb forms. In my experience the following bulbs are especially inclined to this kind of increase: Pink Meadow Onion *(Allium unifolium),* Tuolumne Fawn Lily *(Erythronium tuolumnense),* and Pink Star Tulip *(Calochortus uniflorus).* Year-around watering seems to encourage this kind of reproduction, but reduces the number of flowers, sometimes to none at all. In the wilds, summer dryness halts some offset production, but when grown in a moist garden, these bulbs can be lifted, separated, and replanted every three years or so for better flower production. In my opinion the full use, and ultimate value of many wild bulbs is hardly realized, and many of garden worth remain untried. Suggestions for growing a representative number in each of ten genera will be detailed in this chapter. Rare ones should be left intact and steps be taken to preserve their habitat so that all may enjoy these treasures of the California countryside.

SPECIES DESCRIPTIONS

The following species of native bulbs are a sampling of the possibilities, the majority of them being adaptable to cultivation.

GENUS *ALLIUM:* WILD ONIONS
(Family Amaryllidaceae: Amaryllis)

Thirty-eight species and many varieties of *Allium* are native to California, all having the typical taste and odor of the onion family. Many kinds are found throughout the world and some, including a few native ones, have long provided flavoring for food. Onions grow from small corms, each one tunicated with a different design and pattern. Foliage is basal, linear, and grasslike, but sometimes thick and curved as in the Sickle-Leaved Onion. Flowers are in heads of varying size; colors range through strong to delicate shades of pink, rose, crimson, or purple, and to white. (See Chart 11.)

Propagation and Culture: Most wild onions grow readily from seed, requiring three to five years to reach maturity, although a few seem to need more time. Seeds may be planted in autumn in a friable, gritty mixture in deep pots, and left intact until they reach flowering size. The native habitat of each must be kept in mind when they are planted in the garden. Most species grow in dry, open foothill or mountain regions, and sometimes desertlike conditions, while others are native to meadows and moist fields. The latter are adaptable to sun with regular watering all through the year. The drought-resistant kinds should be planted in sunny, semi-dry borders, accom-

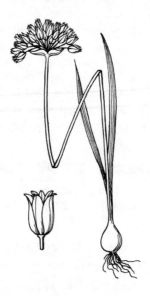

Figure 39 *Allium serratum,* Pom-Pon Onion

CHART 11 *Allium:* Wild Onions

Plant	Height	Flowers	Culture	Remarks	Distribution
A. *unifolium* Pink Meadow Onion	2-6 dm (6-24 in)	Open umbel, campanulate, pale to rose-pink. April-June.	Sun, water tolerant. Forms lateral rootstocks.	Adaptable for borders, colorful with *Brodiaea laxa.*	Moist or heavy soil, Del Norte to Monterey cos.
A. *validum* Swamp Onion	5-10 dm (19-29 in)	Large umbel, rose to white. July-Sept.	Sun, water tolerant. Vigorous habit.	Garden borders, with plants of similar requirements. Good flavor.	Wet meadow montane coniferous forests to Lake Co.
A. *crispum* Crinkled Onion	1-3 dm (4-12 in)	Many in open umbel, orchid to red-purple. March-May.	Sun, semi-dry, lean soil. Adaptable.	Borders, with bulbs, perennials, very attractive.	Heavy soils inner Coast Ranges and So. Sierra foothills to Kern Co.
A. *serratum* Pom-Pon Onion (See Fig. 39)	2-3.5 dm (8-15 in)	Crowded umbel, rose-pink, crimson. March-May.	Sun, dry, porous soil. Adaptable.	Borders, rock garden, with plants of similar requirements.	Slopes, serpentine, Lake to Merced cos.
A. *praecox* Early Onion	2-5 dm (8-19 in)	Open head, pale purple, dark vein. March-April.	Sun to high shade moderate water, porous soil.	Raised border, with other bulbs, annuals, low perennials.	Canyons, Chapparal, Oak Woodland, so. Calif.

panied by species of *Brodiaea, Calochortus,* perennials, and annuals which require similar conditions. A dormant period is essential for the dry-land species.

Estimate of Garden Value: Serious interest in the wild onions as a source of garden materials to accompany other drought-tolerant natives is developing. The few which I have grown have been dependable and quite persistent if given the correct conditions. Suitable situations in which to show off their performance and color include colonies among hardy perennials, in raised borders with other wild bulbs, and in rock gardens.

GENUS *BLOOMERIA:* Golden Stars
(Family Amaryllidaceae: Amaryllis)

Two species of *Bloomeria* are native to California; both are similar in many ways to brodiaeas and equally adaptable to garden conditions.

Bloomeria crocea
Golden Stars

HABIT: Robust scape from fibrous-coated corm, 1.5–6 dm, 5–24 in. (See Fig. 40.) FOLIAGE: Few, basal, linear. FLOWERS: Many, star-like, in loose, open umbel, orange-yellow. April–June. FRUIT: Capsules, somewhat globose, with black seed. DISTRIBUTION: Dry flats, hillsides, often in heavy soils, south Coast Ranges, Santa Barbara and west Kern counties to Baja California and Channel Islands.

Culture: Golden Stars is propagated from seed which requires three to four years to reach a mature bulb. It prefers full sun, semi-dry conditions, and porous to heavy soil. With compatible companions such as brodiaeas, wild onions, or zigadenus, it is showy; it is further enhanced with a ground cover of blue phacelias. Although it is not well known to home gardeners, it has been cultivated at botanic gardens where it often volunteers abundantly.

Estimate of Garden Value: This species of *Bloomeria* is outstanding for its rich color and ease of culture in a sunny border. It can be used in pure stands as it often occurs in the wilds, or in mixtures of other bulbs, blue-flowered delphiniums, or lupines.

Figure 40 *Bloomeria crocea*, Golden Stars

GENUS *BRODIAEA*: BRODIAEAS
(Family Amaryllidaceae: Amaryllis)

The genus *Brodiaea* is concentrated in the Pacific states and is highly developed in California west of the Sierra Nevada. Twenty-nine of the forty known species are native to California. Most are adaptable to garden cultivation; between them their flowering period extends from February to mid-summer. Each flower is composed of six perianth segments fused at the base to form a tube. The flower is variable: in some species the segments turn back abruptly to form a star shape, while in others they expand into an open, bell-shaped flower. There are also differences in the inflorescences, some forming tight heads, others loose or open umbels. Flower colors range through white, shades of yellow, many tints of blue, into purples, with one species having striking flowers in crimson red. All species have similar, grass-like foliage, generally sparse, and all grow from a relatively small corm, so these features will not be individually described. Brodiaeas inhabit open,

CHART 12 *Brodiaea*: Brodiaeas

Plant	Height	Flowers	Culture	Remarks	Distribution
B. laxa Ithuriel's Spear (See Pl. 4F)	1-7 dm (4-29 in)	Open bells in wide umbel, many shades of blue. April-June.	Watered to semi-dry, sun. Adaptable.	Garden borders, with other bulbs, native perennials.	Heavy soils, mountain ranges, foothills.
B. californica California Brodiaea	2-7 dm (8-29 in)	Bells, in erect, open umbel, lilac. May-July.	Sun, semi-dry, lean soil.	With various calochortus, alliums, native perennials.	Hills, plains, Shasta to Nevada cos.
B. lutea Pretty Face	2-8 dm (8-31 in)	Golden yellow, dark mid-veins. May-Aug.	Sun, semi-dry to moderate moisture.	Border edging, with native annuals, other bulbs.	Sandy soils, San Mateo to San Luis Obispo cos.
B. pulchella Blue Dicks	3-6 dm (12-24 in)	Small, in tight heads, violet with purple bracts. March-May.	Sun, semi-dry. Adaptable, will naturalize.	Open borders, with other native bulbs and perennials.	Common, hills, plains, west of Sierra Nevada.
B. peduncularis Long-Rayed Brodiaea (See Fig. 41)	1-8 dm (4-31 in)	White to violet, long pedicels. May-July.	Sun, semi-dry to moist. Adaptable.	Watered borders, with Blue-Eyed Grass, other bulbs.	Fields, wet in spring, Humboldt to Monterey cos.

Species	Height	Flower	Culture	Use	Habitat
B. hyacinthina White Brodiaea	4-10 dm (15-36 in)	Close umbel, white to pale blue tint. April-July.	Sun, water tolerant. Adaptable, variable species.	Mixed flower border, may naturalize.	Moist places, west Sierra Nevada, Tulare to Del Norte and Modoc cos.
B. bridgesii Bridge's Brodiaea	3-6 dm (12-24 in)	Open umbel, lilac to intense blue. April-June.	Sun, semi-dry. Moderately adaptable.	Open borders, with linanthus, penstemon, small lupines, etc.	Dry bluffs, woods, Shasta to Mariposa cos.
B. elegans Elegant Brodiaea	2-4 dm (6-18 in)	Open umbel, vivid blue-purple. May-July.	Sun, semi-dry, lean soil. Adaptable.	Open borders, edging or raised borders, with native perennials.	Heavy soils, plains, foothills, Monterey and Tulare cos., southern mountains.
B. coronaria Harvest Brodiaea	5-25 cm (2-9 in)	Wide umbel, rich blue-purple. May-June.	Sun, semi-dry to moderate water, with lean soil.	Open borders, with buckwheats etc., or other native bulbs.	Adobe, clay, gravel, Sacramento Valley, Shasta and Modoc cos. Coast Ranges southward.

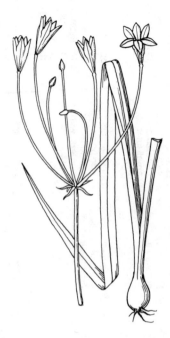

Figure 41 *Brodiaea peduncularis,* Long-Rayed Brodiaea

sunny fields, gravelly slopes, and uplands, light oak woodlands, and a few grow in meadows and places of seasonal
moisture. Many used to be so abundant that they covered
California valleys and hills with tints of blue and purple. (See
Chart 12.)

Culture: Almost all species bear quantities of seed in upright, papery capsules that remain intact until autumn. The
seeds usually germinate readily, and a mature corm is produced
in about three years. Around the base of a mature corm, most
species produce cormlets that take two or three years to reach
flowering size. The corms should be planted three to four
inches deep in mid- to late autumn, and closely spaced to give
a strong splash of color. Of the fourteen species I have grown
in various situations, most have proven adaptable. They prefer
full sun and semi-dry conditions, but may be watered during
their periods of active growth and flowering.

Estimate of Garden Value: Brodiaeas, with very few exceptions, are adaptable to garden cultivation, some making slow increase from seeds or cormlets. Others naturalize readily and have threatened to become pests where garden space is limited. They are dependable and long lived when used in a semi-dry situation, with other bulbs or with some of the drought-resistant native annuals and perennials. Elegant Brodiaea *(B. elegans)* and Azure Penstemon *(Penstemon azureus)* blooming together form a lively and colorful combination. Most species have some distinctive feature and should be more generally cultivated.

Some botanists split this group of plants into several genera, including: *Brodiaea, Hesperoscordum, Triteleia, Dichelostemma,* and *Brevoortia.* The last one includes two rare species: the Firecracker Flower *(Brodiaea ida-maia)* and Rose Firecracker Flower *(Brodiaea venusta).*

GENUS *CALOCHORTUS:* MARIPOSA LILIES OR TULIPS, BUTTERFLY TULIPS, GLOBE TULIPS
(Family Liliaceae: Lily)

Calochortus is restricted to western North America with thirty-seven species native to California. They are among the most beautiful, as well as the rarest bulb plants of the world. Their exquisite beauty comes from a graceful bearing, from the thick, smooth pile of their shapely flowers, and from the intricate designs within the flower bowl of certain species. Plants grow from a slender, coated corm, the coating varying from a thin, onion-like covering to ones of more fibrous texture. In all species the flowers are composed of three petals and three sepals, on plants which may bear one or several blossoms. (See Chart 13.)

Mariposa lilies or tulips: There are botanical differences among the *Calochortus* species, but for the gardener's purpose they can be divided into three categories. First are the large ones with campanulate, or bowl-shaped flowers, known as mariposa lilies or tulips. Foliage of these is thin and grasslike, seldom as long as the scape, normally dying down in early summer. A few have foliage of more substance, and will re-

CHART 13 *Calochortus:* Mariposa Lilies or Tulips, Butterfly Tulips, Globe Tulips

Plant	Height	Flowers	Culture	Remarks	Distribution
C. albus White Globe Lily	4-8 dm (15-31 in)	Globose, nodding, often wine-tinted. April-June.	High shade to sun, water tolerant. Adaptable.	Branched. Shade border, rock garden, with ferns, iris, etc.	Shade, open woods, brush, San Francisco south, and Sierra, Butte to Tuolumne cos.
C. amabilis Golden Fairy Lantern	2-5 dm (8-19 in)	Globose, nodding, deep, clear yellow. April-June.	High shade, semi-dry to moderate water.	Branched. Among trees, shady rock garden.	Dry slopes, brush, or woods, Humboldt and Solano to Marin cos.
C. amoenus Rose Fairy Lantern (See Fig. 42)	2-5 dm (8-19 in)	Nodding globe, vivid rose, wine sepals. April-June.	High, broken shade, friable soil, water tolerant.	Branched. Exquisite in flower color and shape.	Loamy slopes, high shade, western Sierra foothills.
C. tolmiei Tolmie's Pussy Ears	1-4 dm (4-15 in)	Open campanulate, white, lavender, or purple tint. Bearded. April-July.	Broken shade to sun, friable soil. Adaptable.	Shaded borders, rock garden.	Dry, open slope, woods, through Coast Ranges to Santa Cruz Co. and upper Sacramento Valley

C. uniflorus Pink Star Tulip	1-4 dm (3-8 in)	Open, campanulate, white, lilac, dark spot near gland. March-June.	Sun to partial shade, water tolerant. Bulbiferous.	Semi-dry border, raised bed, rock garden.	Wet fields, Coast Ranges, Mendocino to Monterey cos.
C. venustus White Mariposa Lily (See Pl. 4B)	1-8 dm (4-31 in)	Campanulate, wine, white, yellow, red, intricate design. May-July.	Sun, lean, dry soil dormant period late summer. Bulbiferous.	With drought-tolerant natives, other bulbs, perennials, etc.	Sandy, granitic soil, El Dorado to Kern cos. Central Coast Ranges, south.
C. luteus Gold Nuggets or Yellow Mariposa Lily (See Pl. 4D)	2-5 dm (8-19 in)	Shallow bowl, yellow, half-moon gland. April-June.	Sun, semi-dry, porous soil. Adaptable. Bulbiferous.	With brodiaeas, other drought-tolerant natives.	Heavy soils, Mendocino to Santa Barbara, Tehama to Kern cos.
C. vestae Goddess Mariposa Tulip	3-5 dm (12-24 in)	Deep campanulate, white, yellow, brown markings. May-June.	Sun to high shade, lean soil, moderate water. Bulbiferous.	Branched. With alliums, other native bulbs, perennials.	Clay soils, Napa and Sonoma to Humboldt cos.
C. splendens Splendid Mariposa Tulip	2-6 dm (8-24 in)	Campanulate, pale lilac, oval gland. May-June.	Sun, lean soil, moderate water. Not persistent.	Slender. With native mints, scattering of annuals, other native bulbs.	Dry, heavy, or granitic soils, Colusa Co., Baja Calif.

main green through the flowering season. The petals of mariposa tulips are generally fan-shaped, narrow at the base, and wide at the rim, this outer edge often rolled back. Three narrow sepals often contain in miniature the design within the flower, and sometimes curl back, scroll fashion. These designs consist of markings, pencillings, and eye-spots, and are especially pronounced in White Mariposa Lily *(C. venustus)*. Flower colors include pearly whites, several shades of pale to deep yellow, lilac, lavender, rose, wine purple, crimson, and the brilliant vermillion of the desert species, Kennedy's Mariposa Lily *(C. kennedyi)*. Glands of varying shape occur low in each flower cup, but are a conspicuous part of the flower design in the mariposas and are generally fringed with hairs of similar or contrasting colors. The glands may be round, square, oblong, lunate, or A-shaped, and are depressed so that their form is visible on the outside of the flower. Upright, three-sectioned, and pointed capsules almost always bear an abundance of seed.

Star tulips: Star tulips and cats ears are miniatures of the mariposa tulips. They have cup-shaped flowers in white, yellow, pale lilac, pink, or blue, sometimes with tinting of deeper colors. Some of the flowers are smooth within, while others are hairy, either with a light scattering, or densely bearded. All have a wide basal leaf which exceeds the height of the plant. Seed is borne in broad, winged, nodding capsules.

Globe tulips: Four species are known as globe tulips. They are robust, branched plants with a wide, shiny, basal leaf longer than the height of the plant. The lovely, pendant flowers are formed of three petals which meet at the tips, subtended by three shorter sepals. Broad, winged capsules bear an abundance of seeds. All of these small kinds of *Calochortus* are dainty plants, unexcelled for shade borders where their flowers of unusual design will show to advantage.

Culture: All species of *Calochortus* may be grown from seed which germinates readily, and in my experience is best planted in late autumn. Seed can be planted in deep pots, flats, or for large quantities, in an outdoor seed bed. Soil mixture should be porous, with an extra measure of sand or vermiculite for the mariposas, and added leaf mold for the woodland

Figure 42 *Calochortus amoenus,* Rose Fairy Lantern

species. It requires three to five years from seed to a mature corm. Seedlings should be kept evenly moist during the period of active growth, but allowed to dry out when yellowing foliage indicates the need for a dormant period, generally by mid- to late summer. Some find it easier to grow these bulbs in pots, using a friable soil mixture and allowing the pots to dry out after the foliage has died down. Plant the corms about three inches deep and closely spaced, from late September through October. Practically all of the mariposas are drought resistant and should be used in full sun, lean soil, watered only during their period of active growth, and allowed a dormant period in late summer. Star tulips and globe tulips are more adaptable than mariposas, and may be used in lightly shaded borders where water is given for most of the year.

Estimate of Garden Value: Although these are superb plants, their exacting requirements must be met to be successfully cultivated. The star and globe tulips with their spritely bearing are suitable under trees, among ferns and shade plants, or in raised borders with other diminutive plants. The mariposa tulips are sometimes capricious in their behavior, flowering well one year and then resting for the next year or even two before producing blossoms again. The small corms may not accumulate enough nourishment to produce flowers every year. Perhaps growing them in quantity with constant selection of vigorous types will result in a superior strain and more dependable performance. Species of *Calochortus* have continued to be greatly admired, painted, photographed, and enthusiastically described from the time of their initial discovery. However, some vital facts of their life cycle still remain puzzling, and devoted attention to these problems is needed.

The accompanying chart includes one of the small types which is among the most easily cultivated. The last four entries describe the most adaptable mariposa types. The term bulbiferous indicates that the species produces bulblets in the axils of the lower or lowest leaves.

GENUS *CAMASSIA:* CAMAS LILIES
(Family Liliaceae: Lily)

The genus *Camassia* is entirely American, with five species, two of which are native to California. They inhabit wet meadows and waterways, often in such quantities as to form solid masses of rich blue. Plants grow from an oval, coated bulb, with long, slender basal leaves of firm substance. Starlike flowers occur on the upper scape, and the buds open gradually over a long period. Flowers are medium to bright blue with contrasting yellow stamens. Camas bulbs were once an important element of the Indian diet.

Camassia quamash ssp. **linearis**
Common Camas

HABIT: Smooth scape from tunicated bulb, 2–8 dm, 8–31 in. (See Fig. 43.) FOLIAGE: Long, narrow, green on both surfaces. FLOWERS: Open, of 6 unlike segments, divergent,

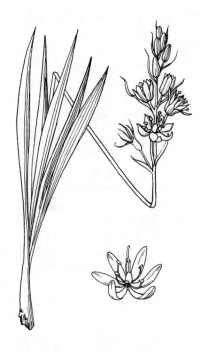

Figure 43 *Camassia quamash* ssp. *linearis,* Common Comas

pale blue to blue-violet. Dense raceme, blossoming from the bottom, with a spire of tight buds above. April–June. FRUIT: Ovoid capsule. DISTRIBUTION: Wet meadows below 2,500 feet elevation, North Coastal Coniferous Forest, Coast Ranges, Del Norte to Marin counties.

Culture: Common Camas lilies are abundant and bulbs are often available so there is little information on seed propagation. These plants can be increased from seed planted in autumn, in a mixture of leaf mold, sand, and gravel. Bulbs should be planted in autumn, in moist soil, about six inches deep, and closely spaced for the maximum effect. A watered flower border with morning sun is the ideal situation. They can be accompanied by scillas, violets, primroses, or such natives as White Brodiaea *(Brodiaea hyacinthina),* Long-Petaled Iris *(Iris longipetala),* or species of *Sisyrinchium.*

Estimate of Garden Value: Common Camas lilies are completely adaptable to garden conditions. While they accept water, they are also accustomed to dryness in late summer and autumn since they sometimes grow where the water source is not constant. The one drawback is the withering flowers which remain on the stem, but which can be removed for enjoyment of the newly opened flowers.

Camassia leichtlinii
Blue Camas

HABIT: Scape growing from bulb, unbranched, 2–13 dm, 8 in.–5 ft. FOLIAGE: Linear, dark green, paler on upper surface. FLOWERS: Open, large, of narrow segments, vivid blue to blue-purple, rarely albino. Petals twist strongly over the developing capsules. FRUIT: Oblong or ovoid capsule. DISTRIBUTION: Mountain meadows of Coniferous Forests, Coast Ranges, Napa County north, Sierra Nevada, Mono and Tulare counties north.

Culture and Estimate of Garden Value: The same as for *C. quamash.*

GENUS *CHLOROGALUM:* SOAP PLANTS
(Family Liliaceae: Lily)

Five species of *Chlorogalum* are native to California, two of them quite rare, and all growing from large, coated bulbs. They are conspicuous for long, tough, wavy-margined leaves, and for widely branched inflorescences, bearing small flowers of white, pink, blue, or purple. Historically *C. pomeridianum* is a plant of multiple uses, known to Indians and early settlers alike.

Chlorogalum pomeridianum
Soap Plant or Amole

HABIT: Tall, erect, from large bulb bearing a coarse, fibrous coating, 7–15 cm, 3–5 in. FOLIAGE: Numerous, long, wavy-margined, light green, 2–7 dm, to 2½ ft. FLOWERS: Of six narrow, spreading segments, oyster white, green or purplish midvein. On firm, branched stem, 6–25 dm, 2–10 ft. Blooms in late afternoon, closes during day. FRUIT: Small

Figure 44 *Chlorogalum pomeridianum,* Soap Plant or Amole

capsule, rounded, black seed. DISTRIBUTION: Dry hills, plains and open woodlands of both mountain ranges from southern Oregon to San Diego.

Culture: Soap Plant may be propagated by seed, and volunteers often occur around established plants. There is also increase by natural division of the bulbs. Should be used in semi-dry, sunny border.

Estimate of Garden Value: Although of coarse appearance, Soap Plant might be cultivated because of its historical significance, if for no other reason. However, the widely divergent and graceful branching and white flowers have an airy effect, and I have found it to be an interesting addition to a border of native shrubs and large perennials. It is suitable for a large garden, among robust plants of similar requirements, and especially where there is a dark background to highlight the white flowers.

Historical Uses: There is a long list of early uses for Soap Plant. Foremost was its cleansing properties. The lather obtained from the crushed bulb was used for bathing, washing clothes, and as a shampoo. Of equal value was its importance as food. After their coating was stripped, the bulbs were wrapped in poison-oak leaves and baked for a long period in pit ovens to drive out the soapy properties. In early spring, young stem shoots were cooked in the same manner and were said to have a sweet taste. The fibrous bulb coating was made into brushes, and early settlers reportedly used these fibers to fill mattresses when nothing else was available. Even the old leaves were used to wrap acorn bread during baking. In addition, crushed bulbs were tossed into dammed streams to stupefy fish for easier catching. The narcotic properties of the soap root affected fish and eels, but not frogs. Several other California native plants produce a soapy lather, but *Chlorogalum* seems to have had the widest use.

GENUS *ERYTHRONIUM:* FAWN LILIES, ADDER'S TONGUES, TROUT LILIES
(Family Liliaceae: Lily)

Twelve species of *Erythronium* are native to California, with the stronghold of this genus in northwestern California and southern Oregon. A few species are quite restricted in their distribution; others are more common and grow in the higher, wooded foothills, in meadows of mountain forests, and in coastal regions. Plants grow from an elongated corm, which is coated and brittle. Corms produce a pair of handsome leaves of thick substance, often glossy and frequently mottled in dark colors. A scape, usually taller than the leaves, bears one to several lily-like blossoms, composed of six similar segments which are slightly reflexed at the tips. Colors include white, several shades of yellow, and delicate tones of pink, lavender, and light purple, sometimes with dark lines at the center. (See Chart 14.)

Culture: Generous quantities of seed are borne in the upright capsules of *Erythronium* species, and these germinate without

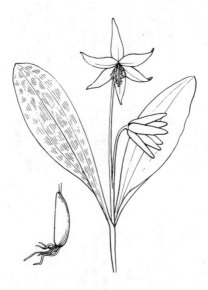

Figure 45 *Erythronium californicum,* California Fawn Lily

any pretreatment. Seeds should be planted in a friable soil composed of sand, loam, and sieved leaf mold or peat, and the container kept in a sheltered place until germination. During the first few years the cormlets produce a narrow, bright green leaf which gradually enlarges until a mature corm has developed in five to seven years. A few species, particularly Tuolumne Fawn Lily *(E. tuolumnense),* increase vegetatively by off-set corms. Members of this genus can safely be watered all through the year, and should have high, or broken shade, and a large proportion of organic material in the soil. They resent being moved, but once recovered from transplanting, and well established, they are likely to flower with increasing abundance for many years. The dainty trout lilies may be used among small ferns, various polemoniums, garden campanulas, and wild irises, in the foreground of shade borders.

Estimate of Garden Value: The fawn lilies have a spritely charm and are generally adaptable to cultivation, but should be used where there is not too much competition from large or

CHART 14 *Erythroniums*: Fawn Lilies

Plant	Height	Flowers	Culture	Remarks	Distribution
E. californicum California Fawn Lily (See Fig. 45 and Pl. 4A)	2–4 dm (8–15 in)	White, pale yellow center. March–April.	High or broken shade, friable soil, water tolerant.	Mottled leaves, scape branched, free-flowering. Under oaks.	Brushy slopes, woods, Colusa to Humboldt cos.
E. helenae Helen's Fawn Lily	2–3 dm (8–12 in)	White, golden yellow center. March–May.	Sun to high shade, friable soil. Vegetative reproduction.	Mottled leaves, scape 1 to several flowered. Shade border.	Volcanic soil, leaf mold, in woods, Mt. St. Helena to Sonoma Co.
E. multiscapoideum Sierra Fawn Lily	2–4 dm (8–15 in)	Cream white, yellow to orange center. March–May.	Open shade to sun. Increase by off-set.	Mottled leaves, many stems each with single flower.	Rich loam, wooded hills, Tehama to Mariposa cos.
E. hendersonii Purple Fawn Lily	1–3 dm (4–12 in)	Lavender, black-purple eye. April–July.	High shade, rich soil, water tolerant.	Dark green leaves mottled with plum-purple.	Wooded slopes, Siskiyou Co. northward.
E. tuolumnense Tuolumne Fawn Lily	2–3 dm (8–12 in)	Clear, bright yellow. March–May.	High, broken shade. Vegetative reproduction.	Leaves bright green unmottled. Shade border.	Woods, base of Sierra Nevada, Tuolumne and Stanislaus cos.

A *Nemophila menziesii*, Baby-Blue Eyes, p. 74

B *Orthocarpus erianthus*, Butter and Eggs or Johnny-Tuck with *Layia* species, Tidy Tips, p. 62

C *Linanthus dianthiflorus*, Ground Linanthus, p. 65

D *Collinsia heterophylla*, Purple Chinese Houses, p. 53

E *Mentzelia lindleyi*, Blazing Star, p. 69

F *Clarkia concinna*, Red Ribbons, p. 50

PLATE 1

A *Mimulus guttatus,*
Common Monkey flower, p. 133

B *Philadelphus lewisii* ssp. *californicus,*
California Mock Orange, p. 313

C *Penstemon heterophyllus* and
Eriophyllum lanatum ssp. *arachnoideum,*
Foothill Penstemon and Dwarf Woolly
Sunflower, pp. 113 and 143

D *Lupinus albifrons,*
var. *flumineus,* Silver Circle Lupine, p. 128

E *Iris innominata,* Golden Iris, p. 118

F *Sisyrinchium bellum,*
California Blue-Eyed Grass, p. 154

PLATE 2

A *Trillium chloropetalum*, Giant Trillium, p. 156

B *Heuchera micrantha*,
Crevice Heuchera, p. 116

C *Arabis blepharophylla*, Rose Rock Cress, p. 92

D *Delphinium herperium*,
Western Larkspur, p. 303

E *Smilacina racemosa*,
Branched Solomon's Seal, p. 317

F *Aquilegia formosa*, Red Columbine, p. 91

PLATE 3

A *Erythronium californicum*,
California Fawn Lily, p. 182

B *Calochortus venustus*, White Mariposa Lily, p. 17

C *Lilium parryi*,
Lemon Lily, p. 188

D *Calochortus luteus*, Gold Nuggets, p. 173

E *Zigadenus fremontii*,
Star-Lily, p. 192

F *Brodiaea laxa*, Ithuriel's Spear, p. 170

PLATE 4

A *Arctostaphylos uva-ursi*
'Radiant,' cultivar, p. 198

B *Arctostaphylos canescens*,
Hoary Manzanita, p. 19

C *Ribes sanguineum*, Red-Flowered Currant, p. 254

D *Cercis occidentalis*, Redbud, p. 218

E *Comarostaphylis diversifolia*,
Summer Holly, p. 224

F *Styrax officinalis*,
var. *californica*,
California Snowdrop Bush, p. 258

PLATE 5

A *Rhamnus californica*,
California Coffeeberry, p. 248

B *Garrya elliptica* 'James Roof,'
cultivar, p. 235

C *Carpenteria californica*, Tree Anemone, p. 208

D *Dendromecon harfordii*,
Island Tree Poppy, p. 231

E *Ceanothus griseus* 'Louis Edmunds'
cultivar, p. 213

F *Ceanothus foliosus*,
Wavy-Leaf Ceanothus, p. 210

PLATE 6

A *Pseudotsuga menziesii*, Douglas Fir, p. 281

B *Sequoia sempervirens*, Redwood, p. 290

C *Acer macrophyllum*, Bigleaf Maple, p. 265

D *Abies bracteata*, Bristlecone Fir, p. 263

E *Arbutus menziesii*, Madrone, p. 270

F *Pinus ponderosa*, Yellow Pine, p. 308
Quercus kelloggii, California Black Oak, p. 288

PLATE 7

A *Aquilegia formosa* (in border), Red Columbine, p. 91

B *Clematis lasiantha*, Pipestem Clematis, p. 97

D *Lilium pardalinum*, Leopard Lily, p.18

C *Vancouveris hexandra*, Northern Inside-Out Flower, p. 158

E *Arctostaphylos glandulosa* var. *cushingiana*, Huckleberry Manzanita, p. 199

F Mixed border of natives (Robert Smaus Garden)

PLATE 8

aggressive plants. Their flowering period begins in March; mountain forms bloom later, but often at the very edge of melting snowbanks. Most species, once well established and left alone, are very long lived. The original few corms of California Fawn Lily planted under the live oak tree in my Los Gatos garden had stems bearing as many as five flowers each season.

GENUS *FRITILLARIA*: FRITILLARIES
(Family Liliaceae: Lily)

Sixteen species of *Fritillaria* are native to California, ten of which are endemic. The California natives represent almost half of the known species in this interesting, exciting, and challenging genus. Fritillary bulbs are composed of fleshy appearing scales, and in some species, bear tiny, rice-grain bulblets around the lower rim. From the bulb an erect stem bears leaves which are mostly narrow and sessile and either scattered along the stem, in tiers, or in a basal whorl. Attractive flowers with a quaint charm occur along the upper stem, generally nodding, but upfacing in a few species. They are bell-shaped to funnelform, composed of six alike segments, and variously lined and freckled. Flower colors include clear deep yellow, a wide range of amber, medium to dark brown, shades of green, dull purple, and one of striking bright red. Erect, conspicuous capsules contain an abundance of flat, roundish seed. (See Chart 15.)

Culture: Rock gardeners greatly admire fritillaries and are foremost in experimenting with their culture. Fritillaries are not always easy to grow. All species should have attention to soil, exposure, amounts of moisture, and habitat. Most of them grow readily from seed, requiring four to five years to produce a mature bulb. Professional growers recommend a friable soil mixture containing loam, peat moss, and sand, both for the seed bed and for pot culture of those species which do not do well in open borders. In my experience, coarse leaf soil well mixed with sharp sand is adequate for most woodland species. Fritillaries from serpentine areas or talus slopes should have coarse soil and perfect drainage. Blooming begins in February for some, extending into May, and then into early summer for

CHART 15 *Fritillaria:* Fritillaries

Plant	Height	Flowers	Culture	Remarks	Distribution
F. lanceolata Mission Bells	3-8 (or 12) dm (12-32 [or 48] in)	Deep bowl, nodding, brown-purple to greenish yellow. Feb.-June.	High shade, friable soil, water tolerant. Forms rice-grain bulblets.	Adaptable, variable size and flower color.	Brush and woods, Coast Ranges, Ventura to Siskiyou cos.
F. atropurpurea Purple Fritillary	1.5-6 dm (6-18 in)	Campanulate, purplish green, mottled yellowish. April-July.	High shade, friable soil, moderate water.	Linear leaves, whorled on upper stem.	Under trees, forests, Tulare to Siskiyou cos.
F. pudica Yellow Bells (See Fig. 47)	7-30 cm (3-9 in)	Bells, nodding, yellow aging to red. March-June.	Sun to filtered shade, light, well-drained soil.	Adaptable. Rock gardens, raised borders.	Grassy to wooded slopes, Siskiyou to Sierra cos.
F. recurva Scarlet Fritillary (See Fig. 46)	3-9 dm (12-30 in)	Funnelform, recurved tips, red-yellow mottling. March-July.	Gravelly, humus sun to high shade, semi-dry.	Open border, with other bulbs, native perennials, rock garden.	Brush, woods, inner Coast Range, Lake to Nevada cos.

F. pluriflora Adobe Lily	2-4.5 dm (6-16 in)	Large bells, nodding, pinkish purple. Feb.-March.	Sun, semi-dry, coarse, well-drained soil, in open areas.	With small alliums, brodiaeas, and native annuals.	Adobe soil, foothills, Mendocino to Butte cos.
F. liliacea White Fritillary	1-3.5 dm (3-12 in)	Campanulate, white with fine green lines, fragrant. March-April.	Sun, well-drained soil, semi-dry. Endemic to S.F. Bay Area.	With native annuals, perennials, in open borders.	Heavy soils, hills, fields, Sonoma and Monterey cos.
F. biflora Chocolate Lily	8-18 cm (5-10 in)	Nodding, dark brown, greenish bronze. Feb.-June.	Sun to high shade, coarse soil, from few fleshy scales. Rare in nature.	Lightly shaded rock garden, raised border.	Heavy soils, slopes, mesas, Mendocino to San Diego cos.

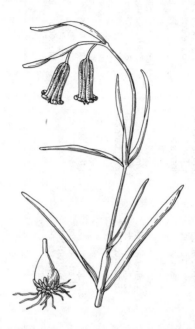

Figure 46 *Fritillaria recurva,* Scarlet Fritillary

the high-mountain species. Practically all members need a summer dormant period when water should be withheld. In my experience, Mission Bells *(F. lanceolata)* has been the most adaptable and persistent, increasing at a moderate rate to form colonies in the shade of deciduous trees. Most species may be watered during their periods of active growth.

Estimate of Garden Value: Although not all of the fritillaries are adaptable, many gardeners find the bell flowers with their quiet, subdued colors to be desirable for a shady nook, and to respond well when suitable conditions are provided. Woodland species may be used in a shade border, or in a raised bed to ensure good drainage. Those native to more arid places can be grown in pockets of coarse soil in rock gardens.

GENUS *LILIUM:* LILIES
(Family Liliaceae: Lily)

Thirteen species and several varieties of *Lilium* are native to California. All are handsome, refined plants suitable to garden

Figure 47 *Fritillaria pudica,* Yellow Bells

culture, and several have long been popular garden materials. At least five are of restricted distribution, and are native to the northwest coastal and low-mountain regions. Others, such as Leopard Lily *(L. pardalinum),* are more widely distributed, growing along watercourses and in meadows. Stout stems of lilies grow from scaly bulbs, with foliage in whorls or scattered along the stems. Large flowers are formed of six alike segments, these reflexed in most species, but less so in some and forming a trumpet-shaped blossom. The six stamens are conspicuous with large anthers, and the stigma is three-lobed. Generous quantities of seed are borne in large, erect capsules. These lilies are plants of fine bearing, with beautiful flowers in a range of bright, lively colors. (See Chart 16.)

Horticultural History: Native lilies have had considerable attention over the years, and horticultural forms of a few species have been selected out, but these are not always well known. During the 1920s, there was a mass crossing of Humboldt Lily *(L. humboldtii),* Lemon Lily *(L. parryi),* and *L. pardalinum,* and some of the resulting lilies came to be known as the Bellingham hybrids. These are still available today in an

CHART 16 *Lilium*: Lilies

Plant	Height	Flowers	Culture	Remarks	Distribution
L. pardalinum Leopard Lily (See Pl. 8D)	10-25 (or more) dm (40-80 plus in)	Nodding, recurved, orange-yellow, red on outer tips. May-July.	Sun to high shade, water tolerant, humus in soil.	Adaptable, forms colonies, variable in nature.	Moist places, Humboldt to Santa Barbara and Kern to San Diego cos.
L. humboldtii Humboldt Lily (See Fig. 48 and cover photo)	9-20 dm (36-96 in)	Segments revolute, orange-red, maroon spots. June-July.	Sun or filtered shade, water tolerant.	Adaptable, naturalizes.	Dry forest, Butte to Fresno cos.
L. humboldtii var. *bloomerianum* Bloomer's Tiger Lily	9-15 dm (36-72 in)	Nodding, spotted, free-flowering. June-July.	Same as species.	Borders or among trees and shrubs.	Open flats, San Diego Co.
L. parryi Lemon Lily (See Pl. 4C)	6-15 dm (24-72 in)	Trumpet, lemon yellow, spotted, fragrant. July-Aug.	Sun to high shade, rich, moist soil, among trees, shrubs.	Borders with meadowrue, campanulas.	Moist soil, San Gabriel Mts. to San Diego co.

L. washingtonianum Washington Lily	6-18 dm (24-84 in)	White trumpet, aging lavender, fragrant. July-Aug.	Semi-dry, sun to high shade, porous soil.	Bulb of large, non-jointed scales.	Dry to loam soil, Fresno to Siskiyou cos.
L. washingtonianum var. *purpurascens* Cascade Lily	6-10 dm (24-42 in)	White trumpet, aging dark rose, fragrant. July.	Semi-dry, sun to high shade, among shrubs.	Relatively adaptable.	Dry forests, Humboldt to Siskiyou cos.

Figure 48 *Lilium humboldtii,* Humboldt Lily

assortment of colors from catalogs, and all are dependable and easily grown plants. When grown from seed, the greatest number will be the Leopard type, some will be similar to the Humboldt Lily, and a small proportion will be the fragrant Lemon Lily. Although there is a wide assortment of garden lilies available today, Californians can be proud of these native plants which have a grace and charm of their own.

Culture: Almost all species of native lilies may be grown from seed which germinates readily. Seedlings may be left in beds or containers until the second year and then transplanted into fresh soil. Most species require three or more years to reach maturity. During this time the seedlings should be kept evenly moist. Most lilies tolerate year-round watering but must have well-drained soil into which organic materials have been incorporated. The majority prefer high, filtered shade, although the adaptable ones will grow in any sunny, well-

watered flower border. For the few which grow in light woodlands or chaparral, such as Washington Lily *(L. washingtonianum),* coarse sand can be used in the planting hole to
ensure sharp drainage. Vigorous species like the Leopard Lily
soon form large clumps and may be divided every four or five
years.

Estimate of Garden Value: Native lilies are worthy of a
place in gardens, if bulbs or seed are available. A few, which
are rare in nature and now threatened with extinction, should
be left intact. Others, such as the Lemon, Humboldt, and
Leopard lilies, flourish under cultivation and persist for many
years. In my mountain garden the Leopard Lily provides a few
volunteer plants each year in a moist, partially shaded area of
deciduous trees and shrubs. A few Lemon Lilies have also
continued to grow and flower each year, although not with the
great number of blossoms recorded for wild forms in the mountains of southern California. The Coast Range form of the
Washington Lily, the Cascade Lily *(L. washingtonianum* ssp.
purpurascens) has performed very well on an east-facing
slope, which gets sun for most of the day, and in coarse soil
with a yearly mulch of leaf mold. This subspecies is said to be
more adaptable than the species, although it is a smaller plant
with fewer flowers.

GENUS *ZIGADENUS:* ZYGADENES
(Family Liliaceae: Lily)

Seven species of *Zigadenus* are native to California, in a
group of plants which lend a quiet charm with their stalks of
cream white, star-shaped flowers. In some cases these plants
are called death-camas because of poisonous alkaloides; *Z.
venenosus* is considered to be the most poisonous.

Culture: Species of *Zigadenus* are grown from seed which
requires three-months stratification for germination. It takes
about four years of steady growth for a mature bulb to be
produced. This camas should have full sun, porous and well-
drained soil, and semi-dry conditions. It can be planted in
mixtures of native bulbs, perennials, and annuals, or may be
used with cultivated bulbs, such as daffodils or grape hyacinths
for the interesting contrast of its starlike flowers.

Estimate of Garden Value: Zygadenes are not much cultivated because they are poisonous, but no harm will be done if
the bulbs are handled with care. Zygadenes appear to be adaptable when used correctly, and are especially valuable for their
spring flowers which may begin in early February. This species
has persisted for many years in a botanical garden.

Zigadenus fremontii
Fremont's Camas

HABIT: Smooth stem, 3–10 dm, 1-3 ft. FOLIAGE: Basal,
long, slender, folded in, arched. FLOWERS: Open, of 6
pointed segments, cream white, yellow center. March–May.
(See Pl. 4E.) FRUIT: Capsule. DISTRIBUTION: Dry grassy
or brushy slopes, Coast Ranges from Butte to San Diego
counties.

Culture and Estimate of Garden Value: See generic description above.

8. GROWING
NATIVE SHRUBS

A wide range of shrubs, within many genera, is native to California. Some are entirely indigenous to the state. There are shrubs for every season and for every garden situation, large and small, common and elegant, evergreen and deciduous. Probably more work has been done to discover the ornamental qualities of native shrubs than for any other category of wild plants. This work has been accomplished by botanic gardens, by a few horticultural institutions, and by dedicated amateur gardeners. Investigation has been on a relatively small scale since there is no large institution devoted entirely to sustained testing of native plants. Practically all of the shrubs now available to the gardener possess natural adaptability, and were selected from crosses of wild forms in which vigor and superior traits are evident, or are the results of deliberate crosses. Further crosses will be needed to achieve heightened ornamental features, greater durability under cultivation, and prolonged seasons of usefulness. Already western landscaping has been greatly enriched by native shrubs, both in home gardens and by their use in freeway and other large-scale landscaping.

SPECIES DESCRIPTIONS

The native shrubs described in the following pages include about thirty genera, out of an estimated two hundred or more which could be used for ornamental purposes.

GENUS *AMELANCHIER:* SERVICE BERRIES
(Family Rosaceae: Rose)

Four species of *Amelanchier* are native to California, mostly of montane coniferous forests. Some species which are noted for white flowers in spring and edible, dark purple berries, have long been cultivated elsewhere.

Amelanchier pallida (A. alnifolia)
Pallid Service Berry

HABIT: Erect, rigid, branching above, slender, deciduous, 1–3 or 6 m, 3–12 or 16 ft. (See Fig. 49.) FOLIAGE: Oval to rounded, light, grayish green, serrate toward tips. FLOWERS: Small, white, petals narrowly oblong, plum like, in terminal racemes. April–June. FRUIT: Purple pome with sweet flesh, small seed. August–September. DISTRIBUTION: Dry, rocky slopes and forested flats, near streams, montane coniferous forests, throughout Coast Ranges and from southern Sierra Nevada north to Oregon.

Culture: Seed of Pallid Service Berry requires three-months stratification and even then germination may be spotty. Plants are adaptable to sun or light shade, and tolerant of year-round watering. From a canyon on my mountain property, I dug a small seedling which rapidly grew to about eight feet at the rear of a flower border. Several slender trunks grew from the base, and some of these have been removed. Suckerlike growth

Figure 49 *Amelanchier pallida,* Pallid Service Berry

appears each spring, and new plants may be obtained by removing and potting some of these until a good root system has formed.

Estimate of Garden Value: Pallid Service Berry is a pleasant, open shrub. It tends to sucker too much for most gardens, but is valuable where a close thicket is wanted. Superior, tree-size forms are being developed that may be used in informal gardens for a woodsy atmosphere, and for the early white blossoms and late summer fruits. Fruit is attractive to several kinds of birds, and deer browse on the young foliage. Country housewives use the fruit for jams and jellies or as a substitute for blueberries, and the Indians used the dried berries in making pemmican.

GENUS *ARCTOSTAPHYLOS:* Manzanitas
(Family Ericaceae: Heath)

Forty-three out of fifty known species of *Arctostaphylos* are native to California. One of these, Bear Berry *(A. uva-ursi),* is circumpolar. In the West, members of this genus are commonly known as manzanita, Spanish for little apple, because of the shape of the fruits. Although widely distributed throughout the state, most species are native to arid places. They often occur in almost unbroken masses in chaparral and dry foothills. Other species make firm, dense carpets on coastal bluffs. Pine Manzanita *(A. nevadensis)* is a mountain form which may occur up to 10,000 feet elevation. This genus has exceptional value for horticultural possibilities, and for natural hybrids which occur where several species overlap. (See Chart 17.)

Description: Manzanitas are evergreen, woody shrubs of uniform growth habit. They range in size from low, creeping or mounding plants through medium size, and to large ones which attain tree proportions. They are especially noted for their satiny, richly colored bark of reddish, brown, or mahogany hue which flakes off in late summer revealing tender new bark of pale beige or soft green. In spite of their reputation for having crooked branches, many manzanitas are erect or have curved or arching branches that are always well spaced for a pleasing outline. Foliage is of firm, leathery substance, ranging in color from pale or bright gray-green to darker shades, and generally

CHART 17 Arctostaphylos: Manzanita

Plant	Growth Habit or Size	Flowers	Culture	Remarks	Distribution
A. densiflora Sonoma Manzanita	Low, procumbent	Abundant, white or pink. March-April.	Semi-dry to moderate water. Facer or edging.	Many hybrids, cuttings root freely.	Open hills, Sonoma Co.
A. densiflora 'Howard McMinn' McMinn Manzanita	to 6 dm (24 in) high; 6-8 dm (24-48 in) wide	Abundant, rose-pink. March-April.	Sun, semi-dry, east or north exposure.	Low-branching, dark green leaves.	Cultivar.
A. densiflora James West James West Manzanita	Spreading 9 dm (36 in)	Small, rose-pink. Feb.	Semi-dry, sun to high shade.	Border edging, facer. Versatile.	Cultivar.
A. densiflora 'Sentinel' Sentinel Manzanita	Erect 2-3 m (6½-10 ft)	Large clusters, rose-pink. Feb.-March.	Sun, semi-dry. Borders, specimen.	Open shrub, red bark. May be shaped.	Cultivar.

Name	Size	Flowers	Culture and Uses	Notes	Habitat
A. hookeri Monterey Manzanita	Spreading mounds 4-12 dm (16-38 in)	Small, white to pink. Feb.-April.	Semi-dry, sandy soil. Stems root readily. Cover or edging.	Will grow in heavy soils.	Sand dunes, woods, Monterey Co.
A. hookeri 'Wayside' Wayside Manzanita	1-3.5 m (3-12 ft) wide: 1 m (3½ ft) high	White. Feb.-April.	Sun, semi-dry. Cover, facer, large rock garden.	Leaves dark, glossy green, white flowers.	Variant.
A. glauca Bigberry Manzanita	Erect 2-4 (6) m (6-12 [18] ft)	Large, white, abundant clusters. Dec.-March.	Semi-dry, sun, porous soil. Shrub borders, with ceanothus, etc.	Adaptable.	Chaparral, central to southern Coast Ranges.
A. stanfordiana Stanford Manzanita	Erect, branching 1-2 m (3-6 ft)	Large, pink, in open clusters. Jan.-March.	Semi-dry, sun. Background, specimen, etc.	Leaves bright green, red berries.	Chaparral, Napa to Mendocino cos.
A. insularis Island Manzanita	Erect 1-2.5 (5) m (3½-8 [15] ft)	White, flowers off and on. Jan.-March.	Sun, moderate water in summer, tolerates heavy soil. Borders, etc.	Leaves bright green, reddish berries.	Chaparral, Santa Cruz and Santa Rosa ids.

CHART 17 *Arctostaphylos:* Manzanita *(continued)*

Plant	Growth Habit or Size	Flowers	Culture	Remarks	Distribution
A. obispoensis Serpentine Manzanita	Erect 1-3 (6) m (3½-10 [20] ft)	Large clusters, deep pink. Feb.-March.	Sun, dry soil. Specimen, with other natives.	Outstanding for gray leaves, purple bark.	Foothill Woodland, San Luis Obispo to Monterey cos.
A. pajaroensis Pajaro Manzanita	Erect, compact 1-3 m (3½-10 ft)	White. Dec.-Feb.	Sun, semi-dry. Specimen, borders, background.	Dark red bark, light red berries.	Sandy hills, northern Monterey Co.
A. uva-ursi Bearberry	Trailing, stems rising at tips	Small urns, white to purplish. March-June.	Light shade, moisture, leaf mold in soil. Adaptable.	Shining, oval leaves, red berries. Under trees.	Coast, central California northward.
A. uva-ursi 'Radiant' Radiant Manzanita (See Pl. 5A)	Wide mats	White, edged rose-pink. Feb.-April.	Broken shade, moist, leaf mold in soil. Rapid growth rate.	Shiny leaves, persistent red berries. Rock garden.	Selected form.

A. *edmundsii* Little Sur Manzanita	Semi-prostrate 2.5-3.5 m (8-11 ft) across	Abundant, blush pink. Nov. into spring.	Sun, tolerates moisture and heavy soil.	Bright green leaves, tinged red. Ground cover.	Ocean bluffs, Monterey Co.
A. *glandulosa* var. *cushingiana* forma *repens* Huckleberry Manzanita (See Fig. 50 and Pl. 8E)	Mounding, densely branched 4 m (13 ft) spread	White, Feb.-April.	Sun to light shade, water tolerant.	Red-brown berries. Shaded slopes, edging, large rock garden, etc.	Chaparral Marin, Napa, and Sonoma cos.
A. *nummularia* Ft. Bragg Manzanita	Decumbent or erect 1.5-5 dm (6-24 in)	Small inflorescences, white. March-May.	Acid soil, sun to high shade.	Rock garden, ground cover, with conifers.	Coast, Mendocino and Sonoma cos.
A. 'Dr. Hurd' Dr. Hurd Manzanita	to 4.5 m (15 ft) high; 6 m (20 ft) spread	Pure white in large clusters. March.	Sun, moderate water, porous soil. Adaptable, treelike.	Mahogany bark, red berries. Relatively fast growing, branched framework.	Cultivar. Origin not known.

Figure 50 *Arctostaphylos glandulosa* var. *cushingiana,*
Huckleberry Manzanita

held in a vertical position to the stem. A nice contrast is af-
forded by the new leaves in late winter which are generally
pale, sometimes downy, and in some edged in red or dark rose.
The urn-shaped flowers are borne in terminal racemes or panicles and vary only slightly in size among the species. Flower
colors include white, pale to deep pink, rose, and a purplish
shade; those with large clusters often have a pearly appearance
from their waxen texture. (See Pl. 5B.) A unique trait of this
genus is the ability of some to stump sprout after a fire; eventually, they develop a heavy, basal, burl-like root. Other species
depend upon seed for their regeneration.

Propagation: Species of *Arctostaphylos* may be propagated
both from seeds and from cuttings. Seed is notoriously difficult
to germinate and requires pretreatment, usually of more than
one kind. Soaking the seed in sulphuric acid followed by a
period of cold stratification will hasten the process. Other
methods include burning pine needles over the flat after planting seed, watering thoroughly, and then setting the flat aside to
await the slow, and often erratic germination. A recent method
is to plant the seed in a deep flat of coarse soil, cover with a

mulch of wood shavings (not redwood or cedar) mixed with a compost starter, and then set aside until germination takes place, possibly by the following spring.

Cuttings: Take cuttings from firm, semi-ripe wood of the current year's growth, about four inches long, and with the lower leaves removed. Dip the cuttings in Rootone F which contains a fungicide. Hormodin #2 or Hormex #3 are also satisfactory. Have ready a wooden flat, eight to ten inches square and about four inches deep, filled with equal parts of peat moss and coarse sand. Water thoroughly and allow to drain. Firm this mixture with a wooden block, insert the cuttings, and water lightly to be certain the mixture is well set around the cuttings. Cover the flat with a light frame over which plastic has been attached. This will give a close atmosphere and help to retain moisture; the cuttings should never be allowed to dry out. Put the flat in a sheltered place where there is plenty of light but not direct sunlight. Cuttings may also be planted in a shallow pot or pan; slip the container into a plastic bag and secure it with a rubber band. Cuttings should root in four to eight weeks, and can then be potted in a mixture of peat moss, coarse sand, and loam. The following species root most easily: *Arctostaphylos uva-ursi* and selected forms, Sonoma Manzanita *(A. densiflora)* and cultivars, Little Sur Manzanita *(A. edmundsii),* Monterey Manzanita *(A. hookeri)* and forms, Stanford Manzanita *(A. stanfordiana)* and Morro Manzanita *(A. morroensis).* Young plants may be set out during autumn in well-drained soil, with full sun for those from arid situations and light shade for those from woodlands or from coastal regions. The rooting of cuttings varies among the species, and is generally more certain in hybrids and cultivars. Horticulturists are studying the problems of manzanita propagation along with other aspects of their culture.

Culture: Species and hybrids of *Arctostaphylos* are among the most handsome, enduring, and useful of all native shrubs. Once established they require very little attention, thriving with sun to light shade and very little water. Their distinctive features make them desirable as cultivated plants, and their uses in gardens and large-scale landscaping are extensive. The low, spreading kinds, especially some of the new cultivars, have few equals as ground and slope covers and are especially appropriate under native oaks where very little water should be given. Other kinds are suitable for massed plantings in parking strips, border edgings, facer shrubs, in mixtures with other native shrubs, and also to stand alone as a specimen. The berries, although seldom mentioned, add notes of lively brown, mahogany, and dark to bright red in late summer. Because of their slow rate of growth, manzanitas seldom require pruning but most will accept some thinning with no harm.

Estimate of Garden Value: The garden worth of manzanitas is now fully recognized, and the trend today is toward new and superior forms, as well as to a better understanding of seed germination and plant culture. An intensive study of the variable traits within certain species and the development of hybrids will eventually result in new types suitable for specific landscape needs. Selected natural hybrids have already shown vigor, adaptability, and a more rapid growth rate. Another factor needing more study is the susceptibility of some species to a fungus disease which begins with the dying of limbs and finally the whole plant. Overhead irrigation and incorrect soil conditions are thought to aggravate this disease.

Traditional Uses: Practically all parts of the manzanita bush were used by Indians and early settlers. The berries were considered to be almost as important as a food item as acorns, and were eaten both raw and cooked. Vinegar, brandy, and a pleasant-tasting cider were made from the berries, and country housewives still use them to make a clear jelly. A delicate honey to please all tastes is produced from the flowers, and bee-men place their hives among the warming foothills for the early flowers in late winter. Birds and many other animals eat the fruits. The generic name, which means bear-grape, comes from bears' fondness for the berries. Indians and trappers ground the leaves of certain manzanitas along with those of other shrubs as a substitute for smoking tobacco, known as kinnikinnik, another term which is associated with the genus. Finally, many household items were fashioned from the hard manzanita wood, including pipe bowls, spoons, and pegs used in the place of nails. This large western genus of evergreen shrubs has had a past history of many uses, and holds the promise of giving even more in the way of distinctive cultivated plants.

GENUS *BACCHARIS:*
CHAPARRAL BROOMS
(Family Compositae: Sunflower)

Nine species in *Baccharis,* all shrubby in character and a few broomlike, are native to California. While they are an important element of the natural landscape, only the one described here has been cultivated to any extent. Experiments with seed germination and other forms of propagation were begun in the mid-1930s, and today this species is an important bank and slope cover, useful on road cuts as well as in home gardens.

Baccharis pilularis
Dwarf Chaparral Broom or
Prostrate Coyote-Brush

HABIT: Mat-forming, evergreen, older stems becoming woody, 10–15 cm high, 1–4 m across, 3½–14 ft across. FOLIAGE: Oval or obovate, dark, bright green, thick, resinous. FLOWERS: Discoid head, small, appear fuzzy, off-white, female flowers bear cottony pappus. FRUIT: Achene. DISTRIBUTION: Dunes and headlands along coast, from Russian River to Point Sur, Monterey County.

Culture: Dwarf Chaparral Broom is easily grown from seed which germinates within two weeks, and seedlings can be shifted to four-inch pots in about four months. When well rooted they may be set into their permanent quarters. Because of the fly-away pappus on the female flowers, the most desirable method of propagation is by short, tip cuttings taken from male plants in late fall to early spring. These may be rooted in clean, sharp sand, and then handled in the same manner as seedling plants. Propagation by cuttings perpetuates plants having the best features and foliage color. This baccharis thrives in full sun to very light shade, and tolerates year-round watering. It performs admirably in heavy soils as well as sandy ones. For a close ground cover it is suggested that young plants be rolled and any upright branches be removed.

Estimate of Garden Value: Because of the popularity of *Baccharis pilularis,* new forms have been selected for rich green leaf color and good performance. Some have a honey-like fragrance which attracts many butterflies. This engaging, fast-growing, carpeting plant is now widely used for road sides, other large-scale landscaping, and in home gardens. Two selected forms include *B. pilularis* 'Twin Peaks', an old standby, and the newer *B. pilularis* 'Pigeon Point', noted for its dark green foliage. Both are considered to be fire retardant and are not eaten by deer.

GENUS *BERBERIS:* BARBERRIES
(Family Berberidaceae: Barberry)

Thirteen species of *Berberis* are native to California, all evergreen and outstanding for their crisp, lustrous, toothed leaves, often like a large holly leaf. California species are sometimes known as Mahonia to distinguish them from thorny members of the genus. Because of their conspicuous purple berries, they are also known as holly grapes.

Berberis aquifolium
Oregon Grape

HABIT: Large, branched, evergreen, 1–2 or 3 m, 3½–6½ or 10 ft. FOLIAGE: Glossy, bright green, once pinnate, three, five, or seven leaflets oblong to lanceolate, with slender spines on the margins. FLOWERS: Drooping racemes, small, bright yellow. March–May. FRUIT: Berry, dark blue, glaucous, few-seeded. DISTRIBUTION: Wooded slopes of mountain forests, Humboldt, Trinity, and Modoc counties, northward.

Culture: Seed of Oregon Grape requires three-months cold stratification for good germination. This species, and several others in the genus, spread by underground rootstocks, and may eventually form large clumps. Rootstocks can be cut from established plants and grown in gallon cans until a new root system has formed. Oregon Grape is most handsome in part shade, as a foundation planting on the cool side of buildings, or in a mixture of trees and shrubs, especially with conifers.

It thrives with some leaf mold in the soil and water through the year.

Estimate of Garden Value: The year-round good qualities of this shiny-leaved shrub are undisputed. It has long been a popular garden plant, and is also widely used in large-scale landscaping.

Berberis nevinii
Nevin's Barberry

HABIT: Large, rounded evergreen, stiffly branched, 1–4 m, 3½–14 ft. (See Fig. 51.) FOLIAGE: Pinnately divided, 3–5 lanceolate to lance-ovate leaflets, thick, nonshiny, blue-green. FLOWERS: Typical, bright yellow. March–April. FRUIT: Juicy berry, yellowish red to red. DISTRIBUTION: Sandy or gravelly places in scattered locations, Coastal Sage Scrub or Chaparral of hills, San Bernardino, Riverside, and San Diego counties.

Culture: Seed of Nevin's Barberry requires up to three-months cold stratification. Young plants are held in pots until

Figure 51 *Berberis nevinii,* Nevin's Barberry

about 16 inches high and then set into their permanent place. Most experiences show this mahonia to be easy to handle, and adaptable both to dry and to watered situations. Its compact growth makes it ideal for hedges, dividers, fillers, or for foundation planting.

Estimate of Garden Value: This rare barberry is no longer found in its original home, so it is fortunate that it is propagated and has become a popular garden plant. It is relatively slow growing, and takes full sun and either porous or heavy soils. Gardeners from central to southern California consider it to be an enduring shrub with excellent year-round appearance.

Other Species:

Berberis nervosa, Longleaf Mahonia, is a vigorous species whose leaves come directly from long, underground rootstocks. These may have from 7 to 21 ovate leaflets, of dark, unshiny blue-green, with bristlelike teeth. It looks like a large, leathery fern and forms colonies in its native setting of damp woodlands of north coast coniferous forests. In gardens it is generally slow to become established.

Berberis repens, Creeping Barberry, is a low, spreading type growing from stolonlike stems. Although slow growing, it is a desirable ground and slope cover for shade, and a specimen of great character when successfully cultivated.

Berberis pinnata, Shinyleaf Barberry, is a large, stout, branching shrub. Its leaflets are crowded and have incurved margins and numerous prickly teeth. This dense, prickly shrub makes an impenetrable hedge, or a large-scale ground cover for arid places.

Berberis amplectens × **B. aquifolium** 'Golden Abundance' is a newly introduced form with a vigorous growth habit, and large racemes of golden yellow flowers in February and March. The fruit clusters are like miniature Concord grapes, and are freely produced for a fine autumn effect. This selection is adaptable to normal garden conditions, but does not tolerate heavy shade.

GENUS *CALYCANTHUS*: Sweet Shrub
(Family Calycanthaceae: Sweet Shrub)

Only one species of *Calycanthus,* a vigorous shrub noted for its aromatic foliage, is native to California.

Calycanthus occidentalis
Spice Bush or Sweet Shrub

HABIT: Erect, branching, rounded in outline, deciduous, 1–3 or 6 m, 3½–10 or to 20 ft. (See Fig. 52.) FOLIAGE: Oblong-lanceolate, dark green, firm texture, spicy. FLOWERS: Solitary, sepals and petals similar, linear and curled at the tips, in several series to form large, wine red or maroon flowers. Odor described as being like strawberries, wine, or vinegar. FRUIT: Erect, cuplike vessel enclosing many achenes. DISTRIBUTION: Moist places, canyons and streams, north Coast Ranges, Napa to Trinity counties, and in Sierra Nevada, west base, Tulare to Shasta counties.

Culture: No treatment is required for the large, oblong seed of the Spice Bush, although a short period of stratification may hasten germination which takes from 30 to 60 days. The seed

Figure 52 *Calycanthus occidentalis,* Spice Bush or Sweet Shrub

leaf is large, robust, bright green, and triangular in outline. Seedlings may be transplanted to large pots or cans and set out after their second year of growth. Spice Bush grows rapidly with regular watering, in sun to part shade, and is suitable in a mixture of trees and shrubs, or for a natural, untrimmed hedge or divider. Although this species is native up to 4,000 feet elevation, I have not found it to be tolerant of prolonged cold or of late spring frosts, which damage emerging foliage. This shrub may also be propagated from tip cuttings or from root-crown sections taken from a mature plant.

Estimate of Garden Value: This large, handsome shrub has long been a garden favorite for its dense habit, aromatic leaves, and unusual flowers. Experiences at botanic gardens show it to be long lived.

GENUS *CARPENTERIA:* CARPENTERIA
(Family Saxifragaceae: Saxifrage)

There is only one species in *Carpenteria*. This lovely and adaptable plant is one of California's rarest endemic shrubs.

Carpenteria californica
Tree Anemone or Carpenteria

HABIT: Erect, evergreen, numerous clustered stems, 1–2 or 5 m, 3–7 ft or to 15 ft. May become rangy or sprawling. FOLIAGE: Oblong-lanceolate, thick, dark green, glabrous. FLOWERS: Large, flat, anemone-like, with many yellow stamens in center, in terminal clusters, fragrant. May–July. (See Pl. 6C.) FRUIT: Leathery, conical capsule, numerous seed. DISTRIBUTION: Dry granite ridges, Sierra foothills of Fresno County, between San Joaquin and King rivers, to 4,000 feet.

Culture: Tree Anemone may be propagated from seed, from cuttings made from young stems, or by suckers. Seed should be sown thinly in a mixture of sand and leaf mold, and covered with sphagnum moss to inhibit damping-off. Seedlings may be transplanted when about 2 inches high, and will make rapid growth. They can be set in their permanent quarters when two-years old, and will begin to flower and fruit after the third year. Plants are water tolerant in well-drained soil, and prefer a somewhat sheltered situation with sun for part of the day or high tree shade.

Estimate of Garden Value: The Tree Anemone is a handsome, adaptable shrub, long admired by gardeners throughout the Pacific States and in Europe. The many uses for this shrub include planting as a specimen, with a mixture of trees and shrubs, among oaks or conifers. It has also been trimmed flat and used as a wall shrub, where it eventually reached the eaves. It is a large, quite dense leafy shrub in open situations, while in shade it may become tall and rangy. Although the Tree Anemone is tolerant of some cold, it has not been fully tested where there are prolonged low temperatures, or for damage from late spring frosts.

GENUS *CEANOTHUS:* CALIFORNIA LILACS
(Family Rhamnaceae: Buckthorn)

The large genus *Ceanothus* is confined to North America, and has forty-three species in California. Members grow in several plant communities and at many elevations, but their greatest concentration is in foothill regions. In size they range from creeping or low-mounding habit to almost tree proportions, with most being medium-sized shrubs of dense to rangy outline. With few exceptions, they are evergreen and characterized by rigid, often divaricate and sometimes spinescent branchlets. Foliage tends to be small to medium in size, from less than one inch up to three inches in Catalina Ceanothus *(C. arboreus).* Some are rough textured, others smooth and thinnish, while a few are thick and glossy with undulate and spine-tipped margins. Individually the flowers are small but attractive because of their abundance in panicles or racemes. The inflorescence varies with each species, and may be short, dense clusters, rounded and stalkless in some, while others have large, compound spikes of feathery beauty. Flower color ranges through many shades of blue to blue-purple, white, and rare pinkish shades that sometimes occur in Deer Brush *(C. integerrimus).* Seed vessels are firm, almost globular capsules, bearing tiny horns or crests in a few species, and in color ranging from tan, brown, mahogany red, to black. (See Chart 18.)

CHART 18 *Ceanothus*: California Lilacs

Plant	Growth Habit or Size	Flowers	Culture	Remarks	Distribution
C. thyrsiflorus Blue Blossom	Large, erect 1-6 m (3½-20 ft)	Large trusses, pale to deep blue. March-June.	Sun to high shade, water tolerant. With purple plum, maple, other natives.	Adaptable. Selected forms may be trimmed into small tree.	Woods, Coast Ranges, Santa Barbara Co. north.
C. impressus Santa Barbara Wild Lilac (See Fig. 53)	Compact 5-15 dm (1¾-6½ ft)	Small, dense spike, deep blue. March-April.	Dry border, sun, porous soil. With tall *Ceanothus* spp.	Small, dark green, rugose foilage	Chaparral, Santa Barbara to San Luis Obispo cos.
C. foliosus Wavy-Leaf Ceanothus (See Pl. 6F)	Low to 1 m (½ to 3 ft)	Short, dense spike, dark blue. March-May.	Sun to light shade. Edging, slope, or bank cover	Dark green leaves, undulate margin.	Woods, Coast Ranges, Humboldt to San Diego cos.
C. integerrimus Deer Brush	1-4 m (3-10 ft)	Compound spikes, white, pale to deep blue. May-June.	Sun to light shade, water tolerant. Free-flowering.	Deciduous. Variable, propagate best colors.	Ridges, forests, San Diego Co. north.

Species	Size	Flowers	Culture	Characteristics	Distribution
C. purpureus Hollyleaf Ceanothus (See Fig. 54)	1-2 m (3½-6½ ft)	Rounded clusters, bluish purple. Feb.-April.	Sun, semi-dry, porous soil. Massed planting, slopes, dry borders.	Closely spaced, waxen, holly leaves, dark green.	Dry, rocky hills, Napa Co.
C. gloriosus Pt. Reyes Ceanothus	Spreading 2-3 m (6½-10 ft)	Round clusters, lavender-blue. March-May.	Sun, porous soil, moderate moisture. Ground, slope, rock garden.	Firm, waxen, toothed leaves, dark green.	Coast, Pt. Reyes to Mendocino Co.
C. gloriosus var. *porrectus* Dwarf Pt. Reyes Ceanothus	Mounding 3-5 dm (1-2 ft)	Small, rounded clusters, violet-blue. March-May.	Sun to high shade, water tolerant with porous soil.	Small, hollylike leaves. Ground and slope cover, rock garden.	Woods, Marin Co.
C. prostratus Squaw Mat, Mahala Mats	Prostrate 1-2.5 m (2-10 ft) broad	Small umbels, lavender to violet-blue. April-June.	Dry, well-drained soil. Ground cover. Difficult to grow.	Trailing branches root, form broad mats.	Flats, pine forest, Sierra Nevada, Calaveras Co., west to Siskiyou and Trinity cos.

CHART 18 *Ceanothus*: California Lilacs *(continued)*

Plant	Growth Habit or Size	Flowers	Culture	Remarks	Distribution
C. arboreus Catalina Ceanothus	Tall shrub, tree with trunk 3-7 m (12-20 ft)	Large clusters, pale blue. Feb.-May.	Sun, semi-dry. Specimen, background.	Ovate-elliptic leaves, dull green, white beneath.	Brushy slopes, Channel Ids.
C. spinosus Greenbark Ceanothus	Large shrub 2-6 m (6⅓-20 ft)	Large, fluffy, pale blue. Feb.-April.	Sun, semi-dry, lean soil.	Hedge, background, used in roadside planting.	Near coast, San Luis Obispo Co. southward.
C. griseus Carmel Ceanothus	1-3 m (3-10 ft)	Dense panicles, violet-blue. March-May.	Sun, to high shade, semi-dry. Adaptable, widely spreading.	Broad, dark green leaves. Filler or specimen.	Coastal, Santa Barbara to Mendocino cos.
C. griseus var. *horizontalis* 'Yankee Point'	3-6 dm (1-2 ft)	Cylindrical clusters, flax blue. April-May.	Sun to high shade, semi-dry. Rapid spreader.	Shiny, dark green leaves, dense carpeter.	Selected form, Monterey Co.

Name	Size	Flowers	Culture	Use	Notes
C. griseus 'Louis Edmunds' Louis Edmunds Lilac (See Pl. 6E)	1.5-3 m (5-10 ft)	Abundant, large clusters, sea blue. April-May.	Sun, semi-dry. Rapid growing, dense shrub.	Background, or in mixture of trees, shrubs, large perennials.	Selected form.
C. griseus 'Ray Hartman' Ray Hartman Lilac	3-5 m (10-18 ft)	Compound clusters, bluebird blue. March-April.	Sun, semi-dry. Adaptable, free-flowering.	Large, dark green leaves. Background, divider, specimen, etc.	Probable hybrid with *C. arboreus*.
C. papillosus var. *roweanus* × *C. impressus* 'Julia Phelps'	2-2.5 m (4-8 ft)	Short, dense clusters, cobalt blue. April-May.	Sun, semi-dry, moderately water tolerant.	Dark, furrowed leaves. Adaptable, borders, divider, specimen.	Selected seedling.
C. arboreus 'Theodore Payne' × *cyaneus* 'Gentian Plume'	to 4 m (to 14 ft)	Plumy clusters, dark gentian-blue. March-April.	Sun, semi-dry. Fast growing, wide spread; prune to prevent legginess.	Massed or among other shrubs, mid-border.	Cultivar.
C. oliganthus × *spinosus* or *impressus* 'Blue Buttons'	to 5 m (to 17 ft)	Round clusters, intense blue. Feb.-March.	Sun, semi-dry. Fast growing, rigid branching, free-flowering.	Ultimate shape vase-like; for screening, etc.	Cultivar.

CHART 18 *Ceanothus*: California Lilacs *(continued)*

Plant	Growth Habit or Size	Flowers	Culture	Remarks	Distribution
C. griseus 'Santa Ana'	1.5-2.5 m (5-8 ft)	In short clusters, rich, pure blue. Feb.-April.	Sun, moderate water, coarse soil. Wide spreading habit.	Edging, banks, slopes; good garden tolerance.	Cultivar.
C. papillosus var. roweanus 'Joyce Coulter'	3 dm (12 in) high by 3 m (10 ft.) spread	Dark blue, in profusion. March through summer.	Sun, water tolerant. Vigorous, spreading.	Dark, rugose leaves. Ground, wall cover, rock garden, low hedge.	Cultivar.
C. papillosus var. roweanus X impressus 'Concha'	to 2 m (to 6½ ft)	Tight, round clusters, dark blue. Feb.-April.	Sun, water tolerant. Rapid growing, vigorous.	Free-flowering, background; good garden tolerance.	Cultivar.

Figure 53 *Ceanothus impressus,* Santa Barbara Wild Lilac

Horticultural History: California plant explorers were attracted very early to these blue-flowered shrubs, and several were grown in England in the early 1800s. Others were developed in French and Belgian nurseries in an almost new race of plants, of which the well-known *C.* 'Glorie de Versailles' is one of the most popular. There was very little interest in California until about 1910, except for a few species such as *C. arboreus,* Blue Blossom *(C. thyrsiflorus),* and Greenbark Ceanothus *(C. spinosus).* From then on, several dedicated botanists and horticulturists studied these unique shrubs and disseminated seed and information. Collections of species were begun, and their popularity increased gradually with the selection of superior natural hybrids. In 1942, a book on the genus and garden cultivation of ceanothus was published, but there is enough recent information and history of new cultivars to fill another. About twenty species and sixteen named cultivars are now popular garden plants, all outstanding for adaptability, abundance of flowers, many in rich, intense shades of blue, excellence of leaf texture or color, for usefulness in a specific garden situation. Further refinement continues, along with studies in propagation, adaptability, and uses. Variable traits within the genus, added to the frequency of natural hybrids, leads to the assumption that this genus is still evolving and we can look forward to many new, exciting possibilities.

Propagation: Most species of *Ceanothus* have hard seed coats, making pretreatment necessary. Immersing the seed in hot water, followed by cold stratification usually brings prompt germination. A few seeds will eventually germinate if planted in flats of coarse soil and left to the elements over the winter season. Treated seed is planted in a mixture of about equal parts of coarse sand, loam, and peat moss. After the second or third pair of leaves form, plants may be shifted to three-inch pots, held until a good mass of roots have formed, and then put into gallon cans. Plants will be ready for their permanent quarters in one and one-half to two years, and most begin to bloom during their third year of growth.

Propagation by Cuttings: Many species and cultivars of *Ceanothus* may be increased vegetatively. The best time for taking cuttings appears to vary among the species. Various authorities have suggested taking cuttings almost throughout the year, but especially from mid-spring until December. Cuttings of three to five inches are dipped into a rooting hormone, and put in flats or shallow pots of sharp sand. Containers may be kept in a frame or sheltered place and covered with plastic until rooting occurs. Plants are ready to set out within a year to eighteen months. Professional growers start cuttings in a greenhouse using bottom heat to ensure the greatest percent of rooting. Practically all of the creeping species root naturally when in contact with moist soil, or they may be layered. Paying close attention to experiments in propagation and keeping good records will eventually give the correct method for each individual species.

Culture: Members of the genus *Ceanothus* are among California's prime drought-resistant shrubs. They are ideal for the dry border, but will tolerate moderate amounts of water during their periods of active growth, as long as the soil drains well. Newly set out plants must be watered occasionally until they are well established; thereafter, deep watering once in four or six weeks will keep growth uniform. Too much water, especially with rich soil, is apt to cause rapid top growth with which the root system has not kept pace. California lilacs are also susceptible to water-borne molds which can cause root rot. They should never be planted deeper than they were in a container because water washing against the trunks can encourage the disease. With only a few exceptions, California lilacs prefer full sun. The soil can be slightly enriched by the use of organic materials or rotted sawdust mixed with bone meal, and applied as a mulch in autumn. Longevity varies among species of *Ceanothus;* some don't live beyond four to six years, while others may persist for as many as twenty.

Estimate of Garden Value: Species and cultivars of *Ceanothus* have become popular and important cultivated materials for many reasons. A large number from coastal and foothill regions bloom in early spring, beginning in February, with mountain kinds flowering in May or later. Other attractive features are evergreen foliage, sometimes with an exciting pungency, and an abundance of flowers in many shades of blue

Figure 54 *Ceanothus purpureus,* Hollyleaf Ceanothus

and with honey-like fragrance. Most California lilacs have a uniform growth pattern, but pinching and training can be practiced, along with limb removal when necessary. They have many garden uses. The prostrate types may be used for ground, slope, or terrace covers, hanging down walls or steep banks, large rock gardens, and parking strips. Several of the dense, mounding types have been used as facers, or for roadside planting. Medium to large shrubs may be used in mixtures, as rough hedges or dividers, and a few can become specimen plants with careful early training. There would seem to be a California wild lilac for every possible situation, except perhaps a shady, well-watered city garden, and some cultivar might be developed to suit that condition. Species of *Ceanothus* from coast and foothill regions are not always cold tolerant at elevations above 3,000 or 4,000 feet, but gardeners can make use of those which are native to these regions. Members of this genus, as with the manzanitas, have an immeasurable value in their ability to control erosion, and to provide sweeping covers in arid places of the California countryside.

GENUS *CERCIS:* REDBUD
(Family Leguminosae: Pea)

There is only one California species in *Cercis,* noted for its brilliant flowers in early spring.

Cercis occidentalis
Redbud

HABIT: To small tree, many clustered, erect stems, 2–5 m, 6–18 ft. FOLIAGE: Round to heart-shaped, smooth, bright apple green. FLOWERS: Pea-shaped, in clusters, magenta pink to reddish purple, occasionally white. February–April. (See Pl. 5D.) FRUIT: Long, flat, dark crimson pods containing rounded, compressed seed. DISTRIBUTION: Dry slopes and canyons in foothills, up to 4,500 feet elevation, inner Coast Ranges from Humboldt to Solano counties. In Sierra Nevada foothills from Shasta to Tulare counties, and desert slopes of Laguna and Cuyamaca mountains.

Culture: Redbud seed has an impermeable seed coat plus internal dormancy and requires pretreatment. Seeds should be dropped into water brought to the boiling point, allowed to stand overnight, and then placed in damp peat moss and put in the refrigerator for sixty days. For small quantities of seed, rub gently between two pieces of sandpaper, and then proceed with the stratification. Processed seeds may be planted in fiber pots and later shifted to gallon cans, and held until of a size to set out. Precautions should be taken against damping-off in seedlings. Redbud requires coarse, well-drained soil, full sun, and may be watered during its period of active growth and seed setting. Although grown primarily for its flowers, the foliage is clean and shapely, and shrubs have a neat appearance until the slight yellowing before they drop. At 3,000 to 4,000 feet elevation the foliage turns a bright red and the heart-shaped leaves look like valentines strung along the stems.

Estimate of Garden Value: This large, deciduous shrub provides garden interest through the year from the early, brilliant flowers, the nicely formed leaves, the crimson seed pods, the pale yellow or red autumn color, and finally to the winter framework of smooth, reddish brown trunks. Redbud should be underplanted with ground covers to complement the flowers. The eastern Moss Phlox *(Phlox subulata)* is an excellent choice; native shooting stars *(Dodecatheon)* or the lively color of Rose-Cress *(Arabis blepharophylla)* would be attractive because they bloom at the same time as the Redbud. Several California lilacs which have dark green, rough-textured leaves may be used to complement the Redbud foliage, while the small leaves and open framework of a mountain mahogany give a nice contrast. Redbud may be pruned to suit its situation, or some of the trunks may be removed to form a small, open tree. Although there may be some losses from damping-off and root rot, Redbud tends to be long lived once it is established, and tends to flower more profusely with each passing year.

GENUS *CERCOCARPUS:* MOUNTAIN MAHOGANIES
(Family Rosaceae: Rose)

Cercocarpus is mostly of the western and southwestern United States, with four species and several varieties in California. They are generally slender, evergreen shrubs inhabiting arid places.

Cercocarpus betuloides
California Mountain Mahogany

HABIT: Erect, open, with stiff or spreading terminal branches, 2–7 m, 5–8 or up to 20 ft. (See Fig. 55.) FOLIAGE: Obovate to oval, deeply grooved and serrate toward tips, dark grayish green, less than one inch. FLOWERS: Tiny, in small clusters, ivory white, fragrance of acacia. March–May. FRUIT: Achene, cylindric-fusiform, with silky, plumose tail, conspicuous in late summer. DISTRIBUTION: Common on dry slopes, foothill and Chaparral, cismontane California, to Oregon and Baja California.

Culture: California Mountain Mahogany is readily propagated from seed, and seedlings transplant without difficulty. Volunteer seedlings can be expected from established plants. This species prefers sun and well-drained soil, and tolerates watering and pruning. It is best used where the silky, curled seed tails can show to advantage, as in a thin planting of shrubs, a filler or a background.

Estimate of Garden Value: The slender, open habit of the

Figure 55 *Cercocarpus betuloides,* California Mountain Mahogany

California Mountain Mahogany contrasts nicely with such natives as Redbud, Santa Barbara Wild Lilac *(Ceanothus impressus),* and the large, bright green leaves of Toyon. It grows quickly with regular watering, more slowly in a semi-dry situation, and appears to be a long-lived shrub. Deer often browse on this shrub and cause suckerlike growth from the base, but my watered plant has produced only a few basal shoots and these are easily removed.

Cercocarpus betuloides var. **blancheae**
Alderleaf Mountain Mahogany

HABIT: Erect, open, 2–7 m, 8–20 ft. FOLIAGE: Broadly elliptical, medium green, veins not deeply impressed. FLOWERS: Typical of genus. March–April. FRUIT: Typical of genus, very long, coiled tails. DISTRIBUTION: Chaparral, Santa Rosa, Santa Catalina, and Santa Cruz islands.

Culture: The same as for *C. betuloides.*

Estimate of Garden Value: The Alderleaf Mountain Mahogany is an adaptable small tree with a naturally symmetrical framework that requires very little pruning or training. In my Los Gatos garden it was accompanied by *Ceanothus griseus* 'Louis Edmunds', Woolly Blue-Curls *(Trichostema lanatum),* Summer Holly *(Comarostaphylos diversifolid),* and assorted drought-tolerant perennials and bulbs. There is a record of its having been used on a south-facing wall where it grew to the second story and made an interesting leafy pattern. Much careful pruning would be necessary for this kind of informal espalier.

GENUS *CHILOPSIS:* DESERT WILLOW
(Family Bignoniaceae: Bignonia)

There is only one species in California of *Chilopsis,* a genus that is widely distributed in the temperate regions of the world. It is noted for an exotic appearance with its bright pink, trumpet flowers.

Chilopsis linearis
Desert Willow or Desert Catalpa

HABIT: Large, deciduous, few to many stems with slender twigs, 2–6 m, 10–20 ft. FOLIAGE: Linear to lance-linear, pointed, light green. FLOWERS: Open, funnelform, in short, terminal racemes, fragrant, bright pink, lavender, or white with purple and yellow markings. May–September, with full flowering usually in August. FRUIT: Long, woody, two-valved capsule with numerous winged seed. DISTRIBUTION: Common along washes and water courses, Mojave Desert, Colorado Desert, Imperial, Riverside, and San Bernardino counties, east and south.

Culture: According to experiences at botanic gardens, the Desert Willow is not difficult to grow from seed, although seedlings are somewhat subject to damping-off and rotting. Hardwood cuttings may be rooted individually in small pots, in a mixture of sand and peat moss, and set from there directly into borders. Some losses occur during handling of small plants, but once established this shrub is quite permanent. Plants tolerate summer watering, full sun, and will grow in heavy soils but are not suitable for the coast or for cold climates.

Estimate of Garden Value: The Desert Willow is adaptable to warm, dry climates and moderate amounts of water. It is said to become straggly with old age, but it is a superb plant for desert gardens, and has been successfully cultivated in the warm hills of the Bay Area. Records show that at one time a nurseryman separated out the deepest colors and propagated them for the trade. Among other uses, fence posts and rails have been made from the wood, and a tonic tea from the flowers.

GENUS *CNEORIDIUM:* BUSHRUE OR BERRYRUE
(Family Rutaceae: Rue)

Bushrue, one of four members in California of the Rutaceae, is noted for its aromatic foliage. It is occasionally cultivated in coastal southern California.

Cneoridium dumosum
Bushrue or Berryrue

HABIT: Evergreen, compact, much branched, slight, with grayish bark, purplish red on young stems, 5–15 dm, to 3 ft. Generally erect, but may be drooping on banks or slopes.

FOLIAGE: Opposite to fascicled, narrow, to one inch, strongly scented from glandular dots on lower surface, yellowish green, somewhat cupped in along margins, and resembling mistletoe leaves. FLOWERS: Small, white, four-petaled, solitary or clustered. Begins blooming in winter after a heavy rain, continues into March or April. FRUIT: Globose berry, yellowish pink, aging to crimson, and brown when ripe, one or two dark brown seeds. DISTRIBUTION: Frequent on mesas and bluffs, Chaparral and Coastal Sage Scrub, Orange to San Diego counties and to Baja California.

Culture: Berryrue is propagated from seed which germinates readily. Plants are easy to handle. They need sun for most of the day when growing near the coast, with some shade when grown in warmer interior regions. Plants are water tolerant, and will require the least water if mulched. This small shrub was persistent at Rancho Santa Ana Botanic Garden where it provided many volunteers.

Estimate of Garden Value: Berryrue is considered to be a neat and charming shrub, but is apparently little cultivated away from its habitat. One writer suggested that it be grown with the manzanita-like Mission Manzanita *(Xylococcus bicolor),* whose bright, rich green leaves offer a nice contrast. Further suggestions include its use as a low hedge or divider, or a filler shrub, or where its attractive and persisting berries can be enjoyed.

GENUS *COMAROSTAPHYLIS:* SUMMER HOLLY
(Family Ericaceae: Heath)

One species of *Comarostaphylis* is native to California. It is an adaptable and enduring large shrub, outstanding for handsome foliage and for bright fruits similar to those of the madrone.

Comarostaphylis diversifolia
Summer Holly

HABIT: Large, evergreen, erect to spreading, 2–5 m, to 15 ft. FOLIAGE: Oblong, margins toothed and rolled under, thick, glossy dark green above, tomentulose beneath. FLOWERS: Urn-shaped, white, in long terminal racemes. May–

June. (See Pl. 5E.) FRUIT: Fleshy, globose drupe, warty, bright vermillion red, containing round stone of fused nutlets. DISTRIBUTION: Chaparral and near coast, San Diego County to Baja California.

Culture: Summer Holly is propagated from seed planted in autumn which germinates in a month or two without pretreatment. Young seedlings may be shifted to three-inch pots by early spring, and transferred to gallon cans before they become root bound. Plants are ready for their permanent place after about one year, and should be planted in full sun to light afternoon shade, in well-drained soil. Plants are reported to accept heavy adobe with a minimum of water. Summer water may be given during the first year, but will be unnecessary after the plants are well established.

Estimate of Garden Value: Summer Holly is a neat, adaptable, large shrub which should be considered seriously for its handsome traits. The red fruits from August to October provide color, especially attractive against the dark foliage. It can be used as part of massed plantings, an informal hedge or divider, or as a specimen shrub. In Tilden Park Botanic Garden, several have grown into dense, round-topped trees and have a wealth of berries each autumn. As a roadside shrub, it has grown without water in its naturally upright, quite dense habit.

GENUS *CORNUS:* DOGWOODS
(Family Cornaceae: Dogwood)

Six species of *Cornus* are native to California, one of which is found in streamside thickets all across the United States. The three described here are interesting for their winter limb patterns, their new leaves in spring, and their berries which attract many kinds of birds.

Cornus glabrata
Smooth Dogwood or Brown Dogwood

HABIT: Slender, deciduous, erect or spreading with limber branches, reddish twigs, 1.5–6 m, 5–12 or 18 ft. FOLIAGE: Oblong, thin, light, bright green, acute at each end. May turn soft yellow, ruddy flame, or wine in autumn. FLOWERS: Many, small, cream white in cyme, terminal and along outer stems. May–June. FRUIT: Globose drupe, white to pale slate blue, two-celled and two-seeded stone. DISTRIBUTION: Streams, thickets and shaded areas of low hills, borders of swamps, Mendocino, Tulare to San Diego counties.

Culture: Smooth Dogwood grows readily from seed, and bird-sown volunteers appear frequently from established plants. It is also easily propagated from cuttings or rooted stems at ground level. It is a fast-growing shrub with ample water and sun to high shade, and readily accepts pruning and training. In my Los Gatos garden, I trained one into a spreading, umbrella-shaped small tree by removing some of the lower limbs as it grew. The upper ones became thick and twiggy, and the arching branches had a weeping effect. Many small birds lived and nested in this dogwood, seeming to enjoy the shelter of the twiggy growth. This versatile shrub has also been recommended as a ground cover for a shaded slope where branches may be pegged down, and upright ones removed until a near solid cover is achieved.

Estimate of Garden Value: With careful thinning and cutting, this is a useful and ornamental shrub. Plants take on a new dimension with the spring emergence of tiny, pointed, chartreuse green leaves along the reddish brown, arching branches. In May, limber branches are decorated with round clusters of cream white flowers, somewhat resembling a spiraea. According to one authority, about twenty kinds of birds eat the fruits of this and other varieties of dogwood. In my opinion this is a highly adaptable shrub, of interest through all seasons.

Cornus stolonifera
American Dogwood

HABIT: Spreading, deciduous, forms thickets by rootstocks, 2–5 m, 5–15 ft. FOLIAGE: Ovate, acute at tip, bright green, conspicuously veined, may turn crimson or flame in autumn. FLOWERS: Tiny, cream, in round clusters. May–June. FRUIT: White, globe-shaped drupe enclosing stone. DISTRIBUTION: Moist places, montane coniferous forests, Sierra Nevada, from Siskiyou and Del Norte to Trinity counties. Widely distributed to Alaska and to eastern states.

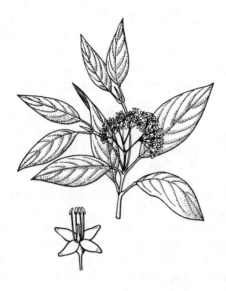

Figure 56 *Cornus stolonifera,* American Dogwood

Culture: Propagation of American Dogwood is from seed, rooted layers, or tip cuttings. This shrub readily accepts water and garden culture, and grows rapidly and vigorously. It should be used with natives of similar requirements, such as other dogwoods, snowberry, hazelnut, and underplanted with trilliums, red columbine, baneberry, and wild iris.

Estimate of Garden Value: The American Dogwood eventually becomes a large, spreading, many-stemmed shrub, especially attractive for the red twigs in winter. It is closely related to the Red Osier Dogwood, which has long been a famous garden plant in many parts of the country. A similar species is Western Dogwood *(Cornus occidentalis),* also of many moist habitats throughout the state.

Cornus sessilis
Black-Fruit Dogwood

HABIT: Spreading, deciduous, green bark, 1.5–4 m, 5–10 or 20 ft. FOLIAGE: Broad, elliptic, jade green, prominently veined, may turn pale to vivid flame in autumn. FLOWERS: Tiny, yellowish, few, in sessile umbels. April–June. FRUIT: Ovoid drupe, color changes from pale green, red, and to glossy black when ripe. DISTRIBUTION: Stream banks, Redwood and Coniferous Forests, Sierra Nevada from Calaveras County north, and in Coast Ranges from Tehama County north.

Culture: Seed of Black-Fruit Dogwood germinates without pretreatment, although it may take some weeks or until the following spring. Cold stratification will hasten the germination period. Seedlings may be transplanted soon after the second pair of leaves have formed, first into three-inch, and later into five-inch pots. Plants generally make sturdy growth and can be planted into a shaded border after one year. This dogwood requires friable soil into which leaf mold or other organic materials have been incorporated, and will accept ample water.

Estimate of Garden Value: Black-Fruit Dogwood is an excellent companion for azaleas, rhododendrons, and huckleberries since all require the same type of soil and exposure. Some of the evergreen foliage plants of redwood forests might be considered as ground covers for these shade lovers. Some examples are species of *Heuchera, Boykinia,* or *Mitella.*

GENUS *CORYLUS:* HAZELNUT
(Family Betulaceae: Birch)

Only one species of *Corylus* is native to California. It is a large shrub which bears edible nuts, although these are seldom abundant.

Corylus cornuta var. **californica**
California Hazelnut

HABIT: Large, spreading, deciduous, 2–6 m, 6–10 ft. FOLIAGE: Rounded to obovate, doubly serrate on margins, veined; medium, bright green with soft-pubescence as they emerge, glabrate in age. FLOWERS: Male is long, slender, tassel-like catkin in winter; female from a scaly bud with two bright red, protruding stigmas. FRUIT: Smooth nut enclosed in pair of joined bracts, twisted together at the tip. DISTRIBUTION: Damp slopes, many plant communities of foothills and mountains. Coast Ranges, Santa Cruz Mountains north, Sierra Nevada from Tulare County north.

Culture: California Hazelnut requires two- to three-months stratification in damp peat moss. The sprouted seed should be planted in friable soil in five-inch pots, and then to gallon cans. Rooted pieces may be detached from the plant and grown in cans until of a size to set in the garden. High, broken shade is ideal; while it accepts water all through the year, it is fairly drought tolerant once established. It may be grown with Big-leaf Maple, pines, and underplanted with wild iris and spring bulbs.

Estimate of Garden Value: Under garden conditions of tree shade and water, California Hazelnut tends to become a large, many-stemmed shrub which may be too large for a small garden. Its period of special attraction comes in winter when the male catkins begin to form, gradually elongating into conspicuous, golden beige tassels. Soon the leaves begin to emerge, distinctive for their soft green enhanced by silken hairs. Although only small quantities of fruit are set, they are greatly relished by several small animals and by birds.

GENUS *CRATAEGUS:* HAWTHORN
(Family Rosaceae: Rose)

There is one California species in the well-known genus of *Crataegus,* noted for its value to wildlife, as well as for ornamental purposes.

Crataegus douglasii
Western Hawthorn or Western Black Haw

HABIT: Branched, thorny, deciduous, 2–10 m, 5–9 or to 20 ft. FOLIAGE: Ovate to obovate, lobed and doubly serrate, dark green. FLOWERS: Small, cream white, in terminal corymb, fragrant. May–June. FRUIT: Drupelike pome, dark red and black when ripe, containing bony nutlets, edible. DISTRIBUTION: Near stream flats, meadows, woods, and forests of mountains, Marin to Siskiyou and Modoc counties, north.

Culture: Seeds of the Western Hawthorn require stratification and are reported to take a year or more for germination. Pulp should be removed from the seed by soaking before plant-

Figure 57 *Crataegus douglasii,* Western Hawthorn or Western Black Haw

ing. Western Hawthorn is common along streams in the north Coast Ranges at about 3,000 feet elevation, and volunteers appear frequently in my garden. Full sun to partial shade suits it equally well, and it grows rapidly when young, about two feet a year. New wood is taffy brown, the outer twigs reddish, and the thorns quite long and sharp. Plants accept pruning and training and may be kept as a shrub or, by some limb removal, as a slender tree.

Estimate of Garden Value: The Western Hawthorn has many seasonal interests, is free-flowering, and its fruits are very attractive to birds, but it may be too rampant for small gardens. Old specimens are apt to become straggly, and large limbs often break off during winter storms. With ample water and loamy soil this hawthorn blooms abundantly. In late autumn the foliage becomes either brilliant yellow or flame orange, resplendent among streamside tangles. The fruits are gone by early autumn and opinions on their taste vary; some describe them as sweet, others as insipid. The Indians used them in making pemmican, and they have also been used in making jams and jellies. The berries are eaten by several kinds of songbirds, upland game birds, and small mammals.

GENUS *DENDROMECON:* TREE POPPIES
(Family Papaveraceae: Poppy)

Two species of *Dendromecon* are native to California. These important plants of chaparral and foothill regions are noted for their long season of bright yellow flowers.

Dendromecon rigida
Bush Poppy or Tree Poppy

HABIT: Open, branched, evergreen, stiff and rounded in outline, 1–3 or 6 m, 2–8 ft. FOLIAGE: Linear-lanceolate to oblong, thick, grayish green. FLOWERS: Open, of four rounded petals, bright yellow, many stamens in center, solitary at ends of short branchlets. April–June. FRUIT: Linear, curved capsule, many seeds. DISTRIBUTION: Common in dry slopes and stony washes, Chaparral in Coast Ranges from Sonoma County to Baja California, and at the base of the Sierra Nevada, Shasta to Tulare counties.

Culture: Seed of the Bush Poppy is difficult to germinate, and burning pine needles or straw over the flats is recommended. Germination should take place in about a month, after which the seedlings are put into small pots, and later to gallon cans. Bush Poppy should have coarse, well-drained soil, full sun, and water only until the plants are established. Companion plants should be chosen from among the drought-tolerant natives, such as species or cultivars of ceanothus, manzanita, fremontia, shrubby salvias, and buckwheats.

Estimate of Garden Value: The Bush Poppy is said to be long lived once it is established and when its requirements for warmth and dryness are met. This unique poppy has a pleasing aspect through most seasons because of the neat, smooth foliage and the long succession of glowing yellow flowers.

Dendromecon harfordii
Island Tree Poppy

HABIT: Rounded, erect, branches spreading or drooping, 2–6 m, up to 20 ft. FOLIAGE: Elliptic to oblong, crowded on branches, smooth, medium dark gray-green. FLOWERS: Open saucers, up to three inches across, numerous. April–July, and intermittently through the year. (See Pl. 6D.) FRUIT: Long, slender capsule. DISTRIBUTION: Brushy slopes, Chaparral, Santa Cruz and Santa Rosa islands.

Culture: The same as for *D. rigida.*

Estimate of Garden Value: The Island Tree Poppy is larger and of more leafy appearance than *D. rigida,* and its extensive blooming period gives it high ornamental value. It is somewhat more water tolerant in well-drained soil, and should be given room to reach its full size.

GENUS *FREMONTODENDRON:*
FREMONTIAS, FLANNEL BUSHES
(Family Sterculiaceae: Cacao)

This genus *Fremontodendron* has two species and several subspecies, entirely of California and Baja California. One of the most colorful of the plants named for John C. Fremont, it is often called the Path Finders Shrub.

Fremontodendron mexicanum
Southern Fremontia

HABIT: Large, evergreen, slender, stiff in appearance, 2–6 m, 6–20 ft. (See Fig. 58.) FOLIAGE: Three- to five-lobed, thick, dark green, densely tawny-hairy beneath. FLOWERS: Five-lobed petaloid calyx, shallowly campanulate, orange-yellow becoming reddish with age, to three inches wide. March–July, off and on during the growing season. FRUIT: Pointed, conical capsule covered with bristly hairs, opening from the tip, and containing shiny black seed. DISTRIBUTION: Dry canyons, Chaparral, Oak Woodlands, mountains of San Diego County and to Baja California.

Culture: Most Southern Fremontias set an abundance of seed and require the hot-water treatment for good germination.

Figure 58 *Fremontonendron mexicanum,* Southern Fremontia

After being soaked overnight, they are planted in a coarse soil mixture in individual four-inch pots, and later shifted to gallon cans until of a size to set out. Seedlings are susceptible to damping-off fungus. The fungicide dexon may be used in soil mix. In my experience, the seedlings are slow growing and sometimes appear to have only a tenuous hold on life. Once they have passed the first year, however, they make greater progress, and when fully established are apt to be long lived. The Southern Fremontia requires full sun, well-drained soil, and water only to become established and maintain steady growth. Nurserymen sometimes propagate these shrubs by tip cutting in the greenhouse.

Estimate of Garden Value: The Southern Fremontia is striking in full flower, especially when accompanied by one of the blue California lilacs such as *Ceanothus* × 'Sierra Blue' or *C.* × 'Ray Hartman'. Their dark green, felted foliage affords a sharp contrast with trees and shrubs, and they are also effective as specimen plants. Unfortunately, this unusual shrub is vulnerable to water-borne disease or to excess water. Water must never be allowed to stand or to wash against the trunks.

Fremontodendron californicum
California Fremontia

HABIT: Spreading, open, evergreen, 1.5–4 or 7 m, 6–15 ft. FOLIAGE: Round to elliptic-ovate, three-lobed, dark green, sparsely pubescent above, tawny-stellate beneath, felted appearing. FLOWERS: Typical, large, clear, bright yellow, on short, lateral, spurlike branchlets. May–June. FRUIT: Ovoid, pointed, densely hairy, dark seed with a brownish caruncle. DISTRIBUTION: Dry, mostly granitic slopes, Chaparral, etc., west base Sierra Nevada in scattered stands, Shasta to Kern and through mountains to San Diego County.

Culture: For California Fremontia the hot-water treatment followed by two- to three-months stratification is recommended for germination. The large, bright green seed leaf is quite different from the true leaves of rugose texture and scalloped margins. California Fremontia is considered to be a little more responsive to cultivation than some others, but there are still losses of seedlings during transplanting.

Estimate of Garden Value: The same as for *F. mexicanum*.

Subspecies: The following subspecies of *F. californicum* are distinctive plants, varying somewhat in size or growth habit, but having typical foliage, flowers, and fruits.

Fremontodendron californicum ssp. **napense,** Napa Fremontia, is a slender plant often with several trunks by which it eventually makes a small clump. In my Los Gatos garden it grew steadily in the semi-dry border and flowered freely from top to bottom every May. The leaves were small and with shallow indentations, but the clear, bright yellow flowers were about two inches across. This plant is native to brushy slopes of Napa, Lake and Yolo counties.

Fremontodendron californicum ssp. **decumbens,** Prostrate Fremontia, is a low type, to 1 m tall and 2–4 m broad, with large flowers in orange to red-brown. This recently discovered subspecies has been difficult to grow in the garden and more experience in its culture is needed.

Fremontodendron mexicanum and **F. californicum,** 'California Glory', is a selected seedling and a presumed hybrid. This tree-sized plant bears an abundance of large, clear yellow flowers.

Fremontodendron mexicanum and **F. californicum** 'Pacific Sunset', is another selected seedling, with dark yellow flowers and greater resistance to disease.

GENUS *GARRYA:* SILK-TASSEL BUSHES
(Family Garryaceae: Silk Tassel)

Six species of *Garrya* are native to California. All are evergreen shrubs noted for their decorative winter catkins on male plants.

Garrya elliptica
Coast Silk-Tassel

HABIT: Evergreen, to 8 m, 5–8 or 24 ft. FOLIAGE: Elliptic to oval, leathery, shining above, felted, woolly hairs below, dark green; margins crisp-undulate and often curled under. FLOWERS: Staminate and pistillate on different plants; male flowers in a series of tiny, cuplike blossoms, pale gray-green, in long, pendulous catkin; female ones, equally small, in less conspicuous catkins. FRUIT: Berry with felted coating, contains one or two hard seed, in short, dense clusters. DISTRIBUTION: Occurs on dry slopes and ridges, in Chaparral and Mixed Evergreen Forests, etc., of outer Coast Ranges from Ventura County to Oregon.

Culture: The bony seeds of Coast Silk-Tassel require three-months cold stratification for good germination. Once they are above ground the seedlings make rapid growth and should be put into containers as soon as they can be handled. This shrub prefers full sun, and is tolerant of both dryness and water in well-drained soil. Some protection should be provided where summer temperatures are high or drying winds prevail. Plants maintain a uniform growth pattern but can be pruned to shape.

Estimate of Garden Value: Coast Silk-Tassel has been a popular garden plant for many years, highly valued for the decorative male catkins which begin to appear in December and remain in fine form until mid-spring. These long tassels are outstanding against the thick foliage, and plants look spectacular trained against a warm wall or fence. They may also be used in mixtures of plants with similar requirements.

G. elliptica 'James Roof' is a selected male form having pendulous, greenish yellow catkins of a foot or more in length beginning in mid-winter. It is a larger plant with an abundance of catkins fringing the entire plant. This cultivar may be propagated by half-hardened terminal shoots. (See Pl. 6B.)

Other Species:

Garrya fremontii, Fremont's Silk-Tassel, is native to mountain areas up to 7,500 feet elevation, and in my experience is adaptable to ordinary garden culture. It is similar in most respects to *G. elliptica,* having large, oval, dark green leaves which are paler on the reverse but not woolly.

Garrya veatchii, Veatch's Silk-Tassel, is native to dry slopes and coastal regions of southern California, from San Luis Obispo County to lower California. The undersides of the leaves are densely hairy as are the tight fruit clusters. It is reported to have flowered and fruited quite well at Rancho Santa Ana Botanic Garden. Most plants take from four to five years to begin flowering.

GENUS *GAULTHERIA:* GAULTHERIAS
(Family Ericaceae: Heath)

Three species of *Gaultheria* are native to California. They are handsome, evergreen shrubs of particular value as ground covers. Branches, especially of Salal, have traditionally been used in sprays and Christmas decorations because of their firm, rich green leaves.

Gaultheria shallon
Salal

HABIT: Slender, spreading, evergreen, almost trailing sub-shrub or upright, 4–20 dm, 1–6 ft. FOLIAGE: Ovate to roundish, serrate on margins, bright rich green, of firm, leathery texture, 3-10 cm, to two inches or more. FLOWERS: Urn-shaped, white or pink, with short, recurved lobes, in axillary or terminal racemes. March–June. FRUIT: Berry-like capsule,

dark purple, edible and containing many seed. DISTRIBU-
TION: Woods, Mixed Evergreen and Closed-Cone Pine
Forests, Redwood Forest, and coastal headlands, from Santa
Barbara County north.

Culture: Salal may be propagated from seed which germinates readily or by rooted underground stems which are freely
produced in moist situations. The underground stems can be
removed and grown in a mixture of leaf mold, sand, and loam
until a good root system has formed. This beautiful shrub will
make relatively rapid growth with shade, humus, acid soil, and
moisture. It will also grow in dry conditions but much more
slowly. It is most useful as a large-scale ground cover, and has
been used to edge the rhododendron dell in Golden Gate Park,
among other places. It is abundant along the redwood highway,
where frequent shearing back has resulted in dense hedges of
great beauty.

Estimate of Garden Value: As long as its requirements are
met, Salal is a superb and highly useful plant. In a shade border
it may be used with plants having similar requirements, as a
slope and bank cover, or as a ground cover under trees. Where
plants are sheared frequently, the reddish twigs and bronzy new
foliage make an interesting contrast to the old leaves. Among
the redwoods it carpets the forest floor, garlands downed logs,
and even grows in the pulpy wood of huge old stumps. Salal
tolerates cold up to 3,000 feet elevation, but does not flower
and fruit there as well as in coastal regions. The Indians made
the berries into a syrup, and also compressed the dried berries
into cakes for storage.

Other Species:

Gaultheria humifusa, Wintergreen, is a matted, woody
plant with firm, oval leaves and red fruits. Rare in California, it
is native to moist situations in the high Sierras from Tulare to
Mariposa counties.

Gaultheria ovatifolia, Oregon Wintergreen, or Western
Teaberry, is found in wet places in the northwest of Humboldt,
Siskiyou, and Del Norte counties, and is abundant north and
eastward. This is a small, spreading shrublet with firm, dark
green leaves. It has red berries in early autumn, which are
eaten raw or made into a jelly. A tea made from the leaves was
used both by Indians and pioneers to reduce fever.

GENUS *HETEROMELES:* TOYON, CHRISTMAS-BERRY
(Family Rosaceae: Rose)

There is one California species in *Heteromeles,* which is closely related to the genus *Photinia,* and in which it was once placed. Toyon is one of the most typical of the foothill plants and has become increasingly popular for gardens and large-scale landscaping.

Heteromeles arbutifolia
Toyon or Christmas-Berry

HABIT: Evergreen, branched, 2–10 m, 6–10 or 25 ft. FOLIAGE: Elliptic to oblong, crisp, thick texture, sharply toothed, dark green. FLOWERS: In large terminal clusters, small, cream white. June–July. FRUIT: Large clusters of bright red, berry-like pomes, persist through winter. DISTRIBUTION: Common on semi-dry, brushy slopes and canyons of foothills and mountains of southern California, north to Humboldt County, and in the Sierra Nevada of Tulare to Shasta counties.

Culture: The Toyon is propagated from seed which germinates readily when fresh. Older seed requires three-months stratification. Plants may be held in containers for the first year and then planted out in the second autumn. They will begin to flower and fruit after the third year. This popular shrub is drought resistant but will accept occasional water in summer with well-drained soil. In the wilds, Toyon is mostly a dense shrub, but tends to be rangy in wooded areas. It is quite amenable to pruning in winter, when berries are cut for seasonal decoration. Toyon may be trained into a small tree by gradual removal of lower limbs, or pruned into a large shrub of several trunks and a full, rounded crown. It is also recommended as an accent plant, as rough hedge or divider, and especially for a mixed border of drought-tolerant native shrubs and perennials. Toyon is sometimes propagated by tip cuttings taken in late summer when the wood is partially hardened. Unfortunately, this fine plant may be attacked by insects which cause honeydew followed by sooty mold, and also by pear blight. These diseases do not occur often and plants should be sprayed as soon as they are noted.

Estimate of Garden Value: Toyon has been in cultivation for at least one hundred years and its value to gardens and large-scale landscaping is well established. The glowing winter berries enliven many miles of freeway where it has been extensively planted. Although in some areas it occurs up to 4,000 feet elevation, Toyon does not seem able to withstand prolonged cold nor abrupt weather changes at higher elevations.

History and Uses: There was once a crusade against the destructive picking of Toyon berries. A law which might have been inspired by the early crusade was passed in the 1920s, making it illegal to pick or dig wild plants. The berries were used as both food and drink by Indians and early settlers, a tannin was once made from the bark, and the flowers are a source of honey. A long list of birds dine on the berries during the autumn and winter months. If Californians ever decide to have an official state shrub, *H. arbutifolia* would be a fitting candidate. It is well known and widely cultivated, is so typical of the vast foothill regions, is highly decorative to the countryside, and belongs almost wholly to California.

H. arbutifolia var. *macrocarpa* of Santa Catalina and San Clemente islands has large berries borne in immense clusters.

GENUS *HOLODISCUS:* CREAM BUSHES
(Family Rosaceae: Rose)

Three species in *Holodiscus,* a genus of delightful plants, are native to California. They are noted for their large sprays of cream white flowers which enhance woodlands and shady garden borders.

Holodiscus discolor
Cream Bush or Ocean Spray

HABIT: Spreading, deciduous, 1.5–6 m, 3–6 ft. FOLIAGE: Broadly ovate, deeply grooved and doubly serrate on margins, medium light green. FLOWERS: Compound, dense plumes of tiny, cream white flowers on slender, pinkish stems. June–August. FRUIT: Achene, one-seeded. DISTRIBUTION: Woods, rocky places, Redwood Forest, Mixed Evergreen Forests, Los Angeles to Del Norte counties, and Santa Catalina and Santa Cruz islands.

Culture: Cream Bush may be propagated from seed and from cuttings, which are reported to root readily. No treatment is required for the seed before planting. This engaging shrub tolerates both moist and dry situations. It sometimes occurs on rocky slopes, but is usually found in tangled woodlands. It shows to best advantage in shrub borders, or among trees, cascading its plumy flower sprays from a dark background. Cream Bush is equally attractive in its pre-blooming period with its many spires of pink-tinted, creamy flower buds. Plants may be pruned to suit their garden situation.

Estimate of Garden Value: Cream Bush is somewhat untidy when its large flower sprays fade and become grayish, but these are easily removed. The plants are said to flower more each year, and they grow large with shade and water.

Other Species:

Holodiscus boursieri, Mountain Cream Bush, is native to montane coniferous forests up to 9,000 feet elevation, and is a low, more compact shrub. The small, grey-green, toothed leaves are somewhat hairy above and whitish below with soft hairs. During the summer months plants have many spires of deep cream flowers, and these are very decorative along benches of streams and on rocky inclines.

GENUS *KECKIELLA:* KECKIELLAS
(Family Scrophulariaceae: Figwort)

Five species in *Keckiella,* a new genus, closely related to the genus *Penstemon,* are native to California. Species in *Keckiella* are shrubby and have other botanical features that separate them from *Penstemon* species.

Keckiella cordifolia
Heart-Leaf Keckiella

HABIT: Loosely branched, sometimes climbing, with arching limbs, 1–3 m, 3½–10 ft. FOLIAGE: Lance-ovate to cordate, serrate or toothed on margins, shiny, dark green, strongly veined. FLOWERS: In compact panicle, drooping and facing downward, slender, tubular, scarlet, the upper lip helmet-like, the lower widely spreading. May–July. FRUIT: Capsule. DIS-

TRIBUTION: Dry slopes and canyons below 5,000 feet, Chaparral, San Luis Obispo County, Channel Islands to Baja California.

Culture: Heart-Leaf Keckiella grows readily from seed, and is known to provide many volunteer plants. It requires sun to broken afternoon shade, and will tolerate moderate amounts of water. Seedlings must be handled carefully to avoid damping-off but, once the plants are established, they require very little attention.

Estimate of Garden Value: This large, vigorous, leafy shrub is very attractive in flower, and is useful among other shrubs or perennials of similar requirements. It is effective as a background in borders, or on slopes and terraces.

Other Species: Two other species of *Keckiella* are considered to be valuable as landscape materials:

Keckiella antirrhinoides, Snapdragon Keckiella, is a large, branched, leafy shrub of 1–2.5 m, 3½–8 ft. Flowers are yellow with brownish tinting, short tubed, with the upper lip strongly incurved, and the lower deeply cleft. This species is native to chaparral regions of southern California.

Keckiella ternata, Whorl-Leaf Keckiella, is a tall, erect shrub with wand-like branches from a woody base, 3–15 dm, 1–6½ ft. The narrow leaves occur in whorls of three, and the scarlet flowers are in elongated terminal clusters. This species is native to dry slopes and canyons below 6,000 feet, in the San Gabriel and San Bernardino mountains, to San Diego County.

All of these shrubby keckiellas tend to become straggly, and may require drastic pruning. All should be allowed space to accommodate their size, and are best used with California lilacs, bush poppies, or some of the tall, blue-flowering *Penstemon* species.

GENUS *LEPTODACTYLON:* SHRUB GILIAS
(Family Polemoniaceae: Phlox)

Three species of *Leptodactylon* are native to California. They are subshrubs, or semi-woody perennials, in a genus confined to the southwestern states. It is sometimes listed as the genus *Gilia*.

Leptodactylon californicum
Prickly Phlox

HABIT: Erect, widely branched, sometimes spreading on slopes, 3–10 dm, 1–3 ft. FOLIAGE: Palmately lobed into needle-like segments, light green, thickly set on stems. FLOWERS: Salverform, in terminal, congested clusters, rose, rose-lavender, or white. March–June, and on and off during year. FRUIT: Capsule, each locule with several seed. DISTRIBUTION: Dry slopes, foothill and Chaparral, San Luis Obispo County to San Gabriel and Santa Ana mountains.

Culture: Prickly Phlox can be grown from seed which germinates reasonably well, and young seedlings are not difficult to handle and transplant. Once established, plants are known to volunteer seedlings. The Prickly Phlox may become a large and widely spreading plant. It requires sun and a semi-dry situation, and is most useful in large rock gardens, dry slopes or terraces, or among boulders.

Estimate of Garden Value: Young plants flower abundantly and present sheets of color in late spring and into early summer. As they age, however, they become somewhat straggly and the old foliage clings to the lower stems giving the plants an untidy appearance. They should probably be replaced with new plants after five years or so. Plants tend to conform to the terrain, and can be trained for specific situations.

GENUS *MYRICA:* WAX MYRTLES
(Family Myricaceae: Wax Myrtle)

Two species of *Myrica,* closely related to the eastern Bayberry family, are native to California. Although usually a shrub, the species described here may attain tree proportions and is an adaptable garden plant.

Myrica californica
Pacific or California Wax Myrtle

HABIT: Evergreen, slender, ascending branches, 2–4 or 10 m, 10–30 ft. (See Fig. 59.) FOLIAGE: Oblong to oblanceolate, glossy, dark green, serrate on margins, resinous fragrance when crushed. FLOWERS: Separate male and female catkins borne in axils. FRUIT: Drupe-like nut of brown-purple, granu-

Figure 59 *Myrica californica,* California Wax Myrtle

lar appearing, covered with whitish wax. DISTRIBUTION: Canyons and moist slopes, Redwood Forest and Coastal Strand, Del Norte County to the Santa Monica Mountains.

Culture: Pacific Wax Myrtle may be grown from seed which requires three-months stratification, but even then germination may be spotty. It is also said to grow from cuttings treated with a strong hormone. This large shrub is especially admired for its glossy, always presentable foliage, and for its usefulness as clipped hedge, screen, specimen, or background. It accepts year-round water, has a moderate growth rate, and may be trained into an upright, leafy tree.

Estimate of Garden Value: By all standards, this is a neat, useful garden plant which thrives with regular watering, and is amenable to pruning and training.

GENUS *PHYSOCARPUS:* NINEBARKS
(Family Rosaceae: Rose)

Two species of *Physocarpus* are native to California, each from a different type of habitat. Both species have clusters of white, spiraea-like flowers.

Physocarpus capitatus
Western Ninebark

HABIT: Deciduous, erect and spreading, with limber branches 1–2.5 m, 3–7 ft. FOLIAGE: Round-ovate, three- to five-lobed, serrate on margins. FLOWERS: Many, small, in terminal corymb. April–July. FRUIT: Follicle, small, pointed, pinkish brown, two- to four-seeded. DISTRIBUTION: Moist banks, north slopes, many plant communities, from Redwood to Red Fir Forests. Sierra Nevada from Tulare County north, Coast Ranges from Santa Barbara County north.

Culture: Seed of Western Ninebark does not need pretreatment, but germination is spotty and propagation by cuttings is recommended. Plants require sun to light shade and tolerate moisture but will do quite well in dry situations. Western Ninebark is a leafy, gregarious plant which looks best among others with similar requirements, and in a shade border with the arching branches brought forward.

Estimate of Garden Value: Western Ninebark is common along streams in many parts of California. Plants may be low and prettily disposed among boulders of mountain streams, or taller in forests. The plants are spiraea-like in full flower, with pink anthers and pinkish stems giving faint color to the flowers. Equally attractive are the tight clusters of light brown, inflated follicles.

GENUS *PRUNUS:* WILD PLUMS
OR WILD CHERRIES
(Family Rosaceae: Rose)

Eight species of *Prunus* are native to California, although several introduced kinds are also included in botany books. The two described here are unique in having evergreen, hollylike foliage and edible fruits. The deciduous kinds are often called bird-cherries, and all species attract many kinds of birds who eat the fruits, as well as small animals who eat twigs, foliage, and bark. In spite of their many attractions, however, these deciduous kinds are considered to be too rampant for city gardens.

Prunus ilicifolia
Hollyleaf Cherry

HABIT: Dense, evergreen, uniformly branched, 1–8 m, 4–7 or to 25 ft. (See Fig. 60.) FOLIAGE: Ovate to roundish, thick, glossy, rich, bright green, spine toothed on margins. FLOWERS: Small, white, in elongated racemes. April–May. FRUIT: Drupe, red to black-purple, thin, sweetish pulp, containing a smooth stone. DISTRIBUTION: Common in dry slopes and flats of foothills, in Coast Ranges from Napa County southward, and on Santa Catalina and San Clemente islands.

Culture: Hollyleaf Cherry is easily grown from fresh seed, and many volunteers occur from fruiting shrubs. Seed may be planted where wanted, or in gallon cans and set out when about

Figure 60 *Prunus ilicifolia,* Hollyleaf Cherry

a foot high. It is inclined to be slow growing at first, moderate to rapid thereafter. Plants prefer porous soil, full sun, and regular watering to get established. Hollyleaf Cherry was first used as material for hedges and it is superb for this purpose. It may be severely clipped once or twice a year for a low hedge, or less often for a tall divider. Other uses include background, specimen, foundation planting, and with other natives of like requirements for foliage contrast, such as California lilacs, fremontias, large buckwheats, etc. This species of *Prunus* is not hardy to cold of high mountain regions.

Estimate of Garden Value: This evergreen, fruiting member of the plum family is distinctively western, a versatile and useful plant that has been cultivated for a hundred years. Seedlings appear in abundance and show a wide range of leaf types, some almost plane, others with crimped edges, often sharply toothed. Several kinds of birds enjoy the fruits, and in the past Indians leached and ground the kernels and cooked them as a gruel. Foliage sprays with the firm-textured, toothed, glossy leaves last for several weeks and are used as a substitute for holly.

Prunus lyonii
Catalina Cherry

HABIT: Usually tree-like, to 15 m, 15–50 ft. FOLIAGE: Narrowly ovate, dark green, plane or undulate margins. FLOWERS: Long racemes of small white flowers. April–June. FRUIT: Fleshy drupe, black, sweet pulp, large stone. DISTRIBUTION: Chaparral and canyons of Santa Catalina, San Clemente, Santa Cruz, and Santa Rosa islands.

Culture: Catalina Cherry seed may be sown where it is wanted, or germinated in plastic bags of moist sand, and then planted in gallon cans. It is not particular as to soil but it must be well drained, and plants will flourish with or without water. The growth rate is moderate, and both of these evergreen cherries are long lived in gardens.

Estimate of Garden Value: As with the Hollyleaf Cherry, this is a clean plant, always presentable, and useful for foundations, large hedges or dividers, or as specimens. The Catalina Cherry hybridizes readily with the Hollyleaf Cherry when they are grown together. There have been some complaints that fruit drop is a nuisance when Catalina Cherry is grown as a street tree.

Other Species:

Prunus subcordata, Sierra Plum, is an admirable, small, fruiting plum, having many thornlike branchlets, an abundance of white, plumlike, fragrant flowers, and round, red-purple fruits. Plants generally occur as thickets because the underground stems emerge every so often and form a new plant. It is a pretty shrub but its fruiting habits are puzzling. In some years the crop is abundant, but in others sparse or none at all. In some areas of northern California it is cultivated for its plums which are said to be plentiful with regular watering. A delectable and tangy preserve can be made from the Sierra Plum.

GENUS *RHAMNUS:* BUCKTHORNS OR COFFEEBERRIES
(Family Rhamnaceae: Buckthorn)

Five species and numerous distinctive subspecies of *Rhamnus* are native to California. This genus is known for evergreen shrubs of fine proportions, and for black fruits giving the name coffeeberry to most species. They range from medium to large, and sometimes spreading shrubs, with a few reaching tree size. Several are notable for their prominently veined leaves, while in others the foliage is glossy, dark green, and verges on being holly-like. All have a berry-like drupe, and in the subspecies of California Coffeeberry *(R. californica)* especially, there is a long ripening period during which several color changes take place. The drupes contain large, oval or oblong nutlets. Several kinds of birds relish the fruits, but especially the wild pigeons and in some areas these shrubs are known as Pigeon Berry Bushes. (See Chart 19.)

Culture: Most of the coffeeberries are propagated from seed which germinates without pretreatment when it is fresh. Stratification is recommended for stored seeds and three-months stratification is necessary for Cascara Sagrada *(R. purshiana)*. Young plants make moderately rapid growth. They may be planted into individual containers and then set out when a year or more of age. Flowering and fruiting will begin

Figure 61 *Rhamnus crocea,* Redberry

after three to five years of growth. Volunteer plants will appear in watered borders where plants are native to the area. With few exceptions, they require sun, coarse soil, and very little water.

Estimate of Garden Value: Species of *Rhamnus* are engaging shrubs of moderate growth habit, presentable foliage, and most of them have large, attractive berries. They accept pruning and training, and a few have been considered as hedge materials, but there remains much to learn about their further uses. They combine well with other natives, including bush salvias, certain of the California lilacs, Toyon, Hollyleaf Cherry, and a few of the large buckwheats. Cascara Sagrada makes a handsome small tree with its well-spaced branching and some removal of lower limbs in its youth. Other uses can be visualized from their performance in the wilds, such as the dark green drapery made by Hollyleaf Redberry on wooded slopes of the central Coast Ranges. Certainly this is a versatile genus with much to offer western gardeners, and with many garden uses yet to be discovered.

CHART 19 *Rhamnus*: Buckthorn

Plant	Growth Habit and Height	Flowers	Culture	Remarks	Distribution
R. californica California Coffeeberry, Pigeon Berry (See Pl. 6A)	Upright 1-4 m (3-14 ft)	Umbels, tiny, greenish. May-July.	Sun, semi-dry, very adaptable. Background, hedge, etc.	Reddish twigs, black fruits, rapid growth.	Coast, Siskiyou to Orange cos.
R. californica ssp. *crassifolia* Velvet-leaf Coffeeberry	Rounded 2-3 m (6-10 ft)	Umbels, tiny, cream. May-July.	Sun, porous soil, moderate water, adaptable.	Leaves velvety, large, black fruits.	Dry slopes, inner north Coast Ranges.
R. californica ssp. *tomentella* Chaparral Coffeeberry	Erect. to 5 m (5-17½ ft)	Umbels, tiny, yellowish. May-June.	Sun, semi-dry. Mixed planting, hedge, divider, etc.	Oblong leaves, tomentose below, abundant fruits.	Dry slopes, inner Coast Ranges, Sierra foothills.
R. californica 'Eve Case' Eve Case Coffeeberry	Compact 1.5-2 m (3½-6½ ft)	Typical. May.	Sun to partial shade, water tolerant with drainage.	Evergreen. Large clusters, fruits. Clipped hedge, specimen.	Cultivar derived from R. c. 'Sea View'

Name	Size	Flowers	Cultivation	Description	Distribution
R. rubra Sierra Coffeeberry	1-1.5 m (3½-5 ft)	Greenish white. May-August.	Sun to high shade, water tolerant. Edging, rock garden.	Semi-deciduous. Reddish twigs, narrow, dark green leaves.	Montane coniferous, Siskiyou to Calaveras cos.
R. purshiana Cascara Sagrada	Large shrub 5-12 m (17½-38 ft)	Small, greenish, in umbels. May-July.	Sun to high shade, water tolerant. Adaptable.	Leaves deciduous. Borders, background, etc.	Moist, Coast Ranges north, Sierra Nevada, Placer Co. north.
R. crocea Redberry (See Fig. 61)	Dense 1-2 m (3½-6½ ft)	Tiny, green, unisexual. March-April.	Sun, semi-dry. Edging, filler, large rock garden.	Evergreen. Oval, glossy, dark green leaves, red fruits.	Dry washes, Lake to San Diego cos.
R. crocea ssp. *ilicifolia* Hollyleaf Redberry	Arborescent 1.5-4 m (5-14 ft)	Tiny, greenish. March-June.	Sun, semi-dry, porous soil. Small red berries Aug.-Sept.	Leaves dark green, toothed or serrate on margins.	Dry slopes, Coast Ranges, Siskiyou Co. south, Sierra foothills.

GENUS *RHUS:* SUMACS
(Family Anacardiaceae: Sumac)

Six species of *Rhus* are native to California, three evergreen and three deciduous shrubs. The nonevergreen ones include the nontoxic Squaw Bush *(R. trilobata)* and Poison Oak *(R. diversiloba),* which causes an allergic reaction in most people, but affords both food and shelter to birds and small animals. The three evergreen species are important elements of the southern foothills, and have long been cultivated.

Rhus integrifolia
Lemonadeberry

HABIT: Rounded, evergreen, aromatic, with reddish twigs, 1–3 m, 3½–10 ft. FOLIAGE: Oblong-ovate, leathery, bright green, entire or with sharp teeth. FLOWERS: Small, in close panicle, white to rose-pink, surrounded by roundish, hairy bracts. February–May. FRUIT: Flattened drupe, pink to dark red, with sticky coating. DISTRIBUTION: Ocean bluffs, canyons, dry places, Santa Barbara County to Baja California, and inland to west Riverside County.

Culture: Seeds of Lemonadeberry germinate well following the hot-water treatment. Seed planted in the fall should be ready to set out from individual containers by the following spring. Plants should be watered during the first season, and thereafter left on their own. They are adaptable to both dry and moist situations. Lemonadeberry is amenable to pruning and has many landscaping uses, including clipped hedges, tall screens, or background. It can be kept low as a leafy ground cover, and may even be espaliered on walls.

Estimate of Garden Value: Lemonadeberry is considered to be one of the most dependable of the ornamental shrubs native to southern California. It may be used with silk tassels, California lilacs, Hollyleaf Cherry, coffeeberries, and many others. Its berries have an acid taste and were made into a drink in the past.

Rhus ovata
Sugar Bush

HABIT: Evergreen, with stout, reddish twigs, 1.5–3 m, 5–10 ft. (See Fig. 62.) FOLIAGE: Ovate, leathery, dark green,

Figure 62 *Rhus ovata,* Sugar Bush

folded along mid-rib. FLOWERS: Dense clusters of small pink-ish flowers from red buds. March–May. FRUIT: Glandular drupes, sticky, reddish. DISTRIBUTION: Dry slopes, mostly in Chaparral, Santa Barbara County to Baja California, to west edge of Colorado Desert, and Santa Cruz and Santa Catalina islands.

Culture: Propagation and culture of Sugar Bush is the same as for the other species, although this one is said not to be amenable for pruning. However it is a sturdy shrub, of moderate growth rate and retains its good proportions. It is also adaptable to inland areas away from the coast.

Rhus laurina
Laurel Sumac

HABIT: Large, rounded shrub or small tree, aromatic twigs, 2–5 m, 6½–17½ ft. FOLIAGE: Lance-oblong, leathery, somewhat folded along mid-rib. FLOWERS: Tiny, white in dense panicles. June–July. FRUIT: Dry, berry-like drupe enclosing the seed. DISTRIBUTION: Dry slopes, coastal slopes, Santa Barbara south to Baja California, and to Riverside County.

Culture: The hard seed of Laurel Sumac requires hot-water treatment for good germination, and soaking for 24 to 48 hours. Germination usually takes place in two to four weeks. The Laurel Sumac is drought resistant but will tolerate moderate amounts of water, and is not particular as to soil composition. Because it is a large rangy shrub, it must have room to grow and is especially recommended for backgrounds and screening.

Estimate of Garden Value: All of the sumacs are considered to be fire resistant and to have year around attraction. The reddish tint of new leaves and twigs in spring makes this species outstanding. The Laurel Sumac is sensitive to frost.

GENUS *RIBES:* CURRANTS, GOOSEBERRIES
(Family Saxifragaceae: Saxifrage)

Of the thirty-one species of *Ribes* native to California, only one is evergreen. This genus includes unarmed kinds, called currants, and those with spines or bristles, known as gooseberries. Some botanists place the latter in the genus *Grossularia*. Foliage tends to be rounded, usually lobed or scalloped, and serrate on the margins, in pale to quite dark shades of green. Flowers of the gooseberries are borne singly, mostly from under the slender or arching branches. Those of the currants are in racemes, usually pendant, and in white, shades of pink, rose, crimson, or yellow. The fruits are pulpy, often highly colored berries, enjoyed by man as well as some small mammals and many kinds of birds. Several species with glutinous foliage have a delightful pungent fragrance well known to those who walk in the woods. In their natural setting the various species grow among boulders, or hang down slopes; an equal number are indigenous to dry places or inhabit light woodlands and streamsides. (See Chart 20.)

Culture: Practically all of the *Ribes* may be grown from both seed and cuttings. Seeds of most germinate without pretreatment, but of those which have been tested, the Golden Currant

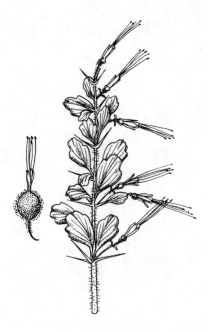

Figure 63 *Ribes speciosum,* Fuschia-Flowered Gooseberry

(R. aureum) and the Red Flowering Currant *(R. sanguineum)*
require three-months stratification. Young seedlings are put
into two-inch pots and later into one gallon cans, and held until
of a size to plant in permanent quarters. Many will begin to
flower and fruit by the third year of growth. Cuttings may be
put into three-inch pots in soil composed of half sand and half
leaf mold, and set into the border when well rooted. With few
exceptions these shrubs prefer morning sun and high shade in
the afternoon, and are water tolerant with well-drained soil.
For those which go dormant in mid-summer, water should be
withheld once their leaves drop. Currants may be used under
trees, on shaded slopes, and in a mixture of plants having
similar requirements.

Estimate of Garden Value: Although five or six species of
Ribes have long been admired and grown by horticulturists,
they have yet to be fully appreciated by the average gardener.

CHART 20 *Ribes*: Currants, Gooseberries

Plant	Growth Habit and Height	Flowers	Culture	Remarks	Distribution
R. sanguineum Red-Flowered Currant (See Pl. 5C)	Erect 1-3 or 4 m (3½-10 ft)	Rose-crimson, in racemes. March-June.	Sun to high shade, water tolerant. Propagated by tip cuttings.	Leaves fragrant, berry blue-black, with bloom.	Moist, Coast Ranges, Del Norte to Santa Clara cos.
R. sanguineum var. *glutinosum* Pink-Flowering Currant	Erect 1-3 m (3-10 ft)	Large clusters, pale to deep pink. Jan.-March.	Sun to high shade. With evergreens. Propagate by tip cuttings.	Leaves with pungent fragrance.	Mountains, Del Norte to San Luis Obispo cos.
R. indecorum White-Flowered Currant	Erect, open 1.5-2.5 m (5-8¼ ft)	White, dense clusters. Jan.-March.	Sunny borders, water tolerant. Winter display.	Fragrant foliage thick, glandular, dark green.	Washes, canyons, Santa Barbara to Baja Calif.
R. aureum Golden Currant	Erect to curved branches 1-2 m (3½-6½ ft)	Small racemes, yellow, fragrant. April-May.	Sun, water tolerant. Provides suckers or may be propagated by cuttings.	Berries orange, red, or black, glossy, light green, thin foliage.	Moist places, Fresno, Inyo cos., east of Sierra Nevada to Modoc and Siskiyou cos.

R. malvaceum Chaparral Currant	Erect, stout 1-2 m (3½-6½ ft)	Drooping racemes, pink to bright rose. Oct.-March.	Sun, well-drained soil, moderate water.	Purple-black berry, rough textured, leaves lobed.	Dry hills, inner and outer Coast Ranges, Marin to Los Angeles cos.
R. speciosum Fuchsia-Flowered Gooseberry (See Fig. 63)	Erect, arching branches 1-2 m (3½-6½ ft)	Bright crimson, pendant from under stems. Jan.-May.	Sun, well-drained soil. In close planting, other natives, evergreens.	Roundish, dark green leaves, prickly stems.	Shaded near coast, Santa Clara to San Diego cos.
R. viburnifolium Evergreen Currant, Catalina Perfume Currant	Trailing to 1 m (2-6 ft); 4 m (12 ft) spread	Small, rose, in raceme. Feb.-April.	Morning sun to high shade, water tolerant. Ground cover, shaded slopes, etc.	Rounded, thick leaves, resinous, stems root readily.	Canyons, Santa Catalina Id. to Baja Calif.

Their early flowers, fragrant foliage, and edible and often well-colored berries give them a long season of interest. And it is easy to visualize some of the low, dense gooseberries as a prickly hedge or divider or in a large rock garden. Certain traits, however, have probably kept some species of *Ribes* from greater popularity. One is their tendency to go dormant in mid-summer. Such species can be used in close plantings of evergreen shrubs where the leafless branches will not be too conspicuous. Some members have exhibited straggly growth and dead limbs, but experiments in botanic gardens were not sufficient to determine whether pruning and greater amounts of water might have resulted in a more acceptable plant. The Evergreen Currant *(Ribes viburnifolium)* is a versatile and adaptable species. It is a perfect ground cover under trees, and has a delightful resinous fragrance.

GENUS *SIMMONDSIA:* SIMMONDSIA
(Family Buxaceae: Box)

One species of *Simmondsia* is native to California. It has had much recent attention because of the useful oil content of its seeds. Although it is not yet grown commercially on a large scale, the possibilities are being considered by several institutions in the southwest.

Simmondsia chinensis
Jojoba, Goatnut, Sheepnut, Hohowi, etc.

HABIT: Rounded, evergreen, with spreading, stiff branches, 1–2 m, 3½–6 ft, or sometimes taller. May become deciduous under extreme heat. FOLIAGE: Oblong-ovate, yellow-green, leathery, opposite in pairs, and erect along the stems. FLOWERS: Dioecious, male and female on separate plants; male flowers in clusters, yellowish from ample pollen; female flowers small, bell shaped, with three pistils from tip of ovary, wind pollinated. February–April. FRUIT: Leathery, nutlike capsule, ovoid, with large oily seeds about the size of a peanut. DISTRIBUTION: Dry, barren slopes below 5,000 feet; Creosote Bush Scrub, Joshua Tree Woodland, Little San Bernardino Mountains, Twentynine Palms to Imperial County;

interior cismontane southern California, to San Diego and Baja California. An endemic plant, in pure stands or scattered among other desert plants.

Culture: No treatment is required for the seeds of Jojoba, and they are reported to germinate in fourteen to eighteen days. Seedlings may be shifted to two-inch pots, using half sand and half loam for the potting soil. Or seeds may be planted in four-inch pots, and then into gallon cans. There may be losses from root rot if the plants are overwatered. Records of experiences at botanic gardens show some difficulty in getting the plants established, but they require very little attention once settled in.

Estimate of Garden Value: Except for records from botanic gardens, little is known of Jojoba under cultivation.

Discussion: S. chinensis is included here because of its economic value. The oil in the seeds is a liquid wax, almost identical to sperm whale oil, and has the potential for many uses in industry. Aborigines were familiar with the oily content of the fruit, and used it as a cosmetic, among other things. The nuts are edible but contain a tannin and are not tasty, although an early naturalist recorded having lunched on them during a field trip. Several institutions concerned with desert plants are trying to determine the most economical way to culture the Jojoba. They are studying propagation techniques, growth requirements, genetic variations, irrigation and fertilization regimes, and the development of high-yield strains. In the past some wild stands have been harvested, but now plantations are being established in California and Arizona. Several other countries with desertlike places are also interested in the Jojoba, including Mexico, Africa, Australia, and Israel.

GENUS *STYRAX:* STORAX OR SNOWDROP BUSH
(Family Styracaceae: Storax)

One species and one variety of *Styrax* are native to foothill regions. The attractive features of this subshrub are only now being realized, even though species from the eastern states and from the Orient have long been in cultivation.

Styrax officinalis var. **californica**
California Snowdrop Bush

HABIT: Erect, small bush, deciduous, 1–4 m, 3½–14 ft. FOLIAGE: Round-ovate to oval, medium green. FLOWERS: Pendant, bell-like from pearly buds, in terminal clusters, fruity fragrance. May–June. (See Pl. 5F.) FRUIT: Oval drupe, persistent calyx attached, single seed. DISTRIBUTION: Dry, rocky places or mixed woodlands, inner Coast Ranges from Shasta to Lake counties, and foothills of Sierra Nevada from Tulare County north.

Culture: California Snowdrop Bush may be grown from seed which will germinate in its own good time. Two-months stratification is recommended to hasten the process. Measures must be taken to prevent damping-off because this shrub is especially susceptible. Young seedlings should be placed in a warm, light, airy place, and watered in the mornings to prevent muggy conditions. Plants grow at a moderate rate, and begin to flower between the third and fifth year of growth. California Snowdrop Bush may be used in light shade to full sun, prefers a porous soil but will grow in clay, and is water tolerant. This subshrub makes a fine underplanting for oaks, or among small shrubs and perennials, and may be used in a normal flower border.

Estimate of Garden Value: California Snowdrop Bush is a neat, small shrub, especially delightful for the fragrant flowers in May to June. Another attractive feature comes in early spring with the emerging leaves and the formative flower buds, which are like pearly white ear-drops. Although it is adaptable and long lived once established, there are losses among seedling plants. My plant was fully grown when I moved it from Los Gatos to my present mountain garden, and it continued to flower in its accustomed manner. It is cold tolerant except for a few late spring frosts which may damage the foliage.

Styrax officinalis var. **fulvescens,** Southern California Snowdrop Bush, is native to slopes and canyons from San Luis Obispo to San Diego counties, and varies from the species in having tawny pubescence on the reverse of the leaves. It is reported to be long lived once established, and is outstanding when grown with low-growing California wild lilacs.

GENUS *TRICHOSTEMA:* TRICHOSTEMAS
(Family Labiatae: Mint)

Ten species of *Trichostema* are native to California, all with a typical, strong mint scent, and some of which are important honey plants. Two species, which are woody in character, have long been used in dry borders.

Trichostema lanatum
Woolly Blue-Curls

HABIT: Many-branched, rounded shrub with woody base, evergreen, 5–15 dm, or 2–6 ft. FOLIAGE: Lance-linear, sessile, yellow-green, thickly set along stems. FLOWERS: Tubular, bright blue, with cleft segments and exserted stamens, in spikes to a foot or more; inflorescence and stems woolly with blue, pink, or whitish hairs. April–August, and intermittently throughout the year. FRUIT: One-seeded nutlet. DISTRIBUTION: Dry slopes, Chaparral, Coast Ranges near coast, Monterey and San Benito to Orange and San Diego counties.

Culture: Woolly Blue-Curls requires full sun and semi-dry conditions with lean, rocky or sandy soil. It will also grow in clay soil as long as it drains thoroughly. Propagation from seed is not difficult except that only a small percent is viable in each seed lot, and the seed should be sown thickly. Leaf mold and sand is a satisfactory seeding and potting mix, over which a layer of sphagnum moss can be spread, the seed sown on this and then covered with perlite. A large assortment of drought-resistant native perennials and shrubs make suitable companions for Woolly Blue-Curls, including the tall St. Catherine's Lace *(Eriogonum giganteum)* and the gray-leaved, pink-flowered Ashyleaf Buckwheat *(E. cinereum)*. In the background, Summer Holly *(Comarostaphylos diversifolia)* and Napa Fremontia *(Fremontodendron californicum* ssp. *napense)* afford nice contrast in foliage as well as in flowers. Two tall perennials are good companions, the Royal Penstemon *(Penstemon spectabilis)* and Cleveland's Penstemon *(P. clevelandii).*

Estimate of Garden Value: Woolly Blue-Curls has been cultivated in botanic and home gardens for many years. It is outstanding for its long flowering season and brilliant flower color against the tinted, woolly stems. Flowering and fruiting begin after the first full year of growth. A plant persisted for many years in my Los Gatos garden, requiring little attention except an annual shearing of the spent flowers. Its average life span is four to eight years, much longer in some instances, but less so in heavy clay soils, especially if the plants receive too much water. The pungent, minty odor is especially noticeable on warm days.

Other Species:

Trichostema parishii, Mountain Blue-Curls, is similar, but has somewhat smaller flowers and the stem wool is not quite so thick. Seed is reported to be more difficult to germinate, hence plants are not as available as are the Woolly Blue-Curls. This species inhabits dry slopes from Los Angeles County to northern Baja California.

GENUS *VACCINIUM:* HUCKLEBERRIES
(Family Ericaceae: Heath)

Eight species of *Vaccinium* are native to California. Some have typical blue berries while others have bright red fruits. California Huckleberry of coastal regions is well known, but there are others, generally of high mountains, having refined traits but seldom cultivated except by a few plant specialists.

Vaccinium ovatum
California Huckleberry

HABIT: Stout, erect, much-branched, leafy, evergreen, 1–2.5 m, 3½–8 ft. FOLIAGE: Ovate to lance-oblong, thick, shiny, dark green, serrate on margins. FLOWERS: Waxy urns, white to pinkish, in clusters, April–May. FRUIT: Berry-like, black, sweet and edible. DISTRIBUTION: Slopes, canyons, and forests, especially near coast, Del Norte to Santa Barbara counties and occasionally southward.

Culture: Seed of California Huckleberry requires three-months stratification, and seedlings are generally slow growing. Cuttings may be easier, and when rooted these should be planted in a friable soil mixture of loam, fine sand, and woods soil or peat moss. Small amounts of aluminum sulfate may be applied to ensure an acid soil, and established plants should be used in a cool, moist, partially shaded situation.

Estimate of Garden Value: The rich, dark green foliage and dense outline of this huckleberry make it a refined and elegant garden plant, suitable to use with azaleas, camellias, and other plants having similar soil and moisture requirements. The fruits have long been used for jelly, jam, and in pies, sauces, and syrups. Except for their slow growth rate and need for acid soil, the huckleberry would probably be more widely cultivated.

Other Species:

Vaccinium parvifolium, Red Huckleberry, is perhaps the most delicate appearing with small, light green leaves on spraylike branches. An interesting pattern results from the angled, green branches, and in autumn the translucent red berries are conspicuous against dark conifers.

Vaccinium caespitosum *(V. nivictum),* Sierra Bilberry, is a self-contained subshrub of great charm, having waxy pink flowers and blue-black fruits. Other species of refined appearance make extensive carpets in mountain bogs and meadows, but are little known except to a few plant specialists, or to rock gardeners.

9. GROWING NATIVE TREES

Trees occupy practically every type of terrain and all but the highest altitudes in California, from the rich forests of high mountains to the windblown cypress of coastal bluffs. They are the most prominent wild plants, and the most highly admired feature of the native landscape. Extensive forests of conifers grow in mountain regions and along the north coast, sometimes in pure stands, but often mingling with broadleafed trees. At elevations just below the forests conifers such as the gray-leaved endemic Digger Pine and oaks give character to low, mountain and foothill regions. Waterways and meadows support maples, poplars, willows, ash, and alder, some of which provide glorious autumn color.

USING NATIVE TREES

From among this wide array of native trees a possible two hundred are likely candidates for gardens, roadsides, and large-scale landscaping. Most of the thirty-five species or varieties described here are already popular as street or garden trees, and the trend now is to look more closely at others which have been ignored as too common. One of these newly prized trees is the Fremont Cottonwood *(Populus fremontii)* whose relatively small size, well-spaced foliage, and whitish trunk makes it valuable for small gardens. Horticulturists are also searching for trees of low stature, or with ornamental features such as unusual leaf forms or textures, or other characteristics of refinement. Our wealth of native trees is being viewed with much more sympathy and understanding as we are coming to recognize their permanent and decorative values for landscaping.

SPECIES DESCRIPTIONS

The following selected native trees are among the best known and most generally cultivated.

GENUS *ABIES:* FIRS
(Family Pinaceae: Pine)

California has five native firs, easily recognized and lovely trees which abound in mountain forests.

Abies bracteata *(Abies venusta)*
Bristlecone Fir or Santa Lucia Fir

HABIT: Large, with spire-like crown, lower branches widely spreading and drooping, 10–30 to 50 m, 75–100 ft. (See Pl. 7D.) FOLIAGE: Flat, rigid, sharply pointed, lustrous dark green, to 2 in. long. CONES: Egg-shaped, about 3 in. long, with slender, needlelike bracts exserted from the cone sections, borne on upper branches; seed dark reddish brown. DISTRIBUTION: Restricted distribution on rocky slopes and canyons of Santa Lucia Mountains of Monterey County, up to 5,000 feet elevation.

Culture: The Bristlecone Fir is propagated from seed which requires three- to four-months stratification. Seedlings should be potted individually, shifted to gallon cans, and held until ready to plant out. Young plants may be kept in pots for several years, and even used as Christmas trees before finally planting in the garden. The growth rate is moderately rapid, about one foot or more a year. There are several mature groves in the San Francisco Bay Area hills from plantings in the 1940s, all now bearing abundant crops of cones. This fir grows equally well on north or east slopes, in open lands, and does not require summer water once established.

Estimate of Garden Value: Although Bristlecone Fir is one of the rarest firs in the world and of restricted distribution, it is quite responsive to handling and cultivation. It is very effective in small groves in parks, for roadside planting, or as a single specimen. As with all firs, the cones are borne in the top branches, and in this species are very pitchy. This balsamic-resinous pitch was once used by Franciscan friars in religious ceremonies.

Abies concolor
White Fir

HABIT: Evergreen, with spire-like crown, stiff, horizontal branches, whitish bark, 15–70 m, 60–200 ft. (See Fig. 64.) FOLIAGE: Needles in flat rows, dark bluish green, whitish or silvery from stomata, often curving upward. CONES: Oblong-cylindric, of closely set scales to give a solid appearance, 3–4 in. long, in upper branches; cones shatter before they fall and the center core is left standing along the limbs; dark brown seed with thin wings. DISTRIBUTION: Dry, rocky places, Yellow and Lodgepole pine forests, from the mountains of San Diego County north through the Sierra, and in the Coast Ranges to Del Norte, Siskiyou, and Modoc counties, and occasionally in desert ranges.

Culture: White Fir is propagated by seed. Germination may be sporadic and stratification for one and one-half months is recommended. Seed is often nonfertile. Plants require regular amounts of water during their early years, and leaf mold or other organic materials added to the soil.

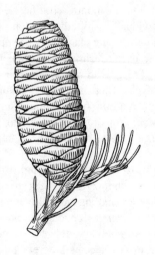

Figure 64 *Abies concolor,* White Fir

Estimate of Garden Value: White Fir is one of the most commonly grown mountain conifers. It is strictly erect and symmetrical and has a pungent fragrance. Its stiff, horizontal branching, dark blue-green needles, and ash white bark makes it stand out in mixed forests. It is satisfactory in a large pot or tub for several years, and may be brought indoors for a Christmas tree. All five of the native firs are probably suitable for large-scale landscaping.

Abies grandis, the Grand Fir, is often used in its home territory, near the coast from Sonoma to Del Norte counties.

GENUS *ACER:* MAPLES
(Family Aceraceae: Maple)

Four species of *Acer* are native to California, mostly near streams and in moist canyons of foothills and mountains.

Acer macrophyllum
Bigleaf Maple or Canyon Maple

HABIT: Round-topped, deciduous, with open branching, and greenish tan bark, 5–30 m, 18–100 ft. FOLIAGE: Roundish, deeply 3- to 5-parted and with a few irregular lobes, 10–25 cm broad, light green, turning pale yellow or golden in autumn, or deeper orange-yellow in mountains. (See Pl. 7C.) FLOWERS: In racemes, tiny, cup-shaped, pale green-yellow; male and female flowers mixed in the raceme, the sepals and petals alike. April–May. FRUIT: Tawny samara, transparent wings at acute diverging angle, seed in the center. DISTRIBUTION: Common on stream banks below 5,000 foot elevation and moist canyons of several plant communities, mostly of cismontane California.

Culture: The seed of Bigleaf Maple requires three-months stratification, but even then germination may be sporadic. Seedlings are potted in a friable soil mixture containing some leaf mold in three-inch pots, and then shifted to gallon containers until of a size to set in borders. Young plants should be watered regularly until well established; they do best with some nearby shade, or in a north or east exposure. Once established they are somewhat drought resistant, especially if an organic mulch is provided once or twice a year. Volunteer seedlings are apt to appear where there is moisture and a light covering of leaves.

Estimate of Garden Value: The Bigleaf Maple is one of California's most useful and fast-growing trees, and is pleasing over long periods because of its seasonal changes. Leaves in spring emerge from large buds enclosed by pinkish bronze bracts, and are bright green to bronzy. Flowers begin to expand at the same time; the raceme spills out and the drooping clusters look like a goldenrain tree, species of *Koelreuteria*. By September the foliage pales to soft yellow, but turns a much richer shade in mountain canyons and flats. Drooping seed clusters are reddish bronze and remain on the tree until autumn when they whirl away. Lower branches of this maple are often pruned to encourage development of a broad, widely spreading crown. Fastigiate maples sometimes develop naturally or may be trained, but I think those with wide branching are the most attractive. In my Los Gatos garden, Bigleaf Maple grew on the edge of the lawn where it attained about twenty-five feet in twelve years. This native maple has not yet achieved the popularity it deserves, probably because a number of others are already in cultivation.

Acer negundo ssp. californicum
Box Elder

HABIT: Round-headed, often slender, deciduous, 6–15 or 20 m, 20–40 ft. FOLIAGE: Pinnately 3-foliate, terminal leaflet the largest, medium pale green. FLOWERS: Sexes separate, the male flowers in clusters of threadlike, pinkish stamens, the female racemose, drooping, and appearing just before the leaves. FRUIT: Small samara, crimson when young, straw colored when mature. DISTRIBUTION: Along streams and bottom lands of many plant communities in cismontane California, from San Jacinto, San Bernardino Mountains, Santa Barbara, Kern, north to Shasta and Siskiyou counties.

Culture: The same as for *A. macrophyllum*.

Estimate of Garden Value: Box Elder is considered by some to be a weed tree which suckers and provides too many volunteers. However, it is fast growing, provides filtered shade, and in my experience persists as a 20- to 30-foot tree for many years. A variegated form with broad, white leaf margins is commonly cultivated in the north Pacific States, less so in California.

Acer circinatum
Vine Maple

HABIT: Deciduous, with slender, reddish twigs, sometimes reclining, or shrubby with several trunks, to a dense, small tree, 1–6 m, 5–20 ft. FOLIAGE: Round-cordate in outline, palmately 5- to 11-lobed to near middle of leaf, medium dark green, with flame or red tints in fall. FLOWERS: Small, red-purple cup, several in corymb, with emerging leaves. April–May. FRUIT: Samara, reddish when mature, wings in line with seed, like a bowtie. DISTRIBUTION: On shaded stream-banks, moist north slopes, and coniferous forests, Yuba, Butte, and Mendocino counties and northward.

Culture: Propagation of Vine Maple is from fresh seed which requires two-months stratification. In its own territory, seed planted in autumn and left to the elements will usually germinate the following spring. Seed leaves are bright, shining green, followed by the typical lobed ones which look like small, unfolding fans. Plants may be held in containers for a year and then planted out in shaded borders. Vine Maple requires water the year around, and will do best where leaf mold or other rich humus has been added to the soil. It will accept pruning and training, but its growth rate is generally slow and plants seldom need cutting.

Estimate of Garden Value: Vine Maple has the delicacy of Japanese Maple *(Acer palmatum),* although it does not have its leaf variations. It is useful in several situations, including a shaded wall, among evergreens or conifers, with azaleas, and with large perennials that need similar conditions of shade and moisture. Foliage color in autumn is red to red-flame, although plants seldom have this intense coloring at lower elevations. Vine Maple is difficult to establish in southern California and the interior valleys unless special conditions of shade and moisture are provided. A sheltered patio in which fuchsias are grown should provide suitable conditions.

GENUS *AESCULUS:* BUCKEYE
(Family Hippocastanaceae: Buckeye)

One species of *Aesculus* is native to California. It is well known for its fragrant flowers and large buckeye balls, which hang on the trees through the autumn season.

Aesculus californica
California Buckeye

HABIT: Broad-headed, deciduous, with open branching, 7–12 m, 15–40 ft. FOLIAGE: Five to 7 leaflets, each oblong-elliptic, enclosed in large bracts, bright green as they unfold. Pale yellow in summer, and drop by early autumn. FLOWERS: Small, cream, packed in a cylindrical thryse, most are stamniate, and the female flowers having thick styles; hawthorne-like fragrance, but sometimes described as being ill-scented. May–July. FRUIT: Capsule; leathery, grayish coating, which splits in autumn to reveal the shiny, mahogany brown seed. DISTRIBUTION: Common on dry slopes and canyons of foothills, Coast Ranges and Sierra Nevada, from Siskiyou and Shasta counties to Kern and Los Angeles counties.

Culture: California Buckeye seed usually sprouts readily when in contact with moist soil, and may be planted where the tree is wanted. The seed can also be planted in large pots or cans and set out when a foot or more high. With well-drained soil it tolerates year around watering and will grow rapidly, as much as two feet a year. It will also accept considerable dryness, but make slower growth. In my Los Gatos garden, a buckeye was planted at the edge of the orchard and watered deeply two or three times during the summer; some inner limbs were removed to eventually form an open, widely spreading tree. The smooth, sand gray bark is especially pleasing, and in the winter has a silvery gray cast. Flowering and seeding begins four to five years after planting.

Estimate of Garden Value: Early yellowing and dropping of the foliage has kept the California Buckeye from being a more popular garden tree. With water, the leaves remain green into early autumn, otherwise they will begin to drop by late June through July. California Buckeye can be planted in a close mixture of other trees or large shrubs where the bare limbs make an interesting pattern against evergreen foliage. Other advantages include rapid growth, large and striking flower spikes, and the buckeye balls which are used in winter decorations. For me the period of greatest interest is the unfolding of the leaf and flower buds when the large bracts fold back like green satin ribbon to reveal the bright green new leaves and the emerging flowers. California Buckeye is not hardy in mountain regions where late frosts prevail. Although the attractive fruits are poisonous, the Indians used them for food after roasting them, and then leaching for long periods in running water.

GENUS *ALNUS:* ALDERS
(Family Betulaceae: Birch)

Four species of *Alnus* are native to California. They are deciduous plants, which may be slender trees or large shrubs. Only one is cultivated to any extent.

Alnus rhombifolia
White Alder

HABIT: Deciduous, whitish or pale gray bark, regular, well-spaced branching, 10–35 m, 35–105 ft. FOLIAGE: Oblong-ovate, coarsely doubly serrate, prominent veining, bright green, 2–3½ inches long. FLOWERS: Catkins, the male pendulous in clusters at branch tips, green-gold; female smaller; both appear in winter. FRUIT: Small, woody cone, containing nutlets. DISTRIBUTION: Widely distributed, mostly in cismontane California, along water courses and in meadows.

Culture: Seed of the White Alder germinates without any pretreatment, and plants are easily handled and transplanted. Vast numbers of seedlings are volunteered in its home territory. This tree is one of the most rapid growing of any native; a well-branched tree of twenty feet or more can be had in about five years. It requires ample amounts of moisture, sun for most of the day, and will tolerate limb removal. This alder is suitable as a lawn tree, background, hedge, or large divider tree.

Estimate of Garden Value: Although the White Alder is a useful and fast-growing tree, it has invasive roots, robs the soil of moisture, and may invade sewer pipes. Deep watering of young plants helps to develop a deep root system rather than surface roots. In my mountain garden I grow small bulbs, wild irises, columbines, and the eastern Blue Phlox *(Phlox divaricata)* under the White Alder. Some horticulturists have suggested the use of alder in groups with removal of a few inner branches. Ground cover plants for such a grouping could include Long-Tailed Wild Ginger *(Asarum caudatum),* or species of alum roots *(Heuchera),* bishop's caps *(Mitella),* boykinias *(Boykinia),* or star flowers *(Lithophragma).* The White Alder grows to 40 or 50 feet in gardens, and its outstanding feature is the fringe of long, golden-beige catkins in the winter months.

GENUS *ARBUTUS:* ARBUTUS OR ARBUTE TREE (Family Ericaceae: Heath)

One species of *Arbutus* is native to California, the well-known and handsome Madrone.

Arbutus menziesii
Madrone or Madroño

HABIT: Widely branched, evergreen, exfoliating cinnamon red bark, tree or many-trunked shrub, 5–40 m, 16–140 ft. FOLIAGE: Elliptic to oblong-ovate, dark green, leathery, shining above, slightly paler beneath, long-petioled. FLOWERS: In panicles, urn-shaped, white, cloying scent. March–May. (See Pl. 7E.) FRUIT: Berry, orange to orange-red, rugose on surface, bony seed. DISTRIBUTION: Wooded slopes and canyons below 5,000 feet elevation, in Redwood and Mixed Evergreen Forests and in scattered mountain localities in southern California. More abundant in north Coast Ranges and also in Sierra Nevada, from Mariposa to Shasta counties and northward.

Culture: Madrone may be grown from seed which will eventually germinate. One-month stratification is recommended, and then seed should be planted in a potting mix that includes peat, sand, and gravel, and then covered with vermiculite. Horticulturists advise that seedlings be sturdy and at least two feet, before planting in their permanent quarters. Water deeply about once a month during the dry season until the young plants are well established. Young plants may be susceptible to fungus from soil, from water washing against the trunks, or from overhead watering. If this occurs, the affected trunk can be cleaned and painted with a bordeaux mixture, and a basin filled with rock can be constructed at the base of the tree. Madrone prefers full sun to some high, afternoon shade and porous, well-drained soil. Once fully established it is quite drought resistant. It looks elegant in a mixture of conifers and broadleafed trees.

Estimate of Garden Value: Madrone is considered to be the most beautiful of California's broadleaf trees. It is seldom recommended for the average home garden, but it can be used in large estates, parks, and roadsides. Leaf drop throughout the year is its worst fault but, if planted as a background or in close groupings with other trees and large shrubs, this feature will not be too noticeable. Growth rate is moderate, and it may take ten years before flowers and fruits are produced. Under cultivation the Madrone may remain a close-branched, small tree, while in forests it is apt to have long, angular, or sometimes beautifully curved branches. In autumn the glowing berries enliven the forests and bring flocks of Robins, Cedar Waxwings, and Bandtailed Pigeons to dine. In former days some large old specimens were known as council tree, and were the meeting place of Indian tribes.

GENUS *CALOCEDRUS:* FALSE CEDAR
(Family Cupressaceae: Cypress)

One species of *Calocedrus,* a genus that is closely related to the true cypress, is native to California. It is one of the most popular of the cultivated conifers.

Calocedrus decurrens
Incense Cedar, Post Cedar, or Red Cedar

HABIT: Slender, evergreen, pyramidal, fluted trunk, shreddy, cinnamon brown bark; upper branches erect, lower sweeping, curved, becoming irregular in age, 25–50 m, 85–160 ft. FOLIAGE: Scale-like, opposite, overlapping in four rows to form flat sprays, dark yellow-green, aromatic. CONES: Small, elongated, of 6 oblong scales, with seed in

between, like duck's bill, mature in one season. DISTRIBU-
TION: Mountain slopes and canyons, Mixed Evergreen and
Yellow Pine Forests, Baja California to Oregon.

Culture: Incense Cedar is propagated from seed that is slow
to germinate. Two-months stratification is recommended.
Seedlings are potted in six-inch containers in a mixture of loam
and sand, and later shifted to gallon cans. They are slow growing at first, but when established, may grow at the rate of two
feet a year. Under controlled conditions of a greenhouse, this
cedar may be propagated by tip cuttings. This cedar is drought
resistant, but will flourish with one deep watering a month
during the dry season. It is useful for a large hedge, wind-
screen, or specimen tree, and for roadsides, parks, and large
gardens.

Estimate of Garden Value: Incense Cedar is highly recommended for its pyramidal habit, clean appearance, and moderately rapid growth rate. It is pest resistant, tolerant of poor
soils, and may be pruned to shape when necessary. The
pungent-resinous fragrance is delightful, and sometimes referred to as spicy. Wood of this cedar has been used for shingles, fence posts, lead pencils, and railroad ties.

GENUS *CHAMAECYPARIS:* FALSE CYPRESSES
(Family Cupressaceae: Cypress)

Two species of *Chamaecyparis* are native to California.
Alaska Cedar *(C. nootkatensis)* occurs only in the far northwestern corner of the state, and north to Alaska. *C. lawsoniana*
is famous for the large number of named forms which have
been derived from it.

Chamaecyparis lawsoniana
Lawson Cypress or Port-Orford Cedar

HABIT: Tall, dense, narrow pyramidal top, full, pendulous
lower branches, 25–60 m, 75–180 ft. FOLIAGE: Scale-like,
dark blue-green, dense on branchlets to form broad, drooping,
fernlike sprays. CONES: Female small, globose, light brown,
like a miniature cone; abundant, contain ample seed, mature in
the autumn of the first season. DISTRIBUTION: Moist slopes,
canyons, serpentine, North Coastal and Mixed Evergreen

Forests, west Shasta, Del Norte, and Siskiyou to Humboldt counties.

Culture: Lawson Cypress may be grown from seed. It will germinate without difficulty, but stratification is generally recommended. Vitality of the seed is said to be transient. There are two seed leaves and the typical leaves form by the second year. The Lawson Cypress is best suited to mild climates and is a superb specimen tree in coastal areas. It prefers some shade and is water tolerant with well-drained soil.

Estimate of Garden Value: Perhaps because the selected forms of Lawson Cypress are so well known, there is scant information on the tree from which they were derived. It is recommended as a windbreak or sun screen, but its soft-appearing foliage and natural symmetry make it an excellent specimen tree. Fruiting begins at about twelve years of age with an abundance of cones which are very decorative on the lower branches.

GENUS *CUPRESSUS:* CYPRESSES
(Family Cupressaceae: Cypress)

Ten species of *Cupressus* are native to California. They are small trees generally of arid, rocky, or serpentine areas. The genus includes the famous Monterey Cypress, a picturesque element of the coast in that county.

Cupressus macrocarpa
Monterey Cypress

HABIT: Evergreen, symmetrical in youth, becoming broad with flat-topped crown, 20–25 m, 70–85 ft. FOLIAGE: Scale-like, opposite, in spray formation, rich green. CONES: Globose, with inconspicuous umbos, green, then brown, and weathering to gray; in clusters clinging to branches, remain closed for many years. DISTRIBUTION: Exposed headlands, dry places, Monterey peninsula.

Culture: Monterey Cypress is grown from seed which is slow to germinate. The seed bed should be allowed to dry out in summer; thereafter the seeds will usually germinate either from winter rains or from applied moisture. This species may also be grown from cuttings started in peat moss and sand.

Young trees are pyramidal with straight trunks and ascending branches to form a pointed crown, quite different from the aged ones which become bent and gnarled.

Estimate of Garden Value: Monterey Cypress is subject to canker fungus, but in spite of this has been widely used for orchard windbreaks. It has also been used in the central coastal regions of California where it seems to be less susceptible to the fungus in the cool, foggy climate. Some trees appear to be resistant to the cypress canker, and cutting material should be taken from these.

Cupressus forbesii
Tecate Cypress

HABIT: Small, with irregular, spreading crown, exfoliating, mahogany brown or cherry red bark, up to 10 m, 15–30 ft. (See Fig. 65.) FOLIAGE: Scale-like, overlapping, tiny, light rich green to dull green. CONES: Globose, umbos inconspicuous, do not open for many years; seed dark brown. DIS-

Figure 65 *Cupressus forbesii,* Tecate Cypress

TRIBUTION: Dry slopes, Chaparral, Santa Ana Mountains in Orange County to peaks in San Diego County.

Culture: The Tecate Cypress is grown from seed which is slow and sporadic in germination. If seed beds are allowed to dry out in summer, more germination can be expected the following spring. Once established this cypress endures wind, heat, dryness, and hard soils. Plants may be trimmed for use in hedges or windbreaks, or used in mixed plantings of other drought-tolerant materials.

Estimate of Garden Value: The Tecate Cypress has long been recommended as a small garden tree where it forms a slender and often irregularly branched specimen, sometimes remaining shrublike. Its green foliage and reddish bark forms a nice contrast with broadleaf materials. This species is not immune to cypress canker disease.

GENUS *JUNIPERUS:* JUNIPERS
(Family Cupressaceae: Cypress)

Four species of *Juniperus* are native to California; one forms mats on mountain peaks, the others are either arborescent shrubs or trees. Many live to 2,000 years or more, and when growing in arid places or in rock fissures become craggy and picturesque in their old age.

Juniperus californica
California Juniper, Desert White Cedar, etc.

HABIT: Arborescent, stout, irregular stems, squat, dark green outline, heavy, fluted trunk; bushy, open, large shrub, 1–4 m, or tree to 10 m, or 3–12 or 35 ft. (See Fig. 66.) NEEDLES: Scale-like, pitted on the back, 3 in a group on stout twigs; pungent fragrance. CONES: Berrylike cone, light red-brown, skin with a bloom, one or two bony seed; mature in autumn of second year. DISTRIBUTION: Dry, arid slopes and flats, below 5,000 feet elevation, deserts from west edge of Colorado to Kern County, and interior cismontane southern California to Tehama County.

Culture: Seeds of the California Juniper are slow to germinate, but may respond if pine needles are burned over the flat after the seed is planted. Seedlings are reported to tolerate

Figure 66 *Juniperus californica,* California Juniper or Desert White Cedar

handling, and to become permanent once the plants are fully established. Plants are erect, and open cone-shaped when young, becoming somewhat open and sprawling in old age. They prefer sun but will tolerate some shade of other trees, are drought resistant, and are not particular as to soil, but will die quickly in standing water.

Estimate of Garden Value: The California Juniper is valuable to the countryside because they persist in dry places where other trees seldom grow. Doubtless they will become important drought-resistant garden materials, useful for background, to train into artistic forms, and for accent as well as specimen trees. In the past Indians made much use of this tree, making a soothing tea from the leaves, eating the berries, and constructing matting and other items from the shreddy bark.

Other Species:

Juniperus communis var. **saxatilis,** Dwarf Juniper, is a low, groundcover type with silvery, blue-green foliage, and is native to high mountain peaks. Probably because of the wide assortment of cultivated junipers available, the native ones have not yet achieved the popularity which they deserve.

Juniperus occidentalis 'glauca', Sierra Juniper, is a columnar form with blue-gray foliage, said to be very adaptable to cultivation.

GENUS *LYONOTHAMNUS:* IRONWOOD
(Family Rosaceae: Rose)

One species with one variety in *Lyonothamnus,* a genus of rare, evergreen trees restricted to the Channel Islands off the coast of southern California, is native.

Lyonothamnus floribundus
Catalina Ironwood

HABIT: Slender, evergreen, red-brown to grayish, exfoliating bark, 5–15 m, 16–50 ft. FOLIAGE: Lance-oblong, entire to serrate on margins, glossy green above, pubescent beneath. FLOWERS: Many, in large, terminal, compound clusters, white. May–June. FRUIT: Pair of woody carpels, flat, oblong, brown, usually four-seeded. DISTRIBUTION: Dry slopes and chaparral, Santa Catalina Island.

Culture: Seeds of Catalina Ironwood require no pretreatment, and germinate in six to eight weeks. Young plants may be shifted to gallon cans, and held until of a size to plant in permanent quarters. This interesting tree requires porous soil, sun for most of the day, and is moderately water tolerant. In landscaping it is suitable as a specimen, in small groves, or in mixtures of conifers, with a foreground planting of manzanitas or with Summer Holly.

Estimate of Garden Value: Although Catalina Ironwood is sometimes planted in parks or for other large-scale landscaping, its variety is much more popular and considered to be an exceptionally handsome specimen.

Lyonothamnus floribundus var. **asplenifolius,** the Fernleaf Ironwood, is similar in all respects to the species except for the foliage. (See Fig. 67.) Its foliage is broadly ovate in outline and divided into two to seven leaflets with oblique-lobed margins. The tree is open and generally spreading, but may be shrublike with several trunks. In its native habitat it integrates freely with the species. The Fernleaf Ironwood is native to Santa Catalina, San Clemente, Santa Rosa, and Santa Cruz islands.

Estimate of Garden Value: This variety is widely planted in

Figure 67 *Lyonothamnus floribundus* var. *asplenifolius,* Fernleaf Ironwood

coastal areas where it is considered to be a distinctive tree. Old flower clusters turn brown and should be removed. Neither this variety nor the species is tolerant of prolonged freezing. They both accept pruning and shaping, and do not seem particular about soil. The tough and close-grained wood has been used for fishing poles and canes by early settlers, and for spear handles and shaft wood by the early Indians. The ironwoods are considered to be relict endemics, but are fortunately available to gardeners for western landscaping.

GENUS *PICEA:* SPRUCES
(Family Pinaceae: Pine)

Three species of *Picea* are native to California, mostly of the northwest coastal areas and northward. The Weeping Spruce *(P. breweriana)* is very rare and occurs only in scattered stands of Del Norte, Trinity, and Siskiyou counties, and into Oregon.

Picea sitchensis
Sitka Spruce or Tideland Spruce

HABIT: Coniferous forests, wide-spreading, rigid branches and drooping branchlets, to 35 m, 80–125 ft. NEEDLES: Flattened, sharp-pointed, spreading from all sides of branchlets, bright green, whitish on upper surface. CONES: Long-oblong, tan to light brown, of closely set, thin, papery-appearing scales. DISTRIBUTION: Moist to swampy places near the coast, from Mendocino County north.

Culture: Sitka Spruce is propagated from seed which is slow to germinate; two- to three-months stratification is recommended. The planting soil should contain forest duff, leaf mold, or decayed wood along with loam and sand. Growth rate is moderate, and garden specimens seldom exceed 40 to 50 feet. Regular watering is necessary for steady growth, and it flourishes in the cool, foggy coastal climate.

Estimate of Garden Value: Although the Sitka Spruce is seldom recommended for gardens away from its home territory, it is included here because I obtained seedling plants many years ago, and they are still growing in a hilltop Berkeley garden. The trees are forty years old, and have borne abundant crops of cones since about their twelfth year. Some lower limbs were removed during their early years so that planting could be done beneath. This spruce is recommended for parks, estates, and roadside planting in coastal areas.

GENUS *PINUS:* PINES
(Family Pinaceae: Pine)

Twenty species of *Pinus* are native to California. (See Pl. 7F.) At least two are endemic and several are quite rare because of restricted distribution. Others are more common and occur in several of the western states. Most of them are members of extensive forests of mountain regions, while some cling to alpine peaks and others grow in coastal areas. Low-elevation pines are the most popular for gardens and large-scale landscaping because they are relatively fast growing and retain a nicely balanced form. Other uses include highway planting, reforestation, erosion control, and bonsai for a few of the small

CHART 21 *Pinus:* Pines

Plant	Height	Cones	Culture	Remarks	Distribution
P. coulteri Coulter Pine (See Fig. 68)	12-25 m (40-80 ft)	Long-oval, incurved spurs.	Adaptable, water tolerant, heat and wind resistant. Screens, highway, large gardens.	Moderate growth rate. Shapely, not cold tolerant.	Dry, rocky slopes, Coast Ranges, Contra Costa Co. to mountains of southern Calif.
P. contorta Beach Pine	3-10 or 16 m (10-35 [or 56] ft)	Ovoid, often clustered, chestnut brown.	Best near coast. Moderate to fast growing.	Compact, dense, dark green needles. Small garden screen, windbreak.	Coastal strand, Mendocino Co. north.
P. muricata Bishop Pine	15-25 m (50-85 ft)	Closed, not symmetrical, brown.	Takes wind, salt air. Rapid growing.	Open to dense and rounded later. Small gardens.	Near coast, Humboldt to Santa Barbara cos.

Species	Height	Cone	Culture	Uses	Habitat
P. torreyana Torrey Pine	10-15 m (35-50 ft)	Broadly ovoid, brown.	Sun, lean soil. Moderately rapid growth.	Broad, open crown, adaptable.	Dry slopes, San Diego Co; to Santa Rosa Id.
P. attenuata Knobcone Pine	2-12 or 15 m (40 ft)	Ovoid, asymmetrical, clinging to trees.	Hardy, drought tolerant. Fast growing, accepts poor soils.	Highways, gardens, parks, screens, or specimen.	Barren, rocky soils, foothills and low mountains, Coast Ranges and Sierra Nevada.

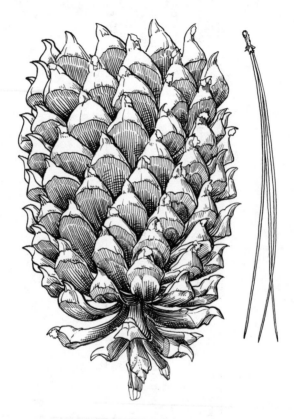

Figure 68 *Pinus coulteri,* Coulter Pine

ones. The sweet, nutritious pine nuts were one of the most important food sources for the Indians. (See Chart 21.)

Propagation: Pines are grown from seed which usually requires stratification before planting. Seedling plants can be potted in five-inch containers, and then into gallon cans until ready for outdoor planting. Some of the pines do well in pots for several years and may be used for Christmas trees.

Culture: A native pine must be carefully chosen for garden use to allow for its growth rate and ultimate height. Rates of growth vary from about six inches to two feet a year, with the height generally less than it is in the wilds. Pines prefer lean and well-drained soil. They may be watered occasionally, but deeply, during the first two summers after planting out. They seldom require pruning except for removal of dead wood. Tip growth or limbs may be cut when necessary, or the trees may be trained for some specific garden purpose. The beautifully sculptured Monterey Pines in the Japanese Tea Garden in Golden Gate Park have had careful and systematic pruning throughout their more than sixty years.

Estimate of Garden Value: In spite of their relatively slow growth rate, many pines are adaptable to cultivation and valuable for their symmetrical habit through all stages of their development. Throughout their lives they afford a dramatic accent to the garden, and provide filtered shade in maturity. The small, slow-growing pines, such as Nut Pine *(P. edulus)* can be used in a rock garden or in other situations where a small, cone-shaped tree is wanted.

GENUS *PSEUDOTSUGA:* FALSE HEMLOCKS
(Family Pinaceae: Pine)

There are two native species of *Pseudotsuga,* the Douglas Fir and the Bigcone Spruce of southern mountains, and both have characteristics of several other conifers.

Pseudotsuga menziesii
Douglas Fir, Douglas Spruce, or Oregon Pine

HABIT: Large, evergreen conifer, full crown, slender, crowded branches, pendulous side branches, to 70 m, 70–250 ft. (See Pl. 7A.) NEEDLES: Straight, bright to blue-green, with white band on either side of midrib beneath, aromatic, with soft appearance. CONES: Pendulous, reddish brown, of thin scales, protruding, 3-pointed bracts. DISTRIBUTION: Moist slopes and mixed forests, below 5,000 feet elevation, coastal regions from Monterey County north. In Sierra Nevada from Fresno County north, and eastward. One of the most important lumber trees.

Culture: Douglas Fir may be grown from seed which requires one- or two-months stratification. Seedlings can be planted in a soil mix containing one-third peat moss or sieved leaf mold, along with sand and loam. Ample water and sun to partial shade will keep this conifer growing steadily, and it probably does best in its home territory or in similar climates. It accepts pruning, and in the north Pacific States is often trimmed into a large hedge.

Estimate of Garden Value: Its rich green needles borne all around the branches give the Douglas Fir a dense, lush quality that makes it one of the most popular for a Christmas tree. It retains its pyramidal form for many years, is moderately fast growing, and the needles have a pleasant aromatic fragrance.

Pseudotsuga macrocarpa
Bigcone Spruce

HABIT: Evergreen conifer, rapidly tapering trunk, lower branches elongated, pendulous side branches, 12–20 m, 40–70 ft. (See Fig. 69.) NEEDLES: Slender, somewhat curved,

Figure 69 *Pseudotsuga macrocarpa*, Bigcone Spruce

growing on all sides of branches, dark green, pointed, but not prickly. CONES: Similar to *P. menziesii,* but almost twice as large. DISTRIBUTION: Dry slopes and canyons to 6,000 feet elevation, mountains from Santa Barbara County to Tehachapi Mountains and to San Diego County.

Culture: Seeds of Bigcone Spruce require one- to two-months stratification. Seedlings are slow growing, but young plants are generally ready to set out by the second year. There is little information on the general behavior of this tree, although it has been cultivated at some of the botanic gardens.

Estimate of Garden Value: The Bigcone Spruce is probably most valuable in its home territory, attaining about 60 feet under cultivation.

GENUS *QUERCUS:* OAKS
(Family Fagaceae: Beech)

Sixteen species of *Quercus,* most with sturdy, often rugged trunks and wide-spread branching, are native to California. They are a pleasing aspect of valleys, foothills, and of mountain ranges to middle elevations. Many species, both deciduous and evergreen, have an asymmetrical balance, several heavy limbs spring from the massive trunk and end in leafy twigginess. Oak trees have been traditionally revered for their majestic form. Ancient rites have been held beneath their sweeping branches, and their leaves and acorns have been chosen as symbols. Oaks and their acorns are important to wildlife. Birds and small animals find food and shelter among their branches. Native deer eat the acorns in autumn to fatten up for the lean winter months. (See Chart 22.)

The Genus: Of the sixteen native species of *Quercus,* five are deciduous trees, four are shrubby types, and the remainder are large, evergreen trees. Foliage is oval to broadly elliptic, some with shallow lobing, others with several divisions, and of firm to leathery texture. Flowers occur in spring catkins; the slender and pendulous staminate ones are conspicuous because of the yellow or orange-yellow color; the pistillate ones are solitary and less showy. Fruits are acorns, which vary in size with species. The nut is set in a cup with scales disposed in a typical manner. Some acorns mature the first year, others re-

Figure 70 *Quercus engelmanii,* Engelmann Oak

quire two years. Oaks are widely distributed and occur at many elevations, from near the coast to the 10,000 feet elevation reached by the rambling Huckleberry Oak *(Q. vaccinifolia)*. California Black Oak *(Q. kelloggii)* occurs from mountain forests to low mountains and foothills in many sections of the state. The Valley Oak *(Q. lobata)* was probably the one most frequently mentioned in early literature, and it still occurs in park-like groves in a few areas. It is also considered to be among the most adaptable and water tolerant of the native oaks. Scrub Oak *(Q. dumosa)* and Leather Oak *(Q. durata)* are typical, evergreen, hard-leaved, large shrubs or small trees of Chaparral or arid foothills.

Culture: All oaks are readily grown from the acorns, after first removing the cup, and inspecting the nuts for plumpness and for insect holes. Acorns may be started by placing in plastic bags of damp peat moss, and then potting when the root begins to sprout, generally in six to eight weeks. Clip or pinch off the root tip to prevent coiling when potted and to aid the formation of feeding roots. Acorns may also be planted in straight-sided cans in friable potting soil, kept moist and shaded until top growth begins, and then brought gradually to the light. Keep oak seedlings in containers for one to two years, or until about two feet in height, and then set in place. Growth rate is slow, but varies somewhat among the species, about one to two feet a year. After planting, they should be watered during the dry months for the first and second years, or until well established and showing signs of vigorous growth. The amount of water will depend upon the type of soil and how fast it drains, but generally slow, deep watering will encourage deep rooting, and a more self-sufficient plant. Good drainage must be provided or the oak will be subject to crown rot or root fungus. Some removal of crossing limbs may be necessary during the early years of growth, and lower limbs may be removed.

Care of Established Oaks: Tragically, many established oaks die in or near construction sites for the following reasons: poor soil drainage; lack of air circulation around roots because of impacted soil, grading too near the trunks, or damage to the tree trunk; changes in natural soil level because of grading and soil or mud washing against the tree. When a change in the grade or soil level is necessary, retaining walls or dry wells may be constructed to keep the original soil line intact. Holes may be dug at about the drip line for watering and fertilizing. Allow water to trickle in order to reach the lower roots. Apply either an organic or a 5–10–10 commercial fertilizer. Some of the fallen oak leaves should be allowed to remain on the ground to form a mulch. Where they have been removed, the soil becomes baked and impervious to moisture. In such cases, a mulch of old manure, ground bark, or other organic materials may be applied. Lawns or other ground covers which require water are not recommended under oaks. There is an assortment of native plants which perform well with a minimum of summer water. Drought-tolerant manzanitas and California lilacs, and other low-growing plants are superb for this purpose.

Estimate of Garden Value: Although no one can expect to see a wide-spread, fully developed oak tree grow in his

CHART 22 *Quercus:* Oak

Plant	Height	Acorn	Culture	Remarks	Distribution
Q. *agrifolia* Coast Live Oak	10-25 m (35-85 ft)	Slender, cup turbinate. 1st season.	By acorn in gallon can, water in dry season.	Evergreen. Slow growing. Street, park, large gardens.	Valleys, slopes, Coast Ranges, Sonoma to San Diego cos.
Q. *lobata* Valley Oak	12-35 m (40-125 ft)	Conicle, in thick cup. 1st season.	By acorn, rapid growth, water tolerant with drainage.	Deciduous. Most adaptable of oaks, graceful lower branches.	Rich loam, Central Valley and borders, inner Middle Coast Ranges to Los Angeles Co.
Q. *engelmanii* Engelmann Oak (See Fig. 70)	5-18 m (16-60 ft)	Thick, in deep cup. 1st season.	Plant acorns where wanted.	Evergreen. Garden or street tree in home range.	Dry foothills, Los Angeles, inland to San Diego Co.

Species	Height	Acorn	Propagation / Growth	Habit	Distribution
Q. kelloggii California Black Oak (See Pl. 7F)	10-25 m (30-80 ft)	Oblong, in large cups. 2nd season.	By acorn, moderate growth. Lobed foilage, fall color.	Deciduous. Large gardens, parks, especially with conifers.	Common, hills and mts., Coast Ranges and Sierra Nevada.
Q. wislizenii Interior Live Oak	10-22 m (30-75 ft)	Cylindric, In deep cup. 2nd season.	By acorn, water tolerant. Good specimen in home area.	Evergreen. Glossy, dark green leaves. Not as massive as Coast Live Oak.	Valleys, slopes, Sierra Nevada and Coast Ranges, Ventura to Siskiyou cos.

lifetime, a well-proportioned, slender tree can be had in ten to fifteen years. Fortunately there is increasing interest in these stately trees, and some areas have laws forbidding their removal. Also there is easily obtainable information on the care of existing oaks listed in the references. They are not always suited to home gardens, but several are being used as street or freeway planting, and in large gardens, parks, and estates.

GENUS *SEQUOIA:* REDWOOD
(Family Taxodiaceae: Taxodium)

There is one species in *Sequoia,* the famous Coast Redwood which has survived from past geological time, with groves still in existence along the California coast. These spectacular trees are a compelling sight, and a heritage in which Californians should take deep pride. The Coast Redwood has long been a popular cultivated tree, widely planted in home gardens and for large-scale landscaping.

Sequoia sempervirens
Coast Redwood

HABIT: Evergreen, with strongly buttressed trunk base, tapering upward, with long, sweeping, and sometimes drooping lower branches; bark thick, reddish, spongy-fibrous; 50–80 or 100 m, 160–280 or 340 ft. (See Pl. 7B.) NEEDLES: Flattish, sharp-pointed, dark green and shining above, forming sprays on slender branchlets. CONES: Male, ovoid, green; female slightly larger, broadly oblong, red-brown, maturing the first season, one inch or less; seed lance-oblong, light brown. DISTRIBUTION: Flats and slopes mostly below 2,000 feet elevation in coastal fog belt, from Santa Lucia Mountains to south Oregon. Important lumber tree because of its resistance to decay, and the wood is light, and straight grained, and easily split.

Culture: Coast Redwood is grown from seed which requires no pretreatment, and takes three to six weeks for germination. Seedlings grow rapidly and should have some shade and protection for the first year. Propagation may also be from cuttings with the use of a rooting hormone, bottom heat, and in sharp sand. Cuttings should be kept in a frame or sheltered place until well rooted, and then potted in friable soil. Young plants should be kept evenly moist. They may be set out in late autumn or early spring, and watered regularly for the first few years, or until firmly established. Sun is acceptable in coastal areas, but shelter and a thick mulch should be provided inland or where drying winds prevail. Young plants may need to be staked for the first year or so. The redwoods are generally pest free. Yellowing of the foliage in summer may indicate iron deficiency and iron sulphate may be applied. The Coast Redwood has been used extensively along freeways, as specimen trees, in groves in parks and golf courses, and even planted in rows and topped for a feathery hedge or large divider.

Estimate of Garden Value: For those who have a special reverence for the Coast Redwood, growing one or several in a group is an exhilarating experience. In my Los Gatos garden I planted four in various sections of the garden so I could watch their progress. Young trees grow rapidly, as much as three to five feet a year with regular watering, but less under semi-dry conditions. The one closest to the house was more sheltered and its growth was especially rapid. At about the eighth year it began to set cones, and in another few years provided volunteer seedlings to give to friends. All phases of the Coast Redwood's growth pattern is fascinating, but especially when the first pale green catkins appear thickly, like delicate scalloping edging the foliage sprays. The foliage has a distinctive, pungent fragrance which is especially noticeable on foggy days. Other young Coast Redwoods were planted in more remote sections of my garden, where they grew more slowly, with less water and attention. The Coast Redwood does not tolerate freezing temperatures of elevations higher than its normal range.

In recent years redwoods have been vegetatively propagated from plants having desirable characteristics such as dense and uniform growth habit, and foliage color which varies from wild forms. *Sequoia sempervirens* 'Aptos Blue' has dense outline and blue-green foliage; and one called 'Soquel' has needles of fine texture in bluish-green. These two forms are also cold tolerant and have been grown at Lake Tahoe for several years without showing any frost damage. These and other named forms are available from nurseries.

GENUS *SEQUOIADENDRON:* GIANT SEQUOIA
(Family Taxodiaceae: Taxodium)

There is one species in *Sequoiadendron,* closely related to the Coast Redwood but now placed in a separate genus. Known also as Big Tree and Sierra Redwood, it is noted for its massive size.

Sequoiadendron giganteum
Giant Sequoia

HABIT: Evergreen with heavy, strongly buttressed trunk; old trees with open crown, a few giant, upturned branches, and often unbranched for 50 m; young trees compact and cone-shaped; bark thick, separating into loose, cinnamon red fibers; 50–80 or 100 m, 160–280 or 325 ft. NEEDLES: Awl-shaped, overlapping, gray-green, pungent fragrance. CONES: Oblong-ovoid, light brown, 5–8 cm, about 2–3 inches long, maturing in two years; seeds light brown. DISTRIBUTION: Giant Sequoia is found in isolated groves, west slopes of Sierra Nevada from Placer to Tulare counties, 4,600 to 8,400 feet elevation. Wood is light and soft but not strong, and was once used in construction for shingles, etc.

Culture: Giant Sequoia is propagated from seeds which require two and one-half months stratification. Young plants should have some shade and protection during their first years of growth. With light shade and occasional watering, plants grow at a steady rate of about two to three feet per year. Giant Sequoia is highly ornamental with other conifers and with broadleafed trees. It is often planted with Coast Redwood for the striking contrast in their foliage pattern and color.

Estimate of Garden Value: This stately tree is attractive at all stages of its growth, especially in the early years when its typical, dense, conical shape is forming. In fifteen to twenty years it is a slender, well-formed tree of dark gray-green. It tolerates a greater range of altitude and temperature than the Coast Redwood. This redwood is most useful in large-scale planting, and has been used in parks, roadsides, golf courses, and large gardens. Colonies have been planted in certain mountain regions to add interest to native mixed forests.

GENUS *UMBELLULARIA:* CALIFORNIA BAY OR LAUREL
(Family Lauraceae: Laurel)

The one species in *Umbellularia* is native to California. The family has several well-known ornamental trees from various parts of the world. California Bay is also known as Bay Laurel or Pepperwood in the north coastal regions and as Myrtle in Oregon.

Umbellularia californica
California Bay or Laurel

HABIT: Evergreen, uniform outline, broad crown, sometimes a large, erect shrub, 30–45 m, 100–165 ft. (See Fig. 71.) FOLIAGE: Oblong, pointed, smooth, dark yellow-green, lustrous, of firm texture, distinctive aromatic fragrance. FLOWERS: Small, bisexual, in rounded umbels, yellow-green. December–May. FRUIT: Rounded drupe, cherrylike, green

Figure 71 *Umbellularia californica,* California Bay

and ripening to dark purple, containing stone, not edible. DISTRIBUTION: Common in canyons and valleys below 5,000 feet elevation, woods and forests of several communities, Coast Ranges, and Sierra Nevada from San Diego County to southwest Oregon.

Culture: Seeds of California Bay do not remain viable for very long. They should be planted fresh and will eventually sprout. Stratification is usually recommended to hasten or improve germination. Seeds may also be placed in plastic bags of moist peat moss until sprouted and then planted in large cans of friable soil. Plants are slow growing, seldom more than one foot per year. This tree is moisture tolerant, does best in deep, loamy soils, and is most luxuriant in the rich soils of the redwood belt. It will, however, accept less favorable conditions. The California Bay is uniform and neat in outline, and may be used as a large specimen, as hedge or windbreak, or clipped into various shapes for a formal garden. Occasionally it is used as a street tree with some thinning of inner branches for a more open effect.

Estimate of Garden Value: In spite of its slow growth rate, the California Bay is being more seriously considered as a cultivated tree, useful in large-scale landscaping, parks, and gardens. Old specimens have often been retained as a garden nucleus where they give shade and enhance other plantings. A few, which have attained tremendous girth and size, are held in high esteem and have been protected. Leaves from the California Bay are used to season food, and the hard, strong wood has been used in many ways. In pioneer times it was used for ship building, interior finish, and furniture. It is still used to make a wide variety of polished artifacts.

GENUS *WASHINGTONIA:* FAN PALM
(Family Palmae: Palm)

Of the two species of *Washingtonia,* one is native to California. The family is well known and widely distributed throughout the temperate climates of the world. California Fan Palm occurs in only a few favored places of southern California and is considered one of the most beautiful palms.

Washingtonia filifera
California Fan Palm

HABIT: Sturdy, unbranched trunk, tufts of large leaves at summit, growing from fibrous roots; trunk usually with thatch of dead leaves, 10–15 or 25 m, 35–50 or 85 ft. FOLIAGE: Large, fan-shaped, of many segments, gray-green, infolded and copiously fibrous. FLOWERS: Many small, whitish, all enclosed by a spathe, in large inflorescence. FRUIT: Berry, oval, hard and black, thin flesh surrounding large seed. DISTRIBUTION: In groves, alkaline spots of seeps, springs, and streams, west and north edge of Colorado Desert, Turtle Mountains, region of Twentynine Palms, eastward, and to Baja California.

Culture: California Fan Palm requires sun and summer water. It is propagated from fresh seed, planted in a friable soil mixture of sand, loam, and peat moss, or vermiculite and peat moss. Seed requires four to fifteen weeks for germination. Soil should be kept evenly moist, and bottom heat will aid in germination. Young plants should be protected from winds and from temperature changes. Seedlings may be shifted to four-inch pots, and later to gallon cans, and held until they are ready for permanent planting. Recent information suggests obtaining seeds from coyote droppings; close to 100 percent germination can be expected from seeds which have passed through the animals' digestive systems. This palm is not cold tolerant, although old, well-established plants are said to withstand low temperatures.

Estimate of Garden Value: Although this is considered to be a handsome palm, the thatch of dead leaves must be removed periodically. Plants are available from several nurseries in southern California, where it is used as a street tree, in parks, and on large estates. It has been used in the central valleys, but is most suitable to the southern coast and desert regions where moisture is available for most of the year.

ADDITIONAL COMMENTS

Besides those already described, there are other native trees with equally attractive features and with possibilities for use in landscaping. Several deciduous trees, especially, have certain outstanding seasonal features, such as flowers, bright fruits, or an interesting limb pattern in winter. The Red Elderberry *(Sambucus callicarpa)* is a well-known small tree of the north coast regions, but adaptable to other areas. Another candidate is Flowering Ash *(Fraxinus dipetala),* a slender, open tree with an abundance of feathery, greenish white flowers in spring followed by pendant clusters of samara fruits in late summer. Both accept water, pruning, and training, and have proven to be adaptable in botanic gardens.

The native Western Sycamore *(Platanus racemosa)* is greatly admired for its graceful branching and mottled trunks. (See Fig. 72.) Unfortunately, it is subject to several pests and a

Figure 72 *Platanus racemosa,* Western Sycamore

blight peculiar to the sycamores, although a breeding program may overcome this problem.

Over the years there has been interest in several of California's rare or unique needle leaf evergreens, such as the California Nutmeg *(Torreya californica),* the dark-needled Pacific Yew *(Taxus brevifolia),* and the rare Gowan Cypress *(Cupressus goveniana),* whose foliage has a pungent, lemony fragrance. These and others should have close attention and be tested under garden conditions for their possibilities in landscaping.

10. SUMMING UP

Many people are working toward bringing more of California's unusual flora into cultivation. A number of handsome shrub cultivars are now available and more are in the experimental stage. Howard McMinn, Lester Rowntree, and many others wrote glowingly of native plants and their possibilities in the 1930s and 1940s. For many of us the glow has continued undiminished. But in the meantime, the influx of population and its problems has kept us occupied, often to the detriment of the land and its proper uses. Two general trends have resulted. First is deep concern for the preservation of native plants with a consequent setting aside of lands on which typical, or endangered species may be safe from further encroachment. Second is a renewed and vital interest in learning more about propagation and cultivation of worthy wild plants and in using them to develop a western landscape style. In their efforts to preserve and to bring order to what has been accomplished in the past, groups of horticulturists, landscape architects, nurserymen, and gardeners meet for round table discussions and to compare experiences. Tentative judgments are made on the merits of some native plants which may have good qualities, but for which there is scant knowledge or testing under garden conditions. The records kept of this sharing of experiences may well become the basis for another book which would be of inestimable value to both novices and professional growers.

Following are some suggestions for future activity in native plant culture, summarizing some points already discussed in this book, and others concerned with methods or procedures for bringing more of California's fine flora into garden use.

1. First recognize that many of the native plants studied in the past were dug from the wilds, a practice which caused problems not necessarily present when the same plants are

propagated from seed. Conclusions about the ease or difficulty of growing plants should not be based on experiences with dug plants.

2. A whole host of plants can doubtless be improved in ornamental qualities as well as in garden response if the species or varieties are crossed, as has already been done with some.

3. For plants which are difficult to propagate, more intensive study and records of procedures are needed.

4. Professional methods of propagation should be used to reduce waste of propagating materials.

5. Larger and more complete collections of living native plants are necessary to provide stock at hand for hybridizing and for study under conditions of cultivation.

6. A complete handbook on propagation and culture of natives is needed, bringing together scattered information from articles, booklets, and other publications.

7. A clearinghouse of information is also greatly needed, and data-processing methods to compile and quickly retrieve accurate information.

8. With the possibility of reduced water supplies in some sections of the state, more attention should be given to drought-resistant plants, and more guidance should be provided for the development of hardy, self-sufficient gardens which will require a minimum of water and attention.

9. There is a need for demonstration gardens displaying specific uses of native plants, such as for hedges, windbreaks, ground covers, etc., and cultural practices such as pruning, training, watering, fertilizing, etc. Some of the botanic gardens have guided tours, and a few demonstrate plant propagation. This kind of program should be more widespread and frequent to reach newcomers who sometimes find native plant culture puzzling.

10. My personal wish is that there will soon be many more publications on how to grow and use native plants. There should be an up-to-date book on shrubs especially, as well as publications on each of the categories discussed in this book.

Like all who are close observers of native plants, I am greatly tempted to praise those that have desirable qualities but have not yet been tested under garden conditions. Every time I see a colony of Purdy's Fritillary *(Fritillaria purdyi)*, with its striking mottled bells, I yearn to see it as an accepted rock garden plant. Snugly at home in a rock crevice is Ridge Sandwort *(Arenaria nuttallii* ssp. *gregaria)*, an intricately branched perennial, appearing to be a piece of veiling liberally sprinkled with tiny white flowers. Many of our charming native plants are small and are hardly noticed by those attuned to showy dahlias and stalwart gladiolus. But in the proper setting and suitably companioned, native plants can greatly enhance special garden spots. Certain of the small bulbs have seldom been used in effective quantities or in the best setting. The White Globe Lily *(Calochortus albus)*, for example, was a prime favorite of many gardeners, including Willis Linn Jepson who used it on the jacket of his *Flowering Plants of California*. Praise was unstinting for the satiny white bells swinging gracefully on sturdy plants. But the temptation to speculate about untested plants must be resisted for now, since few of them are available and their cultural requirements are apt to be a mystery. Today professionals and home gardeners are finding new and exciting uses for native plants. Even more important, they want to learn how to make full use of California's wild plants.

LISTS OF NATIVE PLANTS BY
GARDEN REQUIREMENTS AND USES

The following lists group native plants which have similar garden requirements, and those noted for some special feature or specific garden use. All plants can be placed in one of four main categories, these being sun/dry, sun/water, shade/dry, and shade/water. However, very few will fit completely into just one category since practically every plant will accept conditions a few degrees each way from its presumed norm. Terms such as "drought resistant" and "shade loving" are sometimes relative to other garden conditions, and the term "semi-dry" is used to indicate that water may be necessary to get a plant established, but thereafter may be required only occasionally.

These lists are far from complete. They recapitulate the plants discussed in this book with a few additional ones in each category to indicate the wide choice available. Some lists are brief, such as those for dry shade, because there has been little testing under this combination of conditions. In the list for hedge and background plants, the figures for rate of growth and height are only approximate and may vary according to local conditions, soils, water, and fertilizer. Most useful are the situation categories from which the gardener may choose groupings of plants most apt to grow satisfactorily together.

Note: Throughout these lists, an asterisk (*) indicates that the plant is tolerant of conditions beyond that of the category in which it is placed. A cross (+) indicates that the plant is fully discussed elsewhere in the book.

SUN/DRY SITUATION

SPECIES	COMMON NAME	USES
Annuals		
Eschscholzia caespitosa+	Tufted Poppy	
E. californica+*	California Poppy	
E. lobbii	Lobb's Poppy	massed, borders
Layia chrysanthemoides+	Smooth Layia	
L. glandulosa+	White Layia	
L. pentachaeta+	Sierra Tidy Tips	
L. platyglossa+	Coastal Tidy Tips	
Linanthus androsaceus+*	False Baby Stars	
L. dianthiflorus+	Ground Pink	
L. montanus+	Mustang Linanthus	
Lupinus densiflorus+	Whitebowl Lupine	
Mentzelia lindleyi+	Blazing Star	
Mimulus bicolor+	Yellow and White Monkey Flower	
M. douglasii+	Purple Mouse-ears	
M. kelloggii+	Kellog's Monkey Flower	
M. layneae+*	Layne's Monkey Flower	
Monardella breweri+	Brewer's Monardella	
M. douglasii+	Fenestra Monardella	
M. exilis+	Desert Pennyroyal	
M. lanceolata+	Mustang Mint	
M. leucocephala	Merced Monardella	border, lean soil
Oenothera bistorta+	Southern Sun Cups	
O. deltoides ssp. *cognata*+	Fragrant Evening Primrose	
Salvia columbariae	Chia	borders, with bulbs
Stylomecon heterophylla+	Wind Poppy	
Perennials		
Agastache urticifolia	Horse Mint	also dry shade
Argemone munita	Prickly Poppy	border
Asclepias cordifolia+	Purple Milkweed	
A. solanoana	Creeping Milkweed	edging, slope

SUN/DRY SITUATION

Species	Common Name	Uses
Perennials (continued)		
Delphinium cardinale +	Cardinal Larkspur	
D. hesperium	Western Larkspur	mixed borders
D. luteum	Yellow Larkspur	mixed borders
D. nudicaule	Canyon Larkspur	rock garden
D. parryi	Parry's Larkspur	rock garden
Dicentra chrysantha +	Golden Ear Drops	
Dudleya pulverulenta +	Chalk Dudleya	
Eriogonum arborescens +	Island Buckwheat	
E. cinerum +	Ashyleaf Buckwheat	
E. fasciculatum	California Buckwheat	slope cover
E. giganteum +	St. Catherine's Lace	
E. grande var. *rubescens* +	Red Buckwheat	
E. lobbii +	Lobb's Buckwheat	
E. nudum +	Naked Buckwheat	
E. proliferum ssp. *strictum* +	Proliferous Buckwheat	
E. umbellatum var. *polyanthus* +	Sulphur Buckwheat	
Eriophyllum confertiflorum +	Yellow Yarrow	
E. lanatum ssp. *arachnoideum* +	Dwarf Woolly Sunflower	
E. nevinii	Catalina Silver Lace	borders
Erysimum capitatum +	Douglas Wallflower	
E. concinnum +	Pt. Reyes Wallflower	
E. menziesii	Menzie's Wallflower	border edge
Ipomopsis aggregata	Skyrocket Gilia	mixed borders
Lathyrus splendens	Campo Pea	vine, red flowers
Linanthus nuttallii	Nuttall's Linanthus	rock garden
*Lupinus albifrons**+	Silver Bush Lupine	
L. albifrons var. *flumineus*	Silver Circle Lupine	
L. formosus +	Summer Lupine	
L. leucophyllus	Felted Lupine	border
L. lyalli	Lyall's Lupine	rock garden

SUN/DRY SITUATION

Species	Common Name	Uses
Perennials (continued)		
Mimulus aurantiacus +	Sticky Monkey Flower	
M. clevelandii +	Cleveland's Monkey Flower	
M. longiflorus +	Southern Monkey Flower	
M. longiflorus var. *calycinus* +	Lemon Monkey Flower	
M. longiflorus var. *rutilus* +	Velvet Red Bush Monkey Flower	
M. puniceus +	Red Monkey Flower	
Monardella macrantha +	Red Monardella	
M. odoratissima +	Mountain Monardella	
M. villosa	Coyote Mint	
Oenothera caespitosa +	Tufted Evening Primrose	
Penstemon azureus +	Azure Penstemon	
P. bridgesii	Bridge's Penstemon	rock garden
P. centranthifolius +	Scarlet Bugler	
P. clevelandii +	Cleveland's Penstemon	
P. heterophyllus +	Foothill Penstemon	
P. heterophyllus ssp. *purdyi* +	Blue Bedder Penstemon	
P. heterophyllus ssp. *australis* +	Violet Penstemon	
P. palmeri +	Palmer's Penstemon	
P. parvulus +	Small Azure Penstemon	
P. speciosus	Sagebrush Penstemon	border, rock garden
P. spectabilis +	Royal Penstemon	
Romneya coulteri * +	Matilija Poppy	
R. trichocalyx * +	Ventura Poppy	
R. trichocalyx * × 'White Cloud' * +	cultivar	
Salvia clevelandii +	Cleveland's Sage	
S. dorrii	Great Basin Sage	borders, lean soil
S. leucophylla	Purple Sage	mixed border
S. munzii	Munz's Sage	mixed border
S. sonomensis +	Creeping Sage	

SUN/DRY SITUATION

Species	Common Name	Uses
Perennials (continued)		
Sphaeralcea ambigua	Desert Mallow	border, slopes
Solidago californica	California Goldenrod	border, lean soil
Thermopsis montana	Mountain False Lupine	with penstemon border
Wyethia angustifolia	Narrowleaf Mule Ears	
Zauschneria californica +	California Fuchsia	
Z. cana	Hoary California Fuchsia	dry banks
Bulbs		
Allium crispum +	Crinkled Onion	
A. falcifolium	Sickleleaf Onion	border, lean soil
A. fimbriatum	Fringed Onion	border, lean soil
A. praecox	Early Onion	border, lean soil
A. serratum +	Pom-pon Onion	
Bloomeria crocea +	Golden Stars	
Brodiaea bridgesii +	Bridge's Triteleia	
B. californica +	California Brodiaea	
B. coronaria +	Harvest Brodiaea	
B. elegans +	Elegant Brodiaea	
B. ida-maia	Firecracker Flower	border, lean soil
B. lutea +	Pretty Face	
B. pulchella +	Blue Dicks	
B. venusta	Rose Firecracker Flower	lean soil
Calochortus kennedyi	Kennedy's Mariposa Tulip	desert, specimen
C. luteus +	Gold Nuggets	
C. macrocarpus	Sagebrush Mariposa	lava soil
C. splendens +	Splendid Mariposa Tulip	
C. venustus +	White Mariposa Lily	
C. vestae +	Goddess Mariposa Tulip	
Chlorogalum pomeridianum +	Soap Plant	
*Fritillaria pudica +**	Yellow Bells	
F. recurva +	Scarlet Fritillary	
*Lilium washingtonianum +**	Washington Lily	
Zigadenus fremontii +	Fremont's Camas	

SUN/DRY SITUATION

Species	*Common Name*	*Uses*

Shrubs

Acalypha californica	California Copperleaf	filler
Adenostoma fasciculatum	Chamise	filler
A. sparsifolium	Red Shanks	specimen
Arctostaphylos, most species when established, exceptions noted in other lists.		
Artemesia californica	California Sagebrush	hedge, divider
A. pycnocephala	Beach Sagewort	hedge, divider
Atriplex lentiformis ssp. *breweri*	Quail Bush	hedge, divider
Baccharis pilularis +	Dwarf Chaparral Broom	
Beloperone californica +	Chuparosa	
Berberis dictyota (Mahonia)	California Barberry	facer, edger
B. nevinii + (Mahonia)	Nevin Barberry	
B. pinnata + (Mahonia)	Shinyleaf Barberry	
Ceanothus, most species when established, exceptions noted in other lists.		
Cercis occidentalis +	Redbud	
Cercocarpus betuloides* +	California Mountain Mahogany	
C. betuloides var. *blamcheae +*	Alderleaf Mountain Mahogany	
C. betuloides var. *traskiae*	Island Mountain Mahogany	small tree, background
C. ledifolius	Desert Mountain Mahogany	small tree, filler
Chamaebatiaria millefolium	Fern Bush	specimen, shrub, group
Cneoridium dumosum	Berryrue	hedge, border
Comarostaphylis diversifolia +	Summer Holly	
Cowania mexicana var. *stansburiana*	Cliff Rose	facer, slope, cover, walls
Dendromecon harfordii +	Island Tree Poppy	
D. rigida +	Bush Poppy	

SUN/DRY SITUATION

Species	Common Name	Uses
Shrubs (continued)		
Encelia farinosa+	Brittlebush	
Fremontodendron californicum+	California Fremontia	
F. californicum ssp. *decumbens*	Spreading Fremontia	edging
F. californicum ssp. *napensis*+	Napa Fremontia	
Fremontodendron mexicanum+	Southern Fremontia	
Galvezia speciosa*	Bush Snapdragon	coastal slopes
Garrya elliptica*+	Coast Silktassel	
G. elliptica 'James Roof'+	cultivar	
G. veatchii	Veatch's Silktassel	winter display
Haplopappus linearifolia	Narrowleaf Goldenbush	mix border
Heteromeles arbutifolia+	Toyon	
Isomeris arborea	Bladder Pod	mix border
Leptodactylon californicum	Prickly Phlox	rock garden edging
Nolina parryi+	Parry's Nolina	
Pickeringia montana	Chaparral Pea	shrub border
Prunus ilicifolia*+	Hollyleaf Cherry	
P. lyonii	Catalina Cherry	
P. subcordata	Sierra Plum	deciduous shrub, mixture
Purshia tridentata	Antelope Brush	filler
Rhamnus californica+	California Coffeeberry	
R. californica+ var. *crassifolia*+	Velvetleaf Coffeeberry	
R. californica+ var. *tomentella*+	Chaparral Coffeeberry	
R. californica+ 'Eve Case'+	cultivar	
R. californica+ 'Sea View'+	cultivar	
Rhamnus crocea+	Redberry	
R. crocea + var. *ilicifolia*+	Hollyleaf Redberry	

SUN/DRY SITUATION

Species	Common Name	Uses
Shrubs (continued)		
Rhus integrifolia+	Lemonade Berry	
R. laurina+	Laurel Sumac	
R. ovata+	Sugar Bush	
R. trilobata	Squaw Bush	filler, orange berries
Simmondsia chinensis +	Jojoba	oil-bearing nuts
Trichostema lanatum+	Woolly Blue Curls	
Yucca whipplei+	Our Lord's Candle	
Trees		
Abies bracteata*+	Bristlecone Fir	
Acacia farnesiana	Sweet Acacia	desert, specimen
Aesculus californica+	California Buckeye	
Arbutus menziesii+	Madrone	
Calocedrus decurrens*+	Incense Cedar	
Cercidium floridum	Palo Verde	desert, specimen
Cupressus forbesii+	Tecate Cypress	
C. macnabiana	Macnab Cypress	specimen
C. macrocarpa+	Monterey Cypress	
C. sargentii	Sargent Cypress	specimen, background
Juniperus californica+	California Juniper	
Lyonothamnus floribundus ssp. *asplenifolius+**	Fernleaf Ironwood	
Pinus attenuata+	Knobcone Pine	background
P. coulteri+	Coulter Pine	
P. edulis	Nut Pine	specimen
P. ponderosa	Yellow Pine	street, parks
P. sabiniana	Digger Pine	street, parks
P. torreyana	Torrey Pine	specimen
Prunus lyonii+	Catalina Cherry	
Pseudotsuga macrocarpa+	Bigcone Spruce	
Quercus agrifolia+	Coast Live Oak	
Q. chrysolepis	Canyon Oak	large garden, parks, street
Q. douglasii	Blue Oak	background

SUN/DRY SITUATION

Species	Common Name	Uses

Trees (continued)

Q. engelmannii +	Engelmann Oak	
Q. garryana	Garry Oak	background
Q. kelloggii +	California Black Oak	
Q. wislizenii var. *wislizenii*	Interior Live Oak	parks, street
Sequoiadendron giganteum * +	Giant Sequoia	

SUN/WATER SITUATION

SPECIES	COMMON NAME	USES

Annuals

Abronia villosa +	Desert Sand Verbena	
Clarkia amoena +	Herald-of-Summer	
C. amoena + ssp. *whitneyi* +	Large-Flowered Clarkia	
C. deflexa +	Punchbowl Clarkia	
C. dudleyana +	Dudley's Clarkia	
C. purpurea ssp. *viminae* +	Purple Clarkia	
C. rubicunda	Ruby Chalice Clarkia	borders
C. unguiculata +	Elegant Clarkia	
Collinsia sparsiflora *	Few-Flowered Collinsia	massed
Coreopsis calliopsidea +	Leafystem Coreopsis	
C. douglasii +	Douglas's Coreopsis	
C. stillmanii +	Stillman's Coreopsis	
Downingia concolor +	Fringed Downingia	
D. cuspidata +	Toothed Downingia	
Gilia achillaefolia +	California Gilia	
G. capitata +	Blue-Headed Gilia	
G. tricolor +	Birds-Eye Gilia	
Lupinus bicolor +	Miniature Lupine	
L. nanus +	Douglas's Lupine	
L. subvexus +	Valley Lupine	
L. succulentus +	Arroyo Lupine	

SUN/WATER SITUATION

Species	Common Name	Uses
Annuals (continued)		
Nemophila maculata +	Fivespot	
N. menziesii +	Baby Blue-Eyes	
Phacelia campanularia +*	Desert Bells	
P. ciliata +	Chinese Lantern Phacelia	
P. minor +	California Bells	
P. parryi +*	Parry's Phacelia	
P. tanacetifolia +	Tansy Phacelia	
P. viscida +*	Sticky Phacelia	
Platystemon californicus +	Cream Cups	

Species	Common Name	Uses
Perennials		
Abronia latifolia +	Yellow Sand Verbena	
A. umbellata +	Pink Sand Verbena	
Achillea lanulosa	Woolly Yarrow	mixed borders
Arabis blepharophylla +	Rose Rock Cress	
Aralia californica	California Spikenard	specimen
Armeria maritima var. *californica*	Sea Thrift	mixed borders
Aster adscendens	Narrow-Leaved Aster	borders
A. alpigenus ssp. *andersonii*	Alpine Aster	wet borders
A. chilensis	Chilean Aster	wet border
Asclepias speciosa +	Butterfly Weed	
Caltha howellii	Marsh Marigold	pool edge
Coreopsis gigantea	Tree Coreopsis	specimen
C. maritima +	Sea Dahlia	
Delphinium glaucum	Tower Delphinium	borders
Dodecatheon jeffreyi	Jeffrey's Shooting Star	borders
Erigeron glaucus	Seaside Daisy	mixed border
Epilobium angustifolium	Red Fireweed	mixed border
Fragaria chilensis	Beach Strawberry	ground cover
Helenium bigelovii	Bigelow's Sneezeweed	wet border

SUN/WATER SITUATION

Species	Common Name	Uses
Perennials (continued)		
Iris longipetala +	Long-Petaled Iris	
I. missouriensis +	Rocky Mountain Iris	
I. munzii +	Munz' Iris	
Lobelia cardinalis +	Scarlet Lobelia	
Lupinus latifolius + *	Broadleaf Lupine	
L. latifolius + * ssp. *parishii* +	Canyon Lupine	
L. polyphyllus +	Blue-Pod Lupine	
Mimulus bifidus + *	Azalea-Flowered Monkey Flower	
M. cardinalis +	Scarlet Monkey Flower	
M. guttatus +	Common Monkey Flower	
M. primuloides +	Primrose Monkey Flower	
Parnassia californica	Smooth Grass-of-Parnassus	wet border
Penstemon gracilentus +	Slender Penstemon	
P. procerus +	Pincushion Penstemon	
Rudbeckia californica	Cone Flower	background
Salvia spathacea +	Hummingbird Sage	wet border
Satureja douglasii	Yerba Buena	open cover
Scutellaria siphocamyploides	Narrowleaf Skullcap	ground cover
Sisyrinchium bellum +	California Blue-Eyed Grass	
S. californicum +	Golden-Eyed Grass	
Venegasia carpesioides	Canyon Sunflower	border
Viola adunca	Western Dog Violet	edging
V. pedunculata *	California Golden Violet	edging
V. purpurea *	Mountain Violet	rock garden

Bulbs

Allium unifolium +	Pink Meadow Onion	
A. validum +	Swamp Onion	

SUN/WATER SITUATION

Species	Common Name	Uses
Bulbs (continued)		
Brodiaea hyacinthina+	White Brodiaea	
B. laxa	Ithuriel's Spear	
B. peduncularis+	Long-Rayed Hyacinth	
Calochortus nudus*	Naked Cat's Ear	border edging
C. uniflorus+	Pink Star Tulip	
Camassia leichtlini+	Blue Camas	
C. quamash ssp. *linearis+*	Common Camas	
Fritillaria lilaceae+	White Fritillary	
F. pluriflora+	Adobe Lily	
F. pudica+*	Yellow Bells	
Shrubs		
Amelanchier pallida+	Pallid Service Berry	
Arctostaphylos densiflora 'Howard McMinn'+	cultivar	
Arctostaphylos densiflora 'James West'+	cultivar	
Arctostaphylos densiflora 'Sentinel'+	cultivar	
Carpenteria californica+	Tree Anemone	
Ceanothus papillosus var. *roweanus* × *impressus* 'Concha'	cultivar	dark blue flowers, rugose leaves
C. foliosus var. *vineatus*	Vine Hill Ceanothus	filler, slopes
C. 'Gentian Plume'	cultivar	filler, background
C. griseus+	Carmel Ceanothus	
C. impressus 'Puget Blue'	cultivar	bright, dark blue flowers
C. integerrimus+	Deer Brush	
C. thyrsiflorus+	Blue Blossom	
Cephalanthus occidentalis	Buttonwillow	filler
Chiliopsis linearis+	Desert Willow	
Garrya buxifolia*	Boxleaf Garrya	divider, low hedge

SUN/WATER SITUATION

Species	Common Name	Uses
Shrubs (continued)		
Holodiscus boursieri+	Mountain Cream Bush	
Keckiella antirrhinoides	Yellow Beard-Tongue	filler
K. cordifolia+	Honeysuckle Penstemon	
*Osmaronia cerasiformis**	Oso-Berry	filler
Philadelphus lewisii var. *californicus* (See Pl. 2B)	California Mock Orange	filler
Physocarpus capitatus	Ninebark	facer
Prunus virginiana var. *demissa*	Western Chokecherry	specimen
Ptelea baldwinii var. *crenulata*	Hop Tree	specimen, fragrant flowers
Rhamnus rubra+	Sierra Coffeeberry	
Ribes aureum+	Golden Currant	
R. indecorum	White-Flowered Currant	early flowers
R. sanguineum+	Red Flowering Currant	
R. sanguineum+ var. *glutinosum+*	Pink Flowering Currant	
Spiraea douglasii	Douglas Spiraea	facer
Styrax officinalis var. *californica+*	California Snowdrop Bush	
S. officinalis var. *fulvescens*	Southern Snowdrop Bush	
Trees		
Acer negundo var. *californicum+*	Box Elder	
Betula occidentalis	Water Birch	specimen
Chamaecyparis lawsoniana+	Lawson Cypress	
Fraxinus dipetala	Foothill Ash	filler
F. latifolia	Oregon Ash	background
Picea sitchensis+	Sitka Spruce	

SUN/WATER SITUATION

Species	Common Name	Uses

Trees (continued)

Platanus racemosa	Western Sycamore	specimen
Populus fremontii	Fremont Poplar	filler
*P. tremuloides**	Quaking Aspen	specimen
P. trichocarpa	Black Cottonwood	large specimen
Pseudotsuga macrocarpa+	Bigcone Spruce	
P. menziesii+	Douglas Fir	
Sambucus callicarpa	Red Elderberry	filler
S. caerulea	Blue Elderberry	
Sequoia sempervirens+	Coast Redwood	
Washingtonia filifera+	California Fan Palm	

SHADE/DRY SITUATION

SPECIES	COMMON NAME	USES

Perennials

Dodecatheon hendersonii+*	Henderson's Shooting Star	
Fragaria californica+*	California Strawberry	
*Frasera albicaulis**	Whitestem Frasera	borders
*Heuchera maxima**+	Island Heuchera	
*H. maxima** +× *H. sanguinea* 'Santa Ana Cardinal'+*	cultivar	
H. micrantha+*	Crevice Heuchera	
Iris fernaldii+*	Fernald's Iris	
I. hartwegii+	Hartweg's Iris	
I. hartwegii ssp. *australis*+	Southern Hartweg's Iris	
I. macrosiphon+*	Bowl-Tubed Iris	
I. tenuissima+	Slender Iris	
Lepechina calycina	Pitcher Sage	border

SHADE/DRY SITUATION

Species	Common Name	Uses

Perennials (continued)

Species	Common Name	Uses
Lupinus latifolius + *	Broadleaf Lupine	
L. latifolius + * var. parishii* *	Canyon Lupine	border
Paeonia brownii *	Western Peony	border, cut foliage
Polypodium californicum *	California Polypody	mixer
Silene californica + *	California Indian Pink	
S. hookeri +	Hooker's Indian Pink	
S. hookeri ssp. bolanderi* *	Bolander's Indian Pink	rock garden

Bulbs

Species	Common Name	Uses
Brodiaea ida-maia +	Firecracker Flower	
Fritillaria biflora +	Chocolate Lily	
Lilium washingtonianum +	Washington Lily	
L. washingtonianum var. purpurascens +*	Cascade Lily	

Shrubs

Species	Common Name	Uses
Arctostaphylos nummularia +	Glossyleaf Manzanita	
A. nummularia + var. sensitiva*	Littleberry Manzanita	low hedge
A. hookeri +	Monterey Manzanita	
Berberis pinnata +	Shinyleaf Barberry	
Ribes speciosum + *	Fuchsia-Flowered Gooseberry	
R. viburnifolium + *	Evergreen Currant	
Symphoricarpos mollis *	Trailing Snowberry	slope cover
S. rivularis *	Common Snowberry	filler

Trees

Species	Common Name	Uses
Quercus wislizenii + *	Interior Live Oak	
Sequoiadendron giganteum + *	Giant Sequoia	

SHADE/WATER SITUATION

SPECIES	COMMON NAME	USES
Annuals		
Clarkia concinna+	Red Ribbons	
Collinsia heterophylla+	Purple Chinese Houses	
*C. grandiflora**	Blue Lips	massed, border
*Pholistoma auritum**	Fiesta Flower	border
Perennials		
*Aconitum columbianum**	Monkshood	mixed border
Acteae spicata var. *arguta+*	Western Red Baneberry	
Adiantum capillus-veneris+	Venus Hair Fern	woodlands, borders
A. pedatum var. *aleuticum+*	Five-Finger Fern	
Anemone deltoidea	Glade Anemone	woodland garden
Aquilegia exima+	Van Houtte's Columbine	border
A. formosa+	Red Columbine	
*Aruncus vulgaris**	Goat's Beard	moist woods
Asarum caudatum+	Long-Tailed Ginger	
A. hartwegii+	Hartweg's Wild Ginger	
Athyrium filix-femina var. *californicum*	Lady Fern	woodland garden
Boykinia major	Mountain Boykinia	woodland garden
Clintonia andrewsiana+	Andrew's Clintonia	
C. uniflora	Queen Cup	woods, acid soil
Cynoglossum grande+	Grand Hound's Tongue	
Dicentra formosa+	Pacific Bleeding Heart	
*Disporum hookeri**	Hooker's Fairybells	facer, woods
D. smithii	Smith's Fairybells	facer, woods
Goodyera oblongifolia	Rattlesnake Orchid	woodland garden
Iris douglasiana+	Douglas Iris	
I. innominata	Golden Iris	

SHADE/WATER SITUATION

Species	Common Name	Uses

Perennials (continued)

Linnaea borealis ssp. *longiflora*	Twin Flower	ground cover
*Lithophragma affinis**	Woodland Star	woodland garden
*L. tenella**	Pink Woodland Star	woodland garden
*Mimulus lewisii**	Lewis Mimulus	
Mitella diversifolia	Varied Leaf Mitella	woods border
Oxalis oregana	Redwood Sorrel	ground cover
Polypodium californicum	California Polypody	woods
Polystichum munitum	Western Sword Fern	background
Smilacina racemosa var. *amplexicaulis*	Branched Solomon's Seal	facer (see Pl. 3E)
S. stellata	Star Solomon's Seal	facer
Synthyris rotundifolia	Round-Leaf Synthyris	woods border
Tellima grandiflora	Fringe Cups	woods border
Trientalis latifolia	Pacific Starflower	ground cover
Trillium chloropetalum+	Giant Trillium	
T. ovatum+	Western Trillium	
Vancouveria chrysantha+	Golden Inside-Out Flower	
V. hexandra+	Northern Inside-Out Flower	
V. planipetala+	Redwood Inside-Out Flower	
Viola sempervirens	Redwood Violet	woods garden
Woodwardia fimbriata	Giant Chain Fern	background

Bulbs

Calochortus albus+	White Fairy Lantern	
C. amabilis+*	Golden Fairy Lantern	
C. amoenus+	Rose Fairy Lantern	
C. tolmiei+*	Tolmie's Pussy Ears	
C. uniflorus+*	Pink Star Tulip	
Erythronium californicum+	California Fawn Lily	
E. helenae+	Helen's Fawn Lily	
E. hendersonii+	Henderson's Fawn Lily	
E. multiscapoideum+	Hartweg's Fawn Lily	

SHADE/WATER SITUATION

Species	Common Name	Uses
Bulbs (continued)		
E. revolutum	Coast Fawn Lily	woods border
*E. tuolumnense +**	Tuolumne Fawn Lily	
Fritillaria atropurpurea +	Spotted Mountain Bells	
*F. lanceolata +**	Mission Bells	
*Lilium humboldtii +**	Humboldt Lily	
*L. humboldtii +** var. *bloomerianum +*	Bloomer's Tiger Lily	
*L. maritimum**	Coast Lily	border
L. pardalinum +	Leopard Lily	
*L. parryi +**	Lemon Lily	
*L. parvum**	Alpine Lily	border
Shrubs		
Arctostaphylos edmundsii +	Little Sur Manzanita	
A. hookeri ssp. *franciscana**	San Francisco Manzanita	rockery
A. uva-ursi var. *coactilis*	Sierra Bearberry	slopes
A. uva-ursi 'Radiant' +	cultivar	
Berberis aquifolium +	Oregon Grape	
B. nervosa +	Longleaf Barberry	
Calycanthus occidentalis +	Spice Bush	
Cornus glabrata +	Smooth Dogwood	
C. occidentalis +	Western Dogwood	
C. sessilis +	Black Fruit Dogwood	
C. stolonifera +	American Dogwood	
Corylus cornuta var. *californica +*	California Hazelnut	
Euonymous occidentalis	Western Burning Bush	shrub group
Gaultheria humifusa	Wintergreen	rock garden
G. ovatifolia	Western Teaberry	rock garden
G. shallon +	Salal	
Holodiscus bouriseri	Mountain Cream Bush	facer
*H. discolor +**	Cream Bush	

SHADE/WATER SITUATION

Species	Common Name	Uses
Shrubs (continued)		
Ledum glandulosum	Labrador Tea	acid, humus
Lonicera involucrata	Twinberry	filler
Paxistima myrsinites	Oregon Boxwood	low divider
Rhododendron macrophyllum	California Rhododendron	specimen
R. occidentalis	Western Azalea	specimen (see Pl. 6B)
*Rubus parviflorus**	Thimbleberry	shrub group
R. spectabilis	Salmonberry	shrub group
*Rhamnus purshiana+**	Cascara Sagrada	
Symphoricarpos rivularis	Common Snowberry	shrub group
Vaccinium ovatum+	California Huckleberry	natural garden
V. parvifolium	Red Huckleberry	filler

Trees

Abies concolor+	California White Fir	
A. grandis	Grand Fir	large scale landscaping
Acer circinatum+	Vine Maple	
A. glabrum	Sierra Maple	shelter, water
A. macrophyllum+	Bigleaf Maple	
Alnus rhombifolia+	White Alder	
A. tenuifolia	Mountain Alder	background
Cornus nuttallii	Sierra Dogwood	sheltered area
*Lithocarpus densiflora**	Tanbark Oak	specimen
Picea sitchensis+	Sitka Spruce	
*Quercus lobata**	Valley Oak	specimen
Sequoia sempervirens+	Coast Redwood	
Sorbus cascadensis	Cascade Mountain Ash	shelter
Taxus brevifolia	Western Yew	shelter
Torreya californica	California Nutmeg	background
*Umbellularia californica+**	California Bay	

HEDGES, DIVIDERS, OR WINDBREAKS

SPECIES	COMMON NAME	USES, GROWTH PATTERN
Arctostaphylos densiflora	Sonoma Manzanita	divider, 1-3 ft
A. nummularia var. *sensitiva*	Littleberry Manzanita	divider, 1-2 ft
Artemesia californica	California Sagebrush	clip for dense growth
A. pycnocephala	Beach Sagewort	clip for dense growth
Atriplex lentiformis ssp. *breweri*	Quail Bush	low hedge, 3-5 ft
Berberis nevinii	Nevin's Barberry	hedge, 3-6 ft
Ceanothus impressus	Santa Barbara Ceanothus	3-6 ft
C. thyrsiflorus	Blue Blossom	divider, prune tall
C. verrucosus	Wartystem Ceanothus	rapid, 2-3 ft
Cercocarpus most species	mountain mahoganies	clip to suit
Chamaecyparis lawsoniana	Lawson Cypress	dense, slow growth
Comarostaphylos diversifolia	Summer Holly	divider, tall
Fouquieria splendens	Ocotillo	living fence, to 6 ft
Garrya buxifolia	Box-Leaf Silk-Tassel	slow, 2-3 ft
G. elliptica	Coast Silk-Tassel	rapid, 5-10 ft
Heteromeles arbutifolia	Toyon	tall, prune to suit
Juniperus californica	California Juniper	dense, 20-25 ft
Myrica californica	Pacific Wax Myrtle	rapid, 7 ft or more
Prunus ilicifolia	Hollyleaf Cherry	rapid, prune twice yearly
Rhamnus californica	California Coffeeberry	moderate, 3-5 ft
Rhus integrifolia	Lemonade Berry	moderate, 3-7 ft

GROUND COVERS

The native plants suggested in the following list should not be considered as lawn substitutes, but as hardy plants to give a uniform cover with much less attention, water, and fertilizer than grass. Most will require water to get thoroughly established, followed by several deep waterings during dry periods. The kinds of plants which can be used for ground covers vary widely, from the delicate Twinflower to the tough and often rampant zauschnerias. Little testing has been done on natives which have possibilities as ground, slope, or bank covers. Some of the most handsome, such as Squaw Carpet, grow with frustrating slowness and do not always persist under garden conditions. Experimentation is also needed for some of the low, shrubby-based perennials, or sub-shrubs; there is little information on their persistence, rate of spread, and appearance through the seasons. California Buckwheat has been seeded thickly on large areas and road cuts for massed effects and as a soil binder. There are certainly other native plants equally useful. Drought-tolerant and firm-leaved ground covers tend to complement California's trees, shrubs, and many perennials and, in most circumstances, are more in keeping with the natural landscape than lawns.

SPECIES	COMMON NAME	DESCRIPTION
Perennials		
Sun/Dry Situation		
Eriogonum fasciculatum	California Buckwheat	massed
E. grande var. *rubescens* +	Red Buckwheat	
Lotus argophyllus	Silver Lotus	silvery cover
Monardella macrantha +	Large-Flowered Monardella	
M. odoratissima +*	Mountain Monardella	
M. villosa +	Coyote Mint	
Zauschneria californica +	Hummingbird Trumpet	
Sun With Moderate Amounts of Water		
Abronia latifolia +	Yellow Sand Verbena	
A. umbellata +	Pink Sand Verbena	
Eriophyllum lanatum var. *arachnoideum* +	Dwarf Woolly Sunflower	
*Fragaria californica**	California Strawberry	cover, woods
F. chiloensis	Beach Strawberry	open cover
*Leptodactylon californicum**	Prickly Phlox	slopes, rocks, short lived

GROUND COVERS

Species	Common Name	Description
Perennials (continued)		
Shade With Water		
Asarum caudatum +	Long-Tailed Ginger	
A. hartwegii +	Hartweg's Ginger	
Linnaea borealis spp. *longiflora*	Western Twin Flower	delicate cover
Satureja douglasii * +	Yerba Buena	
Vancouveria chrysantha +	Golden Inside-Out Flower	
V. hexandra +	Northern Inside-Out Flower	
V. planipetala +	Redwood Inside-Out Flower	
Whipplea modesta *	Modesty Flower	trailing, deciduous

Shrubs
Sun/Dry Situation

Species	Common Name	Description
Arctostaphylos hookeri +	Monterey Manzanita	
A. nevadensis *	Pinemat Manzanita	spreads widely
Baccharis pilularis 'Pigeon Point' +	cultivar	
B. pilularis 'Twin Peaks' +	cultivar	
Ceanothus gloriosus var. *porrectus* +	Dwarf Pt. Reyes Ceanothus	
C. hearstiorum	Hearst Ceanothus	low, dense, rapid
C. prostratus var. *occidentalis* +	Western Squaw Carpet	flat, spreading
C. rigidus var. *albus* 'Snowball'	cultivar	dense, not rooting

Sun With Moderate Amounts of Water

Species	Common Name	Description
Arctostaphylos densiflora + 'James West'	cultivar	
A. 'Emerald Carpet'	cultivar, thought to be derived from *nummularia* × *ura-ursi*	low, spreading, rich green

GROUND COVERS

Species	Common Name	Description

Shrubs (continued)

Species	Common Name	Description
A. hookeri 'Monterey Carpet'	cultivar	compact cover
A. 'Ophio-viridis'*	cultivar of uncertain hybrid origin	patterned ground cover
Ceanothus gloriosus+	Pt. Reyes Ceanothus	
C. griseus horizontalis 'Yankee Point'+	cultivar	
C. maritimus	Maritime Ceanothus	carpeting
C. papillosus 'Joyce Coulter'+	cultivar	
Rhamnus californica 'Sea View'+	cultivar	
R. rubra*	Sierra Coffeeberry	draping to erect

Shade With Moderate Amounts of Water

Species	Common Name	Description
Arctostaphylos glandulosa var. cushingiana+	Huckleberry Manzanita	
A. uva-ursi 'Pt. Reyes'*	cultivar	creeping carpet
A. uva-ursi 'Radiant'+	cultivar	
Berberis repens*	Creeping Barberry	open cover
Ceanothus foliosus var. vineatus+	Vine Hill Ceanothus	
Gaultheria shallon+	Salal	
Ribes viburnifolium	Evergreen Currant	

NATIVE PLANTS WITH COLORFUL FRUITS

SPECIES	COMMON NAME	FRUIT COLOR
Actaea rubra ssp. arguta	Western Red Baneberry	shiny red berry
Amelanchier pallida	Pallid Service Berry	purple pome
Aralia californica	California Aralia	purple-black berries

NATIVE PLANTS WITH COLORFUL FRUITS

Species	Common Name	Fruit Color
Arbutus menziesii	Madrone	granular orange-red berry
Arctostaphylos	Manzanita	red, brown, or mahogany berry
Berberis aquifolium	Oregon Grape	dark blue berry
B. nervosa	Longleaf Barberry	dark blue berry
B. nevinii	Nevin's Barberry	orange-red berry
Comarostaphylos diversifolia	Summer Holly	globose red drupe
Cornus glabrata	Smooth Dogwood	slate-blue drupe
C. nuttallii	Mountain Dogwood	scarlet drupe
C. occidentalis	Creek Dogwood	white drupe
Disporum hookeri	Hooker's Fairybell	scarlet berry
Forestiera neomexicana	Desert Olive	blue-black drupe
Garrya elliptica	Coast Silk Tassel	whitish berry
G. fremontii	Fremont Silk Tassel	purplish berry
Gaultheria shallon	Salal	purple, berry-like capsule
Heteromeles arbutifolia	Toyon	red berry
Lonicera ciliosa	Orange Honeysuckle	orange-red berry
L. involucrata	Black Twinberry	shiny black berry
Osmaronia cerasiformis	Oso Berry	black drupe
Prunus emarginata	Bitter Cherry	small, bright red cherry
P. ilicifolia	Hollyleaf Cherry	purple-black drupe
P. subcordata	Sierra Plum	crimson plum
P. virginiana var. *demissa*	Western Choke-Cherry	ruby red cherry
Rhamnus californica	California Coffeeberry	black, berrylike drupe
R. californica var. *crassifolia*	Velvet-Leaved Coffeeberry	black berrylike drupe
Rhamnus crocea	Redberry	red berry
R. crocea ssp. *ilicifolia*	Hollyleaf Redberry	red berry
Rhus integrifolia	Lemonade Berry	reddish drupe
R. ovata	Sugar Bush	reddish drupe
R. trilobata	Squaw Bush	orange-red drupe

NATIVE PLANTS WITH COLORFUL FRUITS

Species	Common Name	Fruit Color
Ribes aureum	Golden Currant	red or black berry
R. malvaceum	Chaparral Currant	purple-black berry
R. speciosum	Fuchsia-Flowered Gooseberry	garnet red berry
Rosa californica	California Rose	red hip
R. gymnocarpa	Wood Rose	ovoid red hip
Rubus parviflorus	Thimbleberry	aggregate fruit, red
R. spectabilis	Salmonberry	aggregate fruit, red or salmon
Sambucus callicarpa	Red Elderberry	red drupe
S. caerulea	Blue Elderberry	blue-black drupe
Smilacina racemosa var. amplexicaulis	Branched Solomon's Seal	spotted red berry
Sorbus cascadensis	Cascade Mountain Ash	red pome

NATIVE PLANTS FOR DESERT REGIONS

Any desert plant that is available, or can be grown from seeds or cuttings, and suits the garden design, should be used. Most desert plants grow in sandy soils, but will benefit from the addition of organic materials that aid in water-holding capacity and add some fertility. Their natural habitat should be followed, and those marked with an asterisk (*) in the following list need occasional watering during the heat of summer. Any local cactus which is suitable to the garden may be used, but cacti are subject to root rot and should be watered sparingly.

SPECIES	COMMON NAME	USES AND CHARACTERISTICS
Annuals		
Abronia villosa+	Desert Sand Verbena	
Coreopsis bigelovii	Bigelow's Coreopsis	large yellow flowers
Gilia aurea	Golden Gilia	yellow flowers
G. dichotoma	Evening Snow	white flowers
G. parryae	Parry's Gilia	purple to violet flowers

NATIVE PLANTS FOR DESERT REGIONS

Species	Common Name	Uses and Characteristics
Annuals (continued)		
Layia glandulosa+	White Layia	
Mohavea confertiflora	Ghost Flower	pale yellow
Oenothera deltoides	Bird-Cage Evening Primrose	borders
Phacelia campanularia	Desert Bells	
P. fremontii	Fremont's Phacelia	lavender-violet
P. parryi	Parry's Phacelia	purple-violet
Perennials		
Agave deserti	Desert Century Plant	accent
Astragalus coccineus	Scarlet Locoweed	difficult to grow
Nolina parryi*	Parry's Nolina	accent
Oenothera primiveris	Large Yellow Primrose	borders
Penstemon eatonii*	Eaton's Penstemon	background
P. palmeri+	Palmer's Penstemon	
Sphaeralcea ambigua	Desert Mallow	border
Stanleya pinnata	Desert Plume	background
Shrubs		
Berberis fremontii	Desert Barberry	screen, specimen
B. nevinii+	Nevin's Barberry	
Chilopsis linearis+*	Desert Willow	
Cowania mexicana var. *stansburiana*	Cliffrose	white flowers
Encelia farinosa	Brittlebush	yellow daisies
Fallugia paradoxa	Apache Plume	white flowers, plumy seeds
Fouquieria splendens	Ocotillo	hedge, background
Isomeris arborea*	Bladder-Pod	borders
Prosopis pubescens	Screw-Bean	deciduous shrub
Prunus lyonii+*	Catalina Cherry	
Simmondsia chinensis+	Jojoba	
Yucca whipplei	Our Lord's Candle	bold accent

NATIVE PLANTS FOR DESERT REGIONS

Species	Common Name	Uses and Characteristics
Trees		
Acacia farnesiana	Sweet Acacia	deciduous, background
*Cercidium floridum**	Palo Verde	yellow flowers
Fraxinus velutina var. *coriacea**	Leatherleaf Ash	shade tree
Juniperus californica	California Juniper	specimen
Olneya tesota	Desert Ironwood	broad tree
*Populus fremontii**	Fremont Cottonwood	light shade
Quercus agrifolia+	Coast Live Oak	
Q. douglasii	Blue Oak	specimen
*Washingtonia filifera**+	California Fan Palm	

NATIVE PLANTS FOR COASTAL AREAS

There is a vast array of plants indigenous to coastal regions. Many are peculiar to certain habitats, such as dunes, bluffs, and coastal marshes. Not all are of value as cultivated materials, but the following list contains a few of the possibilities with some from other areas which have shown a tendency to persist in coastal areas. These plants will grow in sand, but the addition of organic materials will aid in binding the sand, in moisture retention, and will add some fertility to the soil. Many of the shrubs and trees will be blown into sculptured forms by constant winds, but in their early stages they should be staked or protected until their roots are firmly established.

SPECIES	COMMON NAME	USE
Perennials		
Abronia latifolia+	Yellow Sand Verbena	dune cover
A. maritima	Red Sand Verbena	dune cover
Agave shawii	Seacliff Agave	specimen
Armeria maritima var. *californica*	Sea Pink	border accent

NATIVE PLANTS FOR COASTAL AREAS

Species	Common Name	Uses
Perennials (continued)		
Coreopsis gigantea	Tree Coreopsis	accent
C. maritima+	Sea Dahlia	
Dudleya farinosa	Bluff Lettuce	accent
*D. pulverulenta**	Chalk Dudleya	
Erigeron glaucus+	Seaside Daisy	
Eriophyllum nevinii	Catalina Silver Lace	border
Fragaria chiloensis	Beach Strawberry	dune cover
Grindella robusta	Stout Gumplant	border
Lupinus arboreus+	Tree Lupine	
L. chamissonis	Dune Lupine	accent
L. variicolor	Lindley Varied Lupine	edging
Maianthemum dilatatum	False Lily-of-the-Valley	edging
Tanacetum douglasii	Northern Dune Tansy	border
Shrubs		
Arctostaphylos edmundsii+	Little Sur Manzanita	
A. hookeri	Hooker's Manzanita	cover
A. nummularia+	Glossyleaf Manzanita	
A. pumila	Sandmat Manzanita	cover
A. rudis	Shagbark Manzanita	filler
Artemesia californica	California Sagebrush	filler
A. pycnocephala	Beach Sagewort	filler
Atriplex lentiformis ssp. *breweri*	Quail Bush	background
Baccharis pilularis+	Dwarf Chaparral Broom	
Ceanothus dentatus	Cropleaf Ceanothus	filler
C. gloriosus+	Pt. Reyes Ceanothus	
C. griseus+	Carmel Ceanothus	
C. griseus+ var. *horizontalis*+ 'Yankee Point'	cultivar	
Ceanothus rigidus	Monterey Ceanothus	cover
C. thyrsiflorus+	Blue Blossom	
C. thyrsiflorus+ var. *repens*	Creeping Blue Blossom	cover
C. verrucosus	Wartystem Ceanothus	specimen

NATIVE PLANTS FOR COASTAL AREAS

Species	Common Name	Uses
Shrubs (continued)		
Cneoridium dumosum +	Berryrue	
Encelia californica	Brittlebush	border
Gaultheria shallon +	Salal	
Isomeria arborea	Bladder Pod	filler
Lavatera assurgentiflora	Tree Mallow	specimen
Rhamnus californica +	California Coffeeberry	
R. californica + 'Sea View' +	cultivar	
Rhus integrifolia +	Lemonade Berry	
R. laurina	Laurel Sumac	
Sambucus callicarpa	Red Elderberry	specimen
Solanum wallacei	Catalina Nightshade	specimen
Trees		
Myrica californica +	California Wax Myrtle	
Pinus attenuata +	Knobcone Pine	
P. contorta +	Beach Pine	
P. muricata +	Bishop Pine	
P. radiata	Monterey Pine	background
P. torreyana +	Torrey Pine	
Populus trichocarpa	Black Cottonwood	background
Washingtonia filifera +	California Fan Palm	

APPENDIX: PLANT COMMUNITIES

A Plant Community is an aggregation of plant species which grow together where conditions of climate and types of terrain are similar, and where one or more plants are dominant. Botanists have long studied these natural associations of plants, and they are the basis for discussing plant life of the state. Various concepts have been worked out over the years, one of the first being the Life Zone concept of C. Hart Merriam. His theory is now considered inadequate to fully account for plant distribution, and the concept of Plant Communities by Munz and Keck is widely used. In this latter, twenty-nine communities are recognized, and the terms used in this book are based generally on those communities in describing the distribution of plant species.

For readers wishing more complete information on Plant Communities, see the introduction to *A California Flora* by Munz and Keck, or *Terrestrial Vegetation of California* by Barbour and Major.

1. Coastal Strand: sandy beaches, dunes of entire coast. There is a variety of plants, some extending the length of the state.

2. Coastal Salt Marsh.

3. Freshwater Marsh: marshes of interior valleys.

4. Northern Coastal Scrub: a narrow coastal strip between the coastal strand and Redwood Forest, below 500 feet.

5. Coastal Sage Scrub: dry or rocky slopes, south Coast Ranges. Shrubby types.

6. Sagebrush Scrub: deep soils along east base of Sierra Nevada.

7. Shadscale Scrub: heavy soil, mesas and flats, Mojave Desert, Owens Valley, etc. Scattered shrubby types.

8. Creosote Bush Scrub: well-drained soils of slopes, fans, in deserts from south end of Owens Valley to Mexico. Scattered shrubby types, largely dormant between rains.

9. Alkali Sink: poorly drained flats, several kinds of Saltbush.

10. North Coastal Coniferous Forest: outer north Coast Range, dense forests with much undergrowth.

11. Closed-cone Pine Forest: interrupted forest, Mendocino County south to Santa Barbara County, relatively dense forest.

12. Redwood Forest: seaward, outer Coast Ranges, Del Norte to Santa Cruz counties, and scattered along coast to central Monterey County. Dense forests with variety of genera.

13. Douglas-Fir Forest: north Coast Ranges, Mendocino County southward, scattered remnants in Sonoma and Marin counties.

14. Yellow Pine Forest: northern California, Coast Ranges and in Sierra Nevada to southern California. Extensive and continuous forests.

15. Red Fir Forest: north Coast Ranges; Sierra Nevada peaks to 9,500 feet in southern California. Dense forests.

16. Lodgepole Forest, northern California to central Sierra Nevada, up to 9,500 feet. Extensive open forests, meadows scattered through.

17. Subalpine Forest, most boreal forest, northern California up to 11,000 feet, poorly represented in southern mountains.

18. Bristle-Cone Pine Forest: mountains of Inyo and Mono counties.

19. Mixed Evergreen Forest: inner edge of Redwood Forest, north Coast Ranges to Santa Cruz and Santa Lucia Mountains.

20. Northern Oak Woodland: several kinds of oaks, other plants, north Coast Ranges, and in from Redwood Forest to Yolly Bolly Mountains.

21. Southern Oak Woodland: valleys of interior southern California, Los Angeles to San Diego counties, and to San Jacinto Mountains.

22. Foothill Woodland: foothills and valley borders to

3,000 feet. Inner Coast Ranges to Los Angeles County: a composite community with oak parklands.

23. Chaparral: dry slopes and ridges, rocky to gravelly, to fairly heavy soils. Coast Ranges Shasta County south, and below Yellow Pine Forest. Assortment of drought-resistant, evergreen shrubs.

24. Coastal Prairie: temperate hill-grasslands, glades or bald hills.

25. Valley Grassland: Great Central Valley and low valleys of inner Coast Ranges. Open, treeless grasslands, distinctive flora around vernal pools.

26. Alpine Fell-fields: above tree growth, northern California, sparse on high peaks of southern California, up to 10,500 feet. Mostly low, dense perennial plants.

27. Northern Juniper Woodland: Great Basin Plateau, base of Sierra Nevada, Modoc to Mono counties. Open forests on brushy slopes and flats.

28. Pinyon-Juniper Woodland: east base Sierra Nevada, trees in open stands with shrubs between.

29. Joshua Tree Woodland: well-drained mesas and slopes, Owens Valley southward. Joshua Trees scattered, with shrubs and herbs.

REFERENCES, SOCIETIES, AND PLANT SOURCES

BOOKS

Bakker, Elna. *An Island Called California*. Berkeley, Los Angeles: University of California Press, 1971. An ecological tour of California's natural communities, from coast to Sierras. Photos, drawings.

Barbour, Michael G., and Jack Major. *Terrestrial Vegetation of California*, New York, London, Sydney, Toronto: John Wiley, 1977. Articles by many authors on native plant distribution, vegetation map, other maps, and illustrations.

Bowers, Nathan A. *Cone Bearing Trees of the Pacific Coast*. Palo Alto, Ca: Pacific Books, 1956. Description and distribution of conifers, illustrated.

California Native Plant Society. *Native Plants – A Viable Option*. Special publication no. 3, 1977. Several authors. A variety of topics and listings.

Chickering, Allen L. *Growing Calochortus*. Rancho Santa Ana Botanic Garden. Data on growing some members of this genus, color illustrations. (Out of print)

Cornell, Ralph D. *Conspicuous California Plants*. Pasadena, California: San Pasquel Press, 1938. Appraisal of native plants of southern California and Channel Islands. Black and white photos and drawings.

Emery, Dara. *Seed Propagation of Native California Plants*. Santa Barbara Botanic Garden Leaflet, vol. 1, no. 10, 1964. Seed preparation, planting, and germination tables.

Emery, Dara, and J.P. Broughton. *Native Plants for Southern California Gardens*. Santa Barbara Botanic Garden Leaflet, vol. 1, no. 12, 1969. Listings for many situations.

Everett, Percy, C. *The Californian Penstemons*. El Aliso, vol. 2, no 2, 1950. Description and culture for many species of *Penstemon*.

————. *A Summary of the Culture of California Plants*. Claremont, California: Rancho Santa Ana Botanic Garden, 1957. Details of propagating and growing native plants.

Ferris, Roxana. *Native Shrubs of the San Francisco Bay Region*. Berkeley, Los Angeles: University of California Press, 1968. Description of species. Color, black and white illustrations.

Gabrielson, Ira N. *Western American Alpines*. New York: Macmillan Company, 1932. Description and culture for many natives suitable for rock gardens. Black and white photos.

Grillos, Steve J. *Ferns and Fern Allies*. Berkeley, Los Angeles, London: University of California Press, 1971. Description and culture. Illustrated.

Heritage Oaks Committee, *Native Oaks, Our Valley Heritage*. Sacramento: Sacramento County Office of Education, 1976. Description and culture of four native oaks. Illustrated.

Hoover, Robert, and Betty Hoover. *Native Plants in Our Garden*. Blake Printery, 1972. Several categories of plants discussed.

Jepson, Willis Linn. *Flowering Plants of California*. Berkeley: University of California, Associated Students Store, 1925. One of the first complete botanies.

Labadie, Emile L. *Native Plants for Use in the California Landscape*. Sierra City: Sierra City Press, 1978. Selected trees and shrubs described with drawings.

Lenz, Lee W. *Native Plants for California Gardens*. Rancho Santa Ana Botanic Garden, 1956. Cultural information. Illustrated.

Mathias, Mildred E., and Elizabeth McClintock. *A Checklist of Woody Ornamental Plants of California*. California Agricultural Experiment Station and Extension Service, Manual 32, 1963. Lists by common and botanical name.

McMinn, Howard E. *An Illustrated Manual of California Shrubs*. San Francisco: J. W. Stacey, Inc., 1939. A botany with some cultural suggestions. This edition has an article by Fred M. Schumacher on "The Use of California Shrubs in Garden Design."

Milo, Baker Gardener. A leaflet with notes on germination and culture of selected native plants.

Mitchell, Sydney B. *From a Sunset Garden*. Garden City, New York: Doubleday, Doran Company, 1932. General gardening book with a chapter "Native Sons," devoted to an assortment of native plants and their uses.

Mirov, N.T., and Charles J. Kraebel. *Collecting and Handling Seeds of Wild Plants*. Forestry Pub. no. 5. U.S. Dept. of Agric., Washington: Government Printing Office, 1939. Describes process of collecting, storing, growing seeds, with germination tables.

———. *Additional Data on Collecting and Propagating Seeds of California Wild Plants*. Berkeley: California Forest and Range Experiment Station, 1945.

Muller, Katherine K. *Native California Plants for Ground Covers*. Santa Barbara Botanic Garden, vol. 1, no. 9, 1953. Descriptions of a few woody and herbaceous plants for ground covers.

———. *Native Buckwheats*. Santa Barbara Botanic Garden Leaflet, vol. 1, no. 8, 1950.

Munz, Philip A. *A Flora of Southern California*. Berkeley, Los Angeles, London: University of California Press, 1974.

Munz, Philip A., and David D. Keck. *A California Flora*. Berkeley, Los Angeles: University of California Press, 1963.

Niehaus, Theodore F. *Sierra Wildflowers*. Berkeley, Los Angeles, London: University of California Press, 1974. Keys and brief descriptions, color and drawings.

Niehaus, Theodore F., and Charles L. Ripper. *Field Guide to Pacific States Wildflowers*. Boston: Houghton Mifflin Company, 1976. Flowers by color and details of structure to aid in identification. Black and white, color illustrations.

Ornduff, Robert. *California Plant Life*. Berkeley, Los Angeles, London: University of California Press, 1974. Natural history, plant communities, and distribution of native plants. Color illustrations.

Padilla, Victoria. *Southern California Gardens*. Berkeley, Los Angeles: University of California Press, 1961. History of nursery business, and of a few of those concerned with the introduction of native plants. Illustrated.

Peattie, Donald Culross. *A Natural History of Western Trees*. Boston: Houghton Mifflin Company, 1953. Descriptions and uses. Illustrations by Paul Landacre.

Santa Barbara Botanic Garden. *Native Plants for Southern California Gardens*. Leaflet, vol. 1, no. 12, 1969. Lists in 14 categories by cultural and situation categories.

Peterson, P. Victor. *Native Trees of Southern California*.

Berkeley, Los Angeles: University of California Press, 1966. Includes species from the Tehachapi Mountains to the Mexican border, coastal regions from Monterey County south, and Inyo County south. Color and black and white illustrations.

Raven, Peter. *Native Shrubs of Southern California*. Berkeley, Los Angeles: University of California Press, 1970. Descriptions of species. Color and black and white illustrations.

Roof, James B. *Guide to the Plant Species of the Regional Parks Botanic Garden*. East Bay Regional Parks District, 1959. Native plants as they occur in seven broad regions.

Rowntree, Lester. *Flowering Shrubs of California*. Stanford: Stanford University Press, 1939. Garden value and uses of native shrubs. Black and white illustrations.

———. *Hardy Californians*. New York: The Macmillan Company, 1936. Distribution and habitat, few cultural notes for a variety of native plants. Black and white illustrations.

Saunders, Charles Francis. *Western Wild Flowers*. New York: Doubleday Doran Company, 1933. Stories of wild plants, and uses by early settlers and Indians. Illustrated.

———. *The Southern Sierras of California*. Boston, New York: Houghton Mifflin Company, 1923. Outstanding for this region with descriptions of wildlife and some history. Illustrated.

Sharsmith, Helen K. *Spring Wildflowers of the San Francisco Bay Region*. Berkeley, Los Angeles: University of California Press, 1965. Brief descriptions of representative native plants. Illustrated.

Smith, Arthur C. *Natural History of the San Francisco Bay Region*. Berkeley, Los Angeles: University of California Press, 1959. Black and white, color illustrations.

Sudworth, George B. *Forest Trees of the Pacific Slope*. U.S. Dept. of Agric., Washington: Government Printing Office, 1908. Descriptions and large illustrations.

Sunset Western Garden Book. Menlo Park: Lane Magazine and Book Company, 1967. Native plants included, with all garden materials and climate maps for western states.

Thomas, John Hunter, and Dennis R. Parnell. *Native Shrubs of the Sierra Nevada*. Berkeley, Los Angeles, and London: University of California Press, 1974. Illustrated.

University of California Agricultural Extension Service. *Native California Plants for Ornamental Use*. Leaflet 2831, 1966. Several authors. Lists of trees and shrubs.

Van Dersal, William R. *Ornamental American Shrubs*. New York, London, Toronto: Oxford University Press, 1942. Description and culture, including many native to California. Illustrated.

Van Rensselaer, Maunsell, and Howard E. McMinn. *Ceanothus*. Santa Barbara: Santa Barbara Botanic Garden, 1942. Part 1 has descriptions and culture; part 2 has key to the species. Illustrated.

Wiley, Leonard. *Rare Wild Flowers of North America*. Portland, Oregon: Leonard Wiley, 1969. Discussions of many rare plants, including forty species native to California.

PERIODICALS

American Horticulturist. American Horticultural Society, Mount Vernon, Virginia. Six issues a year, wide variety of subjects, occasional ones on native plants.

California Garden. San Diego Floral Association, Balboa Park, San Diego. Bi-monthly, variety of material including occasional articles on native plants.

Flower and Garden Magazine, Western edition. Kansas City, Mo. Monthly, occasional material on growing native plants.

Four Seasons. Edited by James B. Roof, former director of Regional Parks Botanic Garden, Berkeley. An occasional journal devoted to knowledge of California native plants.

Fremontia. California Native Plant Society. Quarterly, all phases of native plant concern with a column on native plants for gardens in each issue.

Golden Gardens. California Garden Clubs, Inc. Long Beach. Bi-monthly, a variety of topics, some on native plants.

Pacific Horticulture. Pacific Horticultural Foundation, San Francisco. Quarterly journal, a wide variety of subjects, many articles on native plants.

Sunset Magazine. Menlo Park. Monthly, with garden section and occasional articles on culture of native plants.

PLANT SOCIETIES AND BOTANIC GARDENS

American Fern Society
Dean P. Whittier, Treasurer
Dept. of Biology, Vanderbilt
  Univ.
Nashville, TN. 37235

American Horticultural
  Society
Mount Vernon, VA. 22121

American Iris Society
Missouri Botanical Garden
Clifford W. Benson,
  Secretary
2315 Tower Grove Ave.
St. Louis, MO. 63110

American Penstemon Society
Orville M. S. Steward
P.O. Box 450
Briarcliff Manor, N.Y. 10501

Balboa Park
San Diego, CA. 92101

California Horticultural
  Society
% California Academy of
  Sciences,
Golden Gate Park
San Francisco, CA. 94118

California Native Plant
  Society
2380 Ellsworth St.
Berkeley, CA. 94704

Descanso Gardens
1418 Descanso Drive
La Canada, CA. 91011

C.M. Goethe Arboretum
Sacramento State College

6000 Jay Street
Sacramento, CA. 95819

Huntington Botanical
  Gardens
1151 Oxford Road
San Marino, CA. 91108

International Plant
  Propagators Society
Department of Pomology
Dr. Hudson Hartmann, Editor
  of Proceedings
University of California
  Davis
Davis, CA. 95616

Joseph McInnes Memorial
  Botanical Gardens
Mills College
Seminary Ave. and
  MacArthur Blvd.
Oakland, CA. 94613

Moorten's Desertland
  Gardens
Palm Springs, CA. 92262

North American Lily Society
Mrs. Betty Clifford,
  Executive Secretary
Rt. 1, Box 395
Colby, WI. 54421

Rancho Santa Ana Botanic
  Garden
1500 N. College Ave.
Claremont, CA. 91711

Regional Parks Botanic
  Garden
Tilden Regional Park
Berkeley, CA. 94708

Santa Barbara Botanic
  Garden
1212 Mission Canyon Road
Santa Barbara, CA. 93105

Strybing Arboretum and
  Botanical Gardens

Golden Gate Park
San Francisco, CA. 94122

University of California
  Botanic Gardens
Strawberry Canyon,
Berkeley, CA. 94720

SOURCES OF SEEDS, PLANTS AND INFORMATION

Bay View Gardens
1201 Bay Street
Santa Cruz, CA. 96060
Native iris, exotics

Berkeley Horticultural
  Nursery
1310 McGee Street
Berkeley, CA. 94702
Exotics, natives

Burton's Oak Grove Nursery
2190 Oak Grove Road
Walnut Creek, CA. 94598
Exotics, natives

Christensen's Nursery
935 Old Country Road
Belmont, CA. 94002
Wholesale

Clyde Robin
P.O. Box 2091
Castro Valley, CA. 94546
Seeds

Deigaard Nurseries, Inc.
P.O. Box 582
Monrovia, CA. 91016

Elfinwood Nurseries
Rt. 1, Box 2936
Colfax, CA. 95713
Mostly natives, wholesale

Forest Seeds of California
P.O. Box 561
Davis, CA. 95616

Hortica Gardens
P.O. Box 318
Placerville, CA. 95667
Exotics, natives

Leonard Coates Nurseries,
  Inc.
400 Casserly Road
Watsonville, CA. 95076
Exotics, natives, wholesale

Monrovia Nursery Company
P.O. Box Q; 18331 Foothill
  Blvd.
Azusa, CA. 91702
Wholesale

Native Plant Farm
3350 St. Helena Highway
St. Helena, CA. 94574

Pecoff Brothers Nursery, Inc.
Route 5, Box 215R
Escondido, CA. 92025

Saratoga Horticultural
  Foundation
Box 308
Saratoga, CA. 95070
Wholesale

Siskiyou Rare Plant Nursery
522 Franquette Street
Medford, Ore. 97501
Rock plants, natives

Shop in The Sierra
P.O. Box 1
Midpines, CA. 95345
Natives

Skylark Nursery
6735 Sonoma Highway
Santa Rosa, CA. 95405

Taylor Nursery
547 Carpenteria Rd.
Aromas, CA. 95004

Theodore Payne Foundation
10459 Tuxford Street
Sun Valley, CA. 91352
Seeds, plants, all natives

Wapumne Plant Farm
8305 Cedar Crest Way
Sacramento, CA. 94826

Western Hills Nursery
16250 Coleman Valley Road
Occidental, CA. 95465
Natives, exotics

Yerba Buena Nursery
19500 Skyline Blvd.
Redwood City, CA. 95004
Natives, exotics

ABBREVIATIONS

B.C.: British Columbia
cm: centimeter
co, cos: county, counties
dm: decimeter
elev: elevation
ft: foot
id, ids: island, islands
in: inch
m: meter
mm.: millimeter

mt, mts: mountain, mountains,
no.: number
ref., refs.: reference, references
sp., spp.: species (singular and plural)
ssp., sspp.: subspecies (singular and plural)
var., vars.: variety, varieties

GLOSSARY

acuminate   tapering to a point

adherent   unlike parts in close contact but not fused

adnate   fusion of unlike parts

alpine   plants growing above timberline

achene   small, dry, hard, not splitting, 1-seeded fruit

amplexicaul   clasping the stem, as the base of certain leaves

alternate   arrangement of leaves or other parts along the axis, not opposite or whorled

annual   of one season's or year's duration

anther   the pollen-bearing part of the stamen

anthrocyanous   showing reddish or purplish coloring

anthocarp   a structure in which the fruit is united with the perianth or receptacle, as in *abronia*

apetalous   lacking petals

appendage   any attached supplement or secondary part

appressed   pressed flat against another organ

ascending   rising or curving upward

asexual   sexless

auricle   ear-shaped appendage

awn   a terminal bristle on an organ

axil   upper angle formed by leaf or branch with stem

axis   main line of development, as main stem

barbed   bearing sharp, reflexed points

basal   relating to, or situated at the base

basifixed   attached by the base

beak   a prolonged tip, especially of seed or fruit

berry   a pulpy, indehiscent fruit, few to many seeds

bi or **bis**   prefix signifying two, twice, or doubly bifid, two cleft

bipinnate   doubly or twice pinnate

bilabiate   two-lipped, of calyx or corolla

bisected   completely divided into two parts

biternate   having double groups of three leaflets

blade   an expanded part of leaf or petal

bloom   whitish, fine powder covering surface

bole   trunk or stem of tree

bract   a reduced leaf subtending a flower, usually associated with an inflorescence

bud   an undeveloped shoot, leaf, or flower

bulb   an underground vegetative bud with thickened scales, or leaves, like an onion

bulbel   daughter bulbs arising from mother bulb

calyx   external whorl of flower, the sepals collectively

campanulate   bell-shaped

capitate   head-shaped, aggregated into dense heads

capsule   a dry, dehiscent fruit composed of more than one carpel

carpel   a simple pistil

caudex   woody base of otherwise herbaceous perennial

cauline   belonging to the stem

caespitose   in little tufts or dense clumps

chaparral   a type of vegetation composed of drought resistant, stiff, evergreen shrubs

ciliate   fringed with hairs on margin

cismontane   region of California west of the main Sierran crest

clasping   a leaf partly or wholly surrounding the stem

claw   a narrow petiole-like base of some petals and sepals

column   body formed by union of stamens and pistil in orchids, or of stamens in mallows and milkweeds

complete   having all floral parts, sepals, stamens, petals, and pistils

compound   having two or more similar parts in one organ

concolor   of uniform color

conglomerate   densely clustered

conic   cone-shaped

connate   congenitally united, as fusion of like parts

cordate   heart-shaped, with notch at base and ovate in general outline, as leaf of redbud

coriaceous   leathery in texture

corm   solid, bulblike, underground stem

corolla   inner perianth of flower, composed of colored petals which may be united or almost so

corymb   a flat-topped or convex racemose flower cluster, the lower or outer pedicels longer, their flowers opening first

cultivar   a horticultural or cultivated variety of a plant having fixed and desirable traits, propagated from cuttings or from seeds. Cultivars should be registered with the International Code of Botanical Nomenclature to promote uniformity and accuracy

cuneate   wedge-shaped

cyme   flat-topped or convex paniculate flower cluster with central flowers opening first

deciduous   falling off, as leaves falling from trees in autumn

decumbent   lying down, but with tips ascending

deflexed   turned abruptly downward

dehiscent   opening spontaneously when ripe

deltoid   triangular

dentate   having the margin cut with sharp teeth not directed forward

dichotomous   repeatedly forking in pairs

diffuse   scattered, widely spread

dioecious   having staminate and pistillate flowers on different plants

discoid   disklike. In the Compositae a head without ray flowers

dissected   deeply divided into numerous fine segments

divaricate   widely divergent

divided   separated to the base

downy   closely covered with short, soft hairs

drupe   fleshy, one-seeded fruit containing a stone with kernel

ecotype   those individuals of a species that are fitted to survive in only one kind of environment occupied by the species

elliptic   flattened circle, more than twice as long as broad

emarginate   with small notch at the apex

endemic   native and restricted to a particular region

endosperm   the nutritive tissue surrounding the embryo of a seed

entire   undivided, as continuous leaf margin

erect   upright in relation to ground, or perpendicular to surface of attachment

evergreen   having living leaves throughout the year

exserted   protruding, as stamens projecting beyond corolla

falcate   sickle-shaped

fastigiate   plants which taper to a point, as tree growing erect with parallel branching

fenestrate   with transparent areas, or windowlike openings

fertile   said of pollen-bearing stamens and seed bearing fruits

filament   a thread, especially the stalk of an anther

filiform   thread-like

fleshy   thick and juicy, succulent

flexuous   zigzag

floriferous   bearing flowers

foliate   having leaflets

follicle   a dry, dehiscent, one-carpelled fruit, opening only along the side, as in larkspur and milkweed

frond   leaf of a fern

fruit   ripened pistil with all of its accessory parts, seed-bearing structure

funnelform   gradually widening upward, as some flowers of penstemon and mimulus

gamo   fused

glabrous   without hairs

gland   a depression, protuberance, or appendage on the surface of an organ which secrets a usually sticky fluid

glaucous   whitened with a bloom

globose   spherical or rounded

glutinous   with gluey exudation

habit   general appearance of a plant

habitat   specific environment in which a plant lives

head   dense, globular cluster of flowers arising from the same point on the peduncle

herb   a plant without persistent woody stem, at least above ground

herbaceous   pertaining to an herb, as opposed to woody; dying to the ground

hirsute   rough with coarse or shaggy hairs

hispid   rough with stiff or bristly hairs

hoary   with white down

humus   decayed organic material

hybrid   a cross between two species

imbricate   overlapping

incised   cut rather deeply and sharply

indehiscent   not splitting open, as an achene

indigenous   native to the country

inferior   lower or beneath
inflated   blown up, bladdery
inflorescence   disposition of the flowers on an axis
interrupted   not continuous or regular
involucre   a whorl of bracts surrounding a flower cluster, as in head of compositae

labiate   lipped
laciniate   cut into narrow lobes or segments
lanate   woolly
lanceolate   lance-shaped, longer than broad
leaflet   segment of a compound leaf
legume   superior one-celled fruit of simple pistil having seed attached along one side
linear   long, narrow, of uniform width
lip   one of the two divisions of a two-lipped corolla or calyx
lobe   a division or segment of an organ, usually rounded
lunate   crescent-shaped

macro   prefix, large or long
maculate   spotted or blotched
micro   prefix, small
montane   pertaining to the mountains
multi   prefix, many

node   joint of a stem, the point of insertion of a leaf
nut   hard-shelled, one-seeded fruit

obcordate   inversely cordate
oblong   much longer than broad and with parallel lines
obtuse   blunt, or rounded at end
offsets   short, basal, lateral shoots from which new plants can develop
opposite   set against, as leaves when two at a node
orbicular   approximately circular in outline
orifice   mouthlike opening of a tubular corolla
oval   broadly elliptic, more than twice as long as broad

palmatified   cleft so as to resemble the outstretched fingers of the hand
panicle   a compound racemose inflorescence

papillate   with bumps or protuberances

pappus   crown of bristles or scales on summit of seed

pedicel   stalk of a single flower in a flower cluster

peduncle   stalk of a flower in a cluster of flowers

peltate   shield shape, as a leaf with stalk attached to lower surface instead of at base or margin

pendent   suspended or hanging, nodding

perennial   lasting from year to year

perfect   a flower having both stamens and pistils

perfoliate   with the leaf entirely surrounding the stem

perianth   the floral envelope collectively when calyx and corolla are not clearly differentiated

persistent   remaining attached, as the calyx on a fruit

petal   one of the leaves of a corolla, usually colored

petiole   leaf stalk

pinna   leaflets, or primary division of a pinnate leaf

pinnate   a compound leaf having leaflets arranged on each side of a common petiole; featherlike

plane   surface flat and even, not curved

pod   any dry, splitting fruit; as a legume

pome   an apple-like fruit

procumbent   trailing on the ground but not rooting

prostrate   lying flat on the ground

pubescent   covered with short, soft hairs; downy

pungent   acrid to taste or smell

quadrate   square

raceme   a simple, elongated, indeterminate inflorescence with each flower subequally pedicelled

rachis   the axis of a spike or raceme, or of a compound leaf

radiate   spreading from a common center

radical   belong to or proceeding from a root

ray   a primary branch of an umbel; the ligule of a ray-floret in Compositae

receptacle   that portion of the floral axis upon which the flower parts are borne

refinement   of plants having good seasonal appearance, neat, ornamental, nonrampant

reflexed   abruptly bent downward

regular   said of a flower having radial symmetry, with the parts in each series alike

remote   distantly spaced

reniform   kidney-shaped

reticulate   with a network; net-veined

rhizome   an underground stem or rootstock, with scales at the nodes, producing leafy shoots on the upper side and roots on the lower side

rib   the primary vein of a leaf, or a ridge on a fruit

rotate   wheel-shaped; said of a sympetalous corolla with obsolete tube and with a flat and circular limb

rubellous   reddish; rubescent, turning red

rugose   wrinkled

saccate   furnished with a sac or pouch

sagittate   shaped like an arrow, with the basal lobes turned downward

salverform   a corolla with a slender tube abruptly expanding into a fat limb

samara   an indehiscent winged fruit

scale   any thin scarious bract; usually a vestigial leaf

scape   a leafless stem rising from ground in stemless plant

scarious   thin, dry, and membraneous, not green

scree   a type of planting area composed of rock or sand, with source of underground water

secund   arranged on one side only, unilateral

seed   the ripened ovule

segment   a division or part of a leaf or other organ that is cleft or divided but not truly compound

sepal   a leaf or segment of the calyx

serrate   saw-toothed, the sharp teeth pointing forward

sessile   attached directly by the base; not stalked as a leaf with a petiole

shrub   a woody plant of smaller proportions than a tree, and which usually produces several branches from the base

simple   unbranched, as a stem or hair; uncompounded, as a leaf; single, as a pistil of one carpel

solitary   borne singly

sordid   of dull or dirty hue

spathe   a broad sheathing bract enclosing a spadix, as in the calla

spatulate   like a spatula, a knife rounded above and gradually narrowed to the base

spike   an elongated rachis of sessile flowers or spikelets

spore   the reproductive body of pteridophytes and lower plants, analogous to the seed

spreading   diverging almost to the horizontal; nearly prostrate. spreading hairs: not all appressed, but erect. Spreading lower lip: diverging from the main axis of the flower.

spur   a slender, saclike, nectariferous process from a petal or sepal

stamen   the male organ of the flower which bears the pollen

staminate   having stamens but not pistils; said of a flower or plant that is male, hence not seed bearing

stellate   star-shaped

sterile   infertile, or barren, as a stamen lacking an anther, a flower wanting a pistil, a seed without an embryo, etc.

stigma   the receptive part of the pistil on which the pollen germinates

stipe   the leaf stalk of a fern; the stalk beneath an ovary

stipule   one of the pair of usually foliaceous appendages found at the base of the petiole in many plants

stolon   a modified stem bending over and rooting at the tip; or creeping and rooting at the nodes; or a horizontal stem that gives rise to a new plant at the tip

stone   a bony endocarp of a drupe

striate   marked with fine longitudinal lines or furrows

style   the contracted portion of the pistil between the ovary and the stigma; style-branches may be only in part stigmatic, the remainder then being appendage

sub   prefix meaning somewhat, almost, of inferior rank, beneath

subtend   to be below and close to, as the leaf subtends the shoot borne in its axil

succulent   juicy, fleshy and soft

subulate   awl-shaped

superior   growing above, as an ovary that is free from the other floral organs

symmetrical   said of a flower having the same number of parts in each circle

syn-   prefix, united

taproot   a primary stout vertical root giving off small laterals but not dividing

taxon   (taxa)   any taxonomic unit, as an order, genus, variety, etc.

tendril   a slender, coiling or twining organ by which a climbing plant grasps its support

terete   cylindrical; round in cross-section

ternate   in threes, as a leaf consisting of three leaflets

throat   the orifice of a gamopetalous corolla; the expanded portion between the limb and the tube proper

thryse a compact, ovate panicle; strictly, with main axis indeterminate, but with other axes cymose

tomentose covered with short, densely matted, soft white wool; tomentum: covering of such densely matted woolly hairs

tri- prefix for three

trichotomous three-forked

triternate thrice ternate

tube the narrow basal portion of a gamopetalous corolla, or a gamosepalous calyx

tuber a thickened, solid, and short underground stem, with many buds. Tuberous: bearing a tuber

tubular shaped like a hollow cylinder

tunicate having coats, as a bulb

umbel a flat or convex flower cluster in which the pedicels arise from a common point, like the rays of an umbrella. Umbellate: borne in an umbel

undulate wavy margined

unisexual flowers having only stamens or pistils; of one sex

valve one of the segments into which a dehiscent capsule or legume separates

vein a vascular bundle of a leaf or other flat organ

velutinous velvety; covered with a fine and dense silky pubescence

ventral relating to the inward face of an organ, in relation to the axis: anterior; front

verrucose warty; covered with wartlike excrescenses

versatile an anther attached near the middle and capable of swinging freely on the filament

verticil a whorl, or circular arrangement of similar parts about the same point on the axis. Verticillate: whorled

verpertine flowering in the evening

villous bearing long and soft and not matted hairs, shaggy

viscid sticky; glutinous

whorl a ring of similar organs radiating from a node

wildflower alternate to native plant. Popular: field annuals

wing a thin and usually dry extension bordering an organ, as in seed of elm, ash

woolly having long, soft, entangled hairs

xerophyte a drought-resistant or desert plant

INDEX